KU-778-344

CONTENTS

Page

FOREWORD ix

PREFACE xi

THE GOVERNANCE OF THE UNION 1

EXECUTIVE SUMMARY 3

1. INTRODUCTION 9
   Scope and Objectives of the Paper 9

2. THE INSTITUTIONAL DEBATE OF THE 1970s AND 1980s 11

3. THE SINGLE ACT INHERITANCE 15
   (i) The Creation of a Package 15
   (ii) Institutional Provisions of the Single Act 16
   (iii) Impact of the Single Act in Practice 17

4. THE INTER GOVERNMENTAL CONFERENCES: PROPOSALS FOR CHANGE 25
   (i) The Negotiations 25
   (ii) The Structure of the Union 25
   (iii) The Policy Scope of the Union 26
   (iv) Subsidiarity 32
   (v) Hierarchy of Norms 37
   (vi) Efficiency and Effectiveness of the Union 38
   (vii) The Political Consequences of EMU 42

5. PROSPECTS AND OPTIONS 47
(i) The Prospects for Change 47
(ii) Issues for Ireland 48
(iii) Looking into the Crystal Ball 57

BIBLIOGRAPHY 59

THE LEGITIMACY OF THE UNION 61

EXECUTIVE SUMMARY 63

1. INTRODUCTION 67
(i) The significance of legitimacy for the EC in the 1990s 68
(ii) The wider competence of EC institutions 69
(iii) Enlargement of the EC 69
(iv) The scope and purpose of the paper 70

2. BACKGROUND 71
(i) The evolution of public opinion 71
(ii) Social policy as a reinforcer of EC legitimacy 72
(iii) 'People's Europe' and the Adonnino Report (1985) 73

3. EUROPEAN COMMUNITY CITIZENSHIP 77
(i) The origins and meaning of EC citizenship 77
(ii) The scope of EC citizenship 77

4. THE DEMOCRATIC DEFICIT 81
(i) The Single European Act and the 'democratic deficit' 81
(ii) The European Parliament 81

(iii) The cooperation procedure: problems and prospects 83
(iv) The European Parliament and the national parliaments 84
(v) Parliament's relations with the Commission and the Council 86
(vi) The Commission's accountability to Parliament 88
(vii) The European Parliament and the impact of 'subsidiarity' 89
(viii) Reforms involving major changes 91

5. OPTIONS FOR IRELAND 95
(i) European Community citizenship? 95
(ii) A Community ombudsman? 95
(iii) A European Senate? A European Affairs Committee? 96
(iv) Wider powers for the European Parliament? 96

APPENDICES 98

BIBLIOGRAPHY 102

THE FOREIGN RELATIONS OF THE UNION 105

EXECUTIVE SUMMARY 107

1. INTRODUCTION 113

2. THE EUROPEAN COMMUNITY AS AN INTERNATIONAL ACTOR 115
(i) The European Community's 'external action' 115
(ii) European Political Cooperation 116
(iii) European Political Cooperation after the Act 117

3. FOREIGN POLICY: PROPOSALS FOR CHANGE 121

(i) From 'EPC' to 'CFSP' 121

(ii) The institutional framework 122

(iii) Decision making 125

4. SECURITY POLICY: A SUITABLE CASE FOR DEFINITION 131

(i) What is 'security policy'? 131

(ii) Multilateral security frameworks 132

(iii) Ireland: security and neutrality 134

(iv) Security in European Political Cooperation 136

5. SECURITY POLICY: THE AGENDA OF 'SOFT SECURITY' 139

(i) Towards a new formulation of 'security policy' 139

(ii) The agenda of 'soft security' in 1991 139

(iii) Implications for Ireland 142

6 THE QUESTION OF DEFENCE 145

(i) "With a view to the future" 145

(ii) A commitment to mutual assistance? 146

(iii) Links between the European Community and WEU 149

7. PROSPECTS AND OPTIONS 153

(i) The prospects for change 153

(ii) The basis of choice 154

(iii) Options for Ireland 155

(iv) The context is a moving target 158

BIBLIOGRAPHY 159

THE EXTENSION OF THE UNION 161

EXECUTIVE SUMMARY 163

1. INTRODUCTION 169

2. THE BACKGROUND 175

3. THE POTENTIAL APPLICANTS 187

4. THE ISSUES 199
   - (i) Impact on Community Institutions 201
   - (ii) Economic Issues 205
   - (iii) Political Issues 207
   - (iv) The Acquis Communautaire 215

5. THE AVAILABLE OPTIONS 219
   - (i) Internal Integration and External Partnership 219
   - (ii) A Larger Single Market 220
   - (iii) A New Intergovernmental Structure 220
   - (iv) Multiple Pillars 221
   - (v) Deepening and Sequential Widening 222

6. CONCLUSIONS 225
   - Policy Options for Ireland 229

APPENDIX 231

BIBLIOGRAPHY 234

AN OVERVIEW OF THE COMMUNITY'S INSTITUTIONAL SYSTEM 237

1. INTRODUCTION 239

2. THE INSTITUTIONAL SYSTEM 243

3. THE COMMUNITY'S POLICY STYLE 249

4. CONCLUSIONS 251

APPENDIX 252

BIBLIOGRAPHY 253

LIST OF ABBREVIATIONS 254

AUTHOR'S BIOGRAPHIES 256

FOREWORD

For the third time within a generation, the Government, the Oireachtas, and the public are faced with major decisions in relation to the movement towards European Union. In the negotiations for entry and the referendum result of 1972, the principle of European Union as an objective was accepted. From that time onwards, the question became one of discussing and deciding how quickly and in what manner that ultimate objective should be achieved. In the early 1980s there appeared to be nothing left of the earlier momentum towards either economic or political union but only a state of stagnation characterised by excessive preoccupation with narrow national interests. That stagnation was broken in 1984 by the formulation of a Draft Treaty on European Union by the Institutional Committee of the European Parliament under the chairmanship of Altiero Spinelli, followed by the Report of the *ad hoc* Committee on Institutional Affairs and European Union of personal representatives of Heads of State and Governments on which I represented the Taoiseach. The latter Report was essentially a political document advocating a specific course of action.

The resulting Treaty reforms under the Single European Act, endorsed in this country by the 1987 referendum, restored momentum to the process of Community development. This happened to such an extent that it is already time to consider further steps to bring us even closer to the long-term goal of European Union. What is at issue at present is not whether we now take the final step but rather how much further we go now along the road to the ultimate objective of European Union endorsed in principle by the Irish electorate in the 1972 referendum.

It has sometimes been said that the two previous referenda campaigns consisted largely of a contest in sloganeering between the groups which took part in the debate. This is, in my opinion, too harsh a judgement but there lies behind it an element of truth. Every political decision, whether by a minister in cabinet or by a voter in a referendum, is based on an individual assessment of the facts that constitute the reality of the point at issue. Discussion can reduce the gap between subjective perceptions and objective facts in such a way as to lead to improved decision making. The role of the newly-established Institute of European Affairs is to narrow that gap between subjective participations and objective facts in relation to key European issues. The aim of the present study is to narrow the particular gap between perceptions and facts that exist in relation to political apsects of European Union.

The individual chapters of this book deal with the key issues of political union. Brigid Laffan discusses under the heading *The Governance of the Union* the special features of the unique political system whose structures and procedures characterise the present Community and must be clearly understood if we are to appreciate the significance of any proposed changes in them. Eddie Moxon-Browne discusses *The Legitimacy of the Union* which is a vital element in relation to the acceptance of the central authority in any form of federation or confederation. Patrick Keatinge ranges over the issues of *The Foreign Relations of the Union* which are certain to loom large in our domestic discussion of the new Treaty proposals. Finally, Tony Brown discusses the topic of *The Extension of the Union* which is now a more central issue than it was when this study started some months ago. In a separate publication, Paul Gillespie and Rodney Rice summarise the implications for the Irish voter of the issues discussed in the present book. Those who find this book on first reading to be too detailed, might like to read that publication first before returning to the present work.

Earlier drafts of the individual papers were circulated to members of the Working Group and were discussed by them at meetings in June and July 1991. While the material now published represents the views of the individual authors and is their sole responsibility, these discussions were of considerable value in shaping the final versions so as to make the maximum possible contribution towards an enlightened public debate on the vital issue of the political structure of the future Community.

James Dooge,
Chairperson of the Working Group.

PREFACE

The European Community emerged as the core regional organisation in Europe at the end of the 1980s. The renewed dynamism in the Community owed much to the 1992 Programme and to the impact of the Single European Act (SEA) which was implemented in 1987. The Single Act, representing the first major modification of the Rome Treaties, allowed for an expansion of the Community's policy scope, a re-ordering of its priorities and a strengthening of its decision-making capacity. Renewed confidence in the Community intensified pressures for a deepening of integration and led to the convening of two Inter Governmental Conferences (IGCs) to negotiate an economic and monetary union and a treaty on political union.

The Inter Governmental Conferences are taking place at a time of considerable turbulence in Europe and in international politics more generally. The economic and political order imposed on east/central Europe after World War II started to unravel in 1989. The collapse of communism in the former eastern bloc ended the political division of the continent and the partition of Germany, the centre-piece of the post-war order. The Warsaw Pact and Comecon disintegrated as the Soviet Union retreated from empire; in the summer of 1991 the Soviet Union itself came apart and another communist federation, Yugoslavia, was in the throes of an ugly civil war.

These events have profound consequences for the European Community. For more than forty years the iron curtain allowed western Europe to ignore difficult and sensitive questions about the boundaries of the continent and a possible eastwards enlargement of the Community. However, for Hungary, Poland and Czechoslovakia, rejoining Europe means joining the European Community, a goal likely to be adopted by other newly-liberated states. Even if an eastwards enlargement is not likely to be achieved in the medium term, the Community has a vital interest in developments to its east; political and economic turmoil in eastern Europe would have adverse consequences for the entire continent. Western Europe's importance as a zone of prosperity and stability for the continent as a whole is critical.

Even before the Soviet and Yugoslav crises erupted, the Iraqi invasion of Kuwait in August 1990 had dampened the initial euphoria about the ending of the cold war. The subsequent war in the Gulf highlighted once again Europe's dependence on oil supplies from the Middle East and its geographical proximity to this most unstable part of the globe. The southern shore of the Mediterranean and the Gulf are of critical importance to western Europe. The Gulf War and its aftermath also highlighted the role of the United States, giving renewed urgency to the reassessment of transatlantic relations which began with the collapse of communism.

Turbulence in the international environment has added a host of issues to an already over-crowded internal Community agenda. The Community is attempting to complete the single market, to plan new policies for industry and infrastructure in the post-1992 era, and to negotiate a treaty establishing an economic and monetary union. The external impact of the Single Market programme has led to a reassessment of integration policies in those west European states which had preferred the looser commitments of the European Free Trade Association (EFTA) to that of the European Community. It appears more and more likely that the negotiations on a European Economic Area (EEA) are a prelude to full accession negotiations for most EFTA states sometime in the 1990s. The prospect of an EFTA enlargement is part of the unrevealed agenda of the Inter Governmental Conference on political union.

Meanwhile, the original six member states of the Community, the driving force of west European integration, wish to deepen integration, in order to protect the level of integration achieved so far. However, this desire has been complicated by the changing balance between Paris and Bonn. The speed of German unification has had a major impact on French foreign policy. France, having seen the traditional maxims of its foreign policy eroded by the new Europe, once again looked to west European integration as a means of influencing the new Germany. For Germany, an acceptance of further integration gives substance to its assertion that unification will lead to a European Germany rather than to a German Europe. Thus the Kohl/Mitterrand resolution of 19 April, 1990, calling for an Inter Governmental Conference on political union, was designed to demonstrate that the Paris/Bonn axis had partly overcome the unease created by German unification. Consequently, at the European Council in Dublin in June 1990, a decision was taken under Article 236 of the Rome Treaty (EEC) to open a political union conference on 14 December, 1990, in parallel with the conference on Economic and Monetary Union.

The aim of this volume is to examine the issues confronting the delegations participating in the Political Union Inter Governmental Conference. Although agreement on a new Treaty is not expected before the meeting of the European Council in Maastricht on 9–10 December, 1991, by the halfway stage of the conference the main questions have been identified, and numerous proposals have been tabled by the member states and the Commission. It is therefore possible to see where the opportunities and difficulties lie, and even to speculate on the forces which are being brought to bear on their resolution. It is also possible to tease out the implications for Ireland, and to suggest, albeit in broad terms, the options facing this country. This is not a matter of academic curiosity. The outcome of the negotiations will be an important determinant of public affairs for the rest of this decade, and the terms of the Treaty will have to be submitted to a referendum before the end of 1992.

That will be the third occasion on which Ireland's membership of the European Community is the subject of a popular vote. The first referendum in 1972 followed a sustained public debate concerning the basic question of accession. Although the nature of the political commitment being undertaken was raised at this time, it did not prove to be the central issue in what was for the most part an exchange of contending expectations of economic advantage. The second referendum in 1987, on the Single European Act, was an object lesson in the poverty of political discussion in the Irish political system. An unexpected decision by the Supreme Court found the political world in disarray, and although several relevant issues were aired the debate was confused and ambiguous, attracting the second lowest turnout of 44.1 per cent, for any Irish referendum.

It may be objected that some degree of confusion and ambiguity is inevitable in a popular consultation of this sort. The arcane nature of any treaty text cannot be avoided altogether, and the Single European Act was a legal patchwork which could not be understood without reference to previous Treaties and the political effects of their implementation. The forthcoming Union Treaty will no doubt compound this complexity. Nevertheless, the underlying issues can be explained and put in their political context, and proposed changes can be tested against alternatives. In the belief that such a process ought not be left to the eleventh hour, the authors of the papers in this volume have attempted to open up public discussion at this stage, without waiting for the final treaty text.

What follows, therefore, must not be read as a definitive interpretation of the emerging union. Indeed, this very appellation 'Union' may be a matter of controversy even after political agreement is reached. The term has long been associated with the evolution of the European Community. The preamble of the EEC Treaty of 1957 refers to the goal of "an ever closer union of the European peoples", but the translation of this general aspiration into a particular institutional form has been attended by conceptual, as well as political, disagreement. The most clear-cut and ambitious form of political union is a fully-fledged *federal* union, on the lines of the United States of America, with fiscal, foreign affairs and defence powers unequivocally concentrated in the central (federal) organs of government. The outcome of the Inter Governmental Conference is most unlikely to take that form, but whether, or how far, the member states are prepared to move in that direction is a pertinent question. Whatever the level of agreement at Maastricht, the forces leading to, and obstructing, further integration will remain as significent determinants of our political future.

The approach adopted in this book assumes a basic understanding of the workings of the European Community's institutions. Readers who are unfamiliar with this unique political system are referred to Brigid Laffan's 'Overview of the Community's Institutional System', at the back of this book. In her main paper, on 'The Governance of the Union', Professor Laffan explores the question of political authority in the European Community. This issue is central to the Political Union negotiations; in fact, institutional questions have been part and parcel of the policy of the Community from the outset. So too is the issue of policy scope. There is constant tension between the policy consequences of advanced integration and the desire of some member states to maintain as much authority at national level as possible. The paper discusses in detail proposals for change covering the Community's policy competence, the principle of 'subsidiarity', the efficiency and effectiveness of its institutions and the political consequences of Economic and Monetary Union (EMU). The paper highlights some dilemmas for Ireland, notably those arising from changes to the Community's institutional balance, the issue of 'cohesion', and the consequences of 'variable geometry'.

In his contribution, Edward Moxon-Browne takes up the question of the Union's legitimacy: how far do the citizens of the Community really believe that the Commission, the Council and the Parliament are jointly making decisions based on consultation, grounded in consensus, and open to public criticism? Indeed, how far is it accurate to speak at all of 'European citizens'? Nonetheless, as the Community evolves, these same citizens will be increasingly affected by its expanding legal competence. But will the accountability of the Community's institutions expand as quickly? Surveys of public opinion in the European Community already tell us that there is a 'democratic deficit' — people are not convinced that the Community's institutions are as democratic as they ought to be. Moxon-Browne suggests a number of ways this might be put right: strengthening links between the Oireachtas and the European Parliament; creating a European Senate; or simply giving the European Parliament more legislative power. Whatever choices are made, he argues that Ireland's role in the Community's decision-making process will be affected; so all the options are worth discussing.

Patrick Keatinge examines the 'foreign relations of the union', an aspect of the Inter Governmental Conference which is receiving particular attention because of the many radical changes in international politics. This has brought the existing procedures for the coordination of national foreign policies — the process of European Political Cooperation (EPC) — closer to the main elements of EC integration, and raises the question of whether a truly common foreign policy is possible. The insistence by most member states that 'security' issues be treated more fully in this context requires a more precise definition of what is at stake. In the past this has impinged on one of the major Irish reservations about EC membership, the question of the compatibility between neutrality (itself a policy which merits a closer appraisal) and the possibility of some form of collective defence. Since the orthodoxies of the cold war era are in the throes of transition elsewhere in the international system, it can hardly be expected that Irish foreign policy will not be affected to some degree.

Although the Inter Governmental Conference is not tackling directly the problems related to a further enlargement of the EC, this is probably the most significant background factor, and is certain to become the next major item on the Community's political agenda. Tony Brown reviews the economic and political factors which have led five countries so far to apply for membership, and which have produced forecasts of an expansion of the Community to as many as twenty five member states. The potential applicants are assessed in terms of their preparedness to take on the responsibilities of EC membership. The main issues arising from prospective enlargement are discussed, in particular the major institutional changes needed if the Community is to retain its impetus, and the political and structural problems which must be confronted. Options are considered and it is suggested that the Community is likely to choose the course of continued integration with sequential enlargement, starting with Austria whose application has met with a broadly favourable opinion from the Commission.

One theme runs through all the contributions — the European Community is an increasingly salient element in the political life of all European societies, whether members or not. Partly this is a consequence of economic developments (see Rory O'Donnell (ed.), 'Monetary Union' in the series *Studies in European Union,* IEA, 1991), but it also derives from the most important changes in the patterns of political power and influence in Europe identified above. Thus, the political union which emerges from the Inter Governmental Conference over the coming months, however incomplete or evolutionary in its approach, will have to exist in circumstances which are revolutionary. It is not easy to predict the consequences for this country with any precision, but readers interested in a general appraisal should consult the separate paper by Paul Gillespie and Rodney Rice, 'Political Union' in the series *Implications for Ireland,* IEA, 1991.

The authors are indebted to the Working Group on Political Union, organised by the Institute of European Affairs. Information, encouragement, criticism and even copy-editing were provided by many members. The Dublin Offices of the EC Commission and the European Parliament, and the Secretariat of the Irish Council of the European Movement, were most helpful in providing documentation. The assistance received from those for whom these negotiations are not a matter of academic interest, but who must in the end define and defend Ireland's interests, was particularly appreciated. Odran Reid, Jean Barker, Victor McBrien and Dominic O'Toole ensured that a tight publication schedule was successfully met. The responsibility for errors of fact and for the views expressed in the papers is entirely that of the authors.

Patrick Keatinge

THE GOVERNANCE OF THE UNION

Brigid Laffan

EXECUTIVE SUMMARY

1. Introduction

The European Community (EC) emerged as the core regional organisation in Europe at the end of the 1980s. The success of the single market programme intensified pressures for a deepening of integration among the existing twelve member states. Economic and Monetary Union (EMU) emerged on the Community's agenda as a major issue for the 1990s. Turbulence in the international system arising from the collapse of communism in East/Central Europe and the Gulf War changed the Community's external environment in a very fundamental way. German unification and the need to accommodate the emerging democracies in the former eastern bloc led to renewed interest in the Community's international role and its institutional capacity. On 14 December, 1990, two Inter Governmental Conferences (IGCs) were convened to negotiate a new Treaty on economic and monetary union and political union.

The purpose of this paper is to examine issues arising at the political union negotiations that have a bearing on the governance of the Union, notably political authority and the policy scope of the Community. In the west European tradition of liberal democracy, the acceptance of political authority stems from the accountability of the executive to parliament. A weakness of political authority can undermine the legitimacy of a political system if the system cannot deliver what is expected by the citizenry and a weakness of legitimacy can undermine political authority. In the Community both political authority and legitimacy are highly diffuse.

2. The Institutional Debate of the 1970s and 1980s

Part two of the paper examines the institutional debate of the 1970s and 1980s because questions concerning the locus of policy competence and the Community's institutional balance have been central to the evolution of the Community. Institutional questions are part of the agenda whenever there is a debate on what the Community ought to do. The main tension has been between those advocating increased powers for the supranational elements of the policy process and those wishing to strengthen its intergovernmental characteristics. During the 1970s and early 1980s, the Community's decision-making system was characterised by institutional inertia. Successive enlargements and recession created a turbulent environment for the Community.

3. The Single Act Inheritance

Part three of the paper examines the moulding of a successive package that led to the signing of the Single European Act (SEA), the institutional provisions of the Act, and the impact of the Single Act in practice. The paper concludes that the Single Act has had an important influence on law making in the Community. The increased use of majority voting has increased the efficiency of the decision-making system and the cooperation procedure has altered the institutional balance in the European Parliament's (EP) favour. This section draws attention to the gradual and evolutionary nature of institutional and constitutional change in the Community. There has never been a root and branch overhaul of the Community's political system. The paper suggests that such disjointed incrementalism may not be sufficient to steer the Community through the 1990s because of the need to respond to the new Europe, the prospect of further enlargements and the creation of an economic and monetary union. The question of how to provide a system of government that has sufficient capacity, political authority and legitimacy is not being confronted openly.

4. The Inter Governmental Conferences: Proposals for Change

This section addresses the substantive issues that have arisen at the Inter Governmental Conference, namely, the policy scope of the Union, subsidiarity and a hierarchy of norms, and the efficiency and effectiveness of the institutions. The European Council meeting in Luxembourg in June 1991 took stock of the negotiations to date and concluded that the Draft Treaty of the Union prepared by the out-going Luxembourg Presidency provided the basis for the continuation of the negotiations. This Treaty defines political union on the basis of three pillars: the original Treaties; provisions on judicial cooperation; and provisions on a common foreign and security policy. The fourth pillar of European Union is economic and monetary union. This has given rise to considerable conflict because those states favouring a 'maximalist' outcome from the negotiations want a unified system of policy making under the traditional Community method of the original Treaties. In an attempt to satisfy them, the Draft Treaty includes a reference to "a Union with a federal goal". This in turn drew a strong reaction from the UK; the British Foreign Secretary, indicated that the UK would not sign a treaty that included the word federal. The political storm raised by the inclusion of a reference to federalism in the preamble to the Treaty shows just how difficult it is to confront the question of government in the Community.

An expansion of the Community's policy scope is being actively negotiated at the conference; a total of 21 different policy areas are listed in the proposed Article 3 of the Luxembourg Draft Treaty and a revision of Article 235. Of particular note is the proposed strengthening of the Treaty basis on matters of social policy, economic and social cohesion, R&D and the environment. Proposed new policy areas include education, health, consumer affairs and energy. The Draft Treaty gives separate treatment to judicial cooperation. The long list of policy competences listed in the Draft Treaty may not augur well for policy integration in some respects. There is a real possibility that the

Community's policy reach will extend beyond the capacity of its institutions to deliver effective policies and beyond the capacity of the member states to implement Community policies. Just how much policy competence the Community should wield is a key issue encapsulated in the debate about subsidiarity.

The principle of subsidiarity has acquired a central place in the debate about constitutional reform. Consideration of subsidiarity in the Community concerns the distribution of public authority among different levels of government, a federalist principle. It is generally understood to mean that policy competence and public authority should be exercised at the lowest effective level. Subsidiarity is seen as having a role in placating those who fear an overly powerful Community, in dealing with the impact of integration on government below the level of central government and as a means of preventing the Community's policy process from becoming overloaded.

Subsidiarity is an issue in the political union negotiations and those on economic and monetary union. The main problem is to arrive at a definition of the concept and to agree where the principle should be included in the new Treaty. The Luxembourg Draft Treaty provides for a new Article 3 which establishes that the Community will take action in accordance with the principle of subsidiarity. In its present format, the reference to subsidiarity is justiciable; in other words, Community institutions or a member state could bring cases to the European Court of Justice (ECJ) to test issues relating to policy competence. This means that judicial review will become an even more important aspect of the Community in the future. Subsidiarity may channel the debate on policy competence in the Community but it cannot take the politics out of the relationship between the Community and the member states.

The debate about the efficiency and effectiveness of Community institutions is part of a continuous debate about the role and functions of each institution and the institutional balance. An extension of majority voting is the central issue in relation to the Council. The starting point of the Conference is whether or not majority voting should become the norm, reserving unanimity for constitutional issues. Majority voting would thus be extended to sensitive issues in the social domain, environmental policy, taxation, and R&D. The question of voting on judicial cooperation and foreign policy is particularly delicate. In practice, the Inter Governmental Conference is treating majority voting on a case by case basis.

Three issues dominate discussions on the role of the Commission, namely its size, its method of appointment, and exercise of delegated powers. The idea of reducing the size of the Commission to one Commissioner per member state has considerable support, (and would allow for new member states). Moreover, the Commission wants more freedom in the execution of policy from the constraints of regulatory committees of national civil servants imposed by the Council.

The most contentious issue relates to the powers of the Parliament and the perennial issue of democratic legitimacy within the Community. The European Parliament is looking for the power of co-decision with the Council in the legislative domain. The Luxembourg Draft Treaty makes provision for a limited form of co-decision. The proposed procedure follows the lines of the existing cooperation procedure until the Council's second reading; under the new system provision is made for a process of conciliation between Council and Parliament and the Parliament is given the right to reject the final text in the absence of agreement.

The paper addresses the political consequences of an economic and monetary union because economic management is at the heart of contemporary government. EMU touches both on the substance of public policy making and the process of decision making. It involves a further pooling of sovereignty between the member states. The paper points out that although a parallelism is envisaged between economic union and monetary union, agreement on the latter is being more readily achieved. The broad outline of the monetary institution, a European system of central banks, has been agreed to. There remain difficult issues relating to the relationship between the monetary institution and the Council, the Monetary Committee, the Commission and the Parliament. Furthermore, there is the wider issue of macroeconomic management in EMU. It appears from the negotiating documents, that apart from monetary policy, the preferred model of EMU is characterised by a high degree of decentralisation of economic policy making.

It is argued in the paper that the Luxembourg Draft Treaty does not provide a centre of economic government; its institutional blueprint is based very much on existing institutions, notably the European Council and the EcoFin. The paper questions whether or not such an intergovernmental system will have the capacity to respond effectively to as yet unknown external shocks. There is also concern that there will not be an authoritative executive capable of balancing an independent monetary institution, with its limited but clear goal of price stability.

The paper predicts that the system of budgetary discipline, even if it is voluntary, will have a profound impact on domestic budgetary politics, cabinet government and relations between the social partners. Peer group pressures will enter the 'rules of the game' and the 'norms of behaviour' at national level. If a government is likely to run an excessive budget deficit, it will have to reduce expenditure or raise taxes, the stuff of contemporary politics.

5. Prospects and Options

The paper concludes that there is general convergence at the Inter Governmental Conference on an extension of the Community's policy scope and a strengthening of the Treaty basis for existing policies, that subsidiarity should be included in a substantive article of the Treaty and that there should be some extension of majority voting. Divergence persists concerning the extent of majority voting, on the timing of EMU, the nature of budgetary discipline within an economic and monetary union, the powers of the European Parliament and measures of economic and social cohesion that should accompany an economic and monetary union.

The broad outline of Ireland's policy is well established. Ireland supports an extension of the Community's policy scope provided it is given adequate and appropriate means. There is an acceptance of subsidiarity although without enthusiasm for judicial review and a certain fear of 'government by judges'. A strengthening of Treaty provisions on economic and social cohesion is a primary policy goal. There is a reluctance to alter the Community's institutional balance, especially if this involves strengthening the powers of Parliament. Finally, Ireland wants to avoid a stratified Community or one characterised by extensive 'variable geometry'.

The paper highlights some dilemmas for Ireland, notably the desire for an advanced form of economic integration particularly if this is accompanied by a large and redistributive Community budget. Yet such a Community implies a high degree of solidarity and advanced political integration. Ireland's policies on a common foreign and security policy and on the institutional balance are rather 'minimalist'.

The paper examines the context, issues and proposals for change in the current debate on cohesion. The paper suggests that although there is a commitment to cohesion in the Single Act and in the Communique of the Luxembourg European Council of June 1991, there are widely differing views concerning the responsibility and capacity of the Community to foster cohesion. The politics of redistribution in the Community are becoming more problematic because of the costs of German unification, the demands of the third world and the aftermath of communism in the former eastern bloc. Furthermore, there are no clearcut prescriptions for reducing regional imbalances even within national economies.

A realistic assessment of the debate on cohesion suggests that there will be a Treaty revision but that there is no prospect of automatic regional transfers on a scale that characterises advanced federations. The Community does not have the degree of political cohesion required for this, nor does it require it given its present stage of evolution. The issue will re-surface when the Community attempts to move to the second and final stages of EMU. Detailed consideration must now be given in Ireland to the kinds of policy instruments that are in Ireland's interest. An extension of the existing structural funds will not achieve the goal of economic and social cohesion in the Community.

Ireland has an interest in ensuring that the Community's legislative process can deliver decisions within a reasonable time period. It is not in Ireland's interest that the Community return to the stagnation of the early 1980s. A primary goal of Irish policy makers is also to protect the rights of small states in the system; protecting the role of the Commission in the policy-making process is a manifestation of this. However, on increased powers for the Parliament, Ireland is at the 'minimalist' end of the spectrum. While co-decision is not opposed in principle, Irish policy makers will only endorse the most limited changes to the institutional balance. There are clear fears that Irish interests would not be adequately protected in a system characterised by co-decision. This reflects a political culture that gives primacy to the executive branch of government and to a relatively weak parliamentary tradition. Yet the institutional balance is set to change and the Parliament is likely to become more important in the Community's policy process in the future. Irish political parties must adapt to this change by paying more attention to the European Parliament and European elections.

The final substantive issue raised in this paper relates to 'variable geometry'. While Ireland's European policy has never favoured a multi-speed Europe, differentiated integration is likely to become a more pronounced feature of the Community in the 1990s. Whereas the government has clearly signalled its intention to be a founder member of EMU, the attitude towards a common foreign and security policy is less clear cut. If in the 1990s, the Community develops a responsibility for 'hard security' with its integration with the Western European Union (WEU), Ireland may be faced with a choice of 'opting out' of any such arrangement to protect neutrality. However, 'variable geometry' of a permanent or semi-permanent kind would fundamentally alter the nature of the Community because it would introduce a political hierarchy in the Community. This is not in Ireland's interests.

The issues raised in this paper will remain part of the Community agenda for the 1990s. It is clear that the current Inter Governmental Conferences will not provide a sufficiently tight set of policy, institutional and constitutional rules for the Community as it attempts to finalise arrangements for EMU and as foreign and security policy are revisited in 1996 or soon afterwards. But it is unlikely to be possible for the Community in the next round of negotiations to continue to adopt an incremental and orthodox approach to constitutional change. The question of government will have to be confronted openly if the Community is to have the capacity to respond to the challenges it now faces.

1. INTRODUCTION

Scope and Objectives of the Paper

The central theme of this paper is the governance of the Union. Its purpose is to address issues concerning the political authority and policy scope of the European Community in the light of the political union negotiations. The authority of governments rests on the twin pillars of capacity and legitimacy. The notion of governmental capacity relates to the effectiveness of institutions, the possession of adequate policy instruments and budgetary resources, the ability to promulgate, implement and enforce laws and to administer policies. Political authority is rendered legitimate by representative parliaments, constitutional norms and judicial accountability through the courts.

In the west European tradition of liberal democracy, the rightness of political authority stems from the accountability of the executive to parliament. It is that direct link between the political authority of government and parliament that underpins the legitimacy of our political systems. A weakness of political authority can undermine the legitimacy of a polity if the system does not deliver what is expected by the citizenry and likewise a weakness of legitimacy can undermine political authority. There is therefore a direct link between the substance of this paper and the paper on the political legitimacy of the Union (see Edward Moxon-Browne's *The Legitimacy of the Union,* the following paper in this book). Many of the arguments in this paper are based on the discussion of the Community's institutional system found in *An Overview of the Community's Institutional System,* the last paper in this book.

The remainder of the paper has four sections. Section two examines the institutional debates of the 1970s and 1980s since the issues falling within the terms of this paper have been current since the foundation of the Community. Section three assesses the impact of the Single Act on the Community's legislative process and policy scope. Section four gives detailed examination to the substances of the negotiations, notably the policy scope of the Union, subsidiarity, the efficiency and effectiveness of the Community's institutions, and about the political implications of an economic and monetary union. EMU raises questions about the locus of decision making on monetary, budgetary and other economic policies. This section includes some analysis of the positions of the various states and Community institutions as the negotiations unfold. Finally, section five assesses the main issues for Ireland and attempts to look into the crystal ball.

2. THE INSTITUTIONAL DEBATE OF THE 1970s AND 1980s

Institutions have played an important role in the dynamics of integration from the outset. Questions concerning the locus of policy competence and institutional balance at Community level and between the national and Community levels have been central to the debate on the evolution of the European Community as a political system. According to Morgan, "questions of how it ought to do things have always been inseparable from the question of what things it ought do do". (Morgan, 1989). Put simply, each time the Community attempts to alter its policy competence and deepen the level of integration, institutional questions become part of the negotiating agenda. The main tension in a succession of institutional debates has been between the advocates of increased powers for the supranational elements of the policy process, notably the Commission and the Parliament, and those political forces favouring a strengthening of the intergovernmental attributes of the policy process.

Academic writing on the Community from the 'veto' crisis onwards drew attention to the fact that the institutional blueprint of the Rome Treaties, at the centre of which was the Council–Commission dialogue, had been altered. Community level institutions suffered from a weakness both of authority and legitimacy. A series of official reports focused on institutional issues: the Vedel Report of 1972 examined the powers of the parliament and the question of legitimacy; the Tindemans Report on European Union (1975) dealt both with institutional questions and the Community's policy objectives; the Spierenburg Report (1979) analysed the Commission and the report of the Three Wise Men of the same year extended the analysis to the Community's other institutions. The Genscher–Colombo plan of 1982 also made suggestions about the institutional balance. There is thus a long line of reports which ignore proposals on institutional change in the Community. Yet none of these reports resulted in fundamental modifications to the Treaties.

The academic literature on the Community and the official reports listed above drew attention to weaknesses in the Community's institutional capacity. Its decision-making process was characterised by institutional inertia, *'lourdeur'*, time-consuming negotiations leading at best to agreements based on the lowest common denominator or no agreement at all. If by the beginning of the 1980s the Community was becoming less relevant to the problems facing the member states, this is not to say that all of the Community's problems stemmed from institutional inertia: recession and enlargement created a turbulent environment for the Community.

The practice of searching for unanimity in the Council on almost all issues allowed individual member states to block agreement or to water down the content of proposed laws. The 'veto' led to stagnation in the Council and timidity in the Commission. The growing importance of Coreper and the Presidency of the Council strengthened the intergovernmental character of the Community. The creation of the European Council in 1975 and the intergovernmental nature of European Political Cooperation (EPC) lent further weight to an intergovernmental portrayal of the Community. It is difficult to disagree with the conclusion of the report on the Institutions (Report of the Three Wise Men) that "the balance of power between the Commission and the Council has shifted more and more in the latter's favour and the Commission has lost much of its independent prestige" (Three Wise Men, 1979, p. 64). The Commission itself in 1982 acknowledged that its "political function has been heavily compromised as regards its involvement in the legislative process" (Commission, EC Bulletin, Supplement, 3/82, p. 8).

Moreover, the Commission suffered from a number of internal weaknesses and external constraints arising from the way in which the Community's policy process evolved. As early as 1970, Coombes concluded that the Commission had come to "exercise purely, delegated, administrative functions", because it had become less creative and had compromised its right of initiative (Coombes, 1970, p. 236). Internally, the Commission had too many basic administrative units with a dearth of horizontal linkages among directorates generals. Lines of communication in the Commission were largely vertical and policy coordination was weak or entirely absent. The Spierenburg Report argued that the Commission itself was too large. It advocated one Commissioner per member state (Spierenburg Report, 1979).

Fragmentation in the Commission was symptomatic of an absence of coherence, purpose and direction in the Community's wider political system. *Ad hoc* schemes or solutions were concocted to deal with what were more fundamental problems. The continuous saga of the UK budgetary problem highlighted this. In the early 1980s, the Community lacked the 'big idea', something that would serve to give coherence and political capacity to the system as a whole. An issue of legitimacy arose as the Parliament sought to build on the democratic credentials of its election.

The image of institutional inertia portrayed so far should not blind us to a number of incremental changes in the 1970s. European Political Cooperation, which began with modest ambitions in 1970, proved remarkably robust. By the end of the decade EPC had become a corner-stone of the member states' foreign policies. The establishment of the European Council in 1975 brought the most senior national office holders regularly into the heart of EC politics (see Patrick Keatinge's *The Foreign Relations of the Union,* the third paper in this book). The prestige and authority of the heads of government would in time help restore political direction to the Community. The creation of the European Monetary System (EMS) in 1979 began the slow process of creating a regional currency bloc and a system of joint decision making on monetary matters. The first elections to the Parliament in that same year provided the Community with an institution that had a direct democratic mandate from European citizens rather than from governments and parliaments. These incremental changes paved the way for the Single Act, the first major modification of the original Treaties.

3. THE SINGLE ACT INHERITANCE

(i) The Creation of a Package

Because the Community is again embarking on a process of Treaty reform, it is important to highlight the core issues that arose in the conference that led to the Single Act, and the manner of their resolution. The process of Treaty reform in the 1980s began with the Fontainebleau European Council in 1984 when a decision was taken to establish the Dooge Committee composed of the personal representatives of the heads of government. The Committee was given the task of making "suggestions for the improvement of the operation of European cooperation in both the Community field and that of political, or any other, cooperation" (Keatinge and Murphy, 1987, p. 217). The report of the Ad Hoc Committee might have joined the countless other neglected reports on the development of the Community had Mr. Craxi, the Italian Prime Minister, not called a vote on the convening of an Inter Governmental Conference (IGC) at the Milan European Council in June 1985. By seven votes to three (UK, Denmark and Greece), the European Council agreed to begin the formal process of Treaty negotiations. The outcome of this process was the Single European Act signed in 1986 and ratified by all states by 1987.

The catalyst for successful Treaty change was agreement on the central importance of the 1992 Programme. The completion of the single market gave the Community its 'big idea' for the latter half of the 1980s. The central importance of the programme was guaranteed because of Western Europe's search for renewed competitiveness in an increasingly globalised world economy. A convergence of economic policy around the principles of de-regulation and market liberalisation in the major Community states created the domestic conditions for consensus on the 1992 Programme. The completion of the single market programme in turn required institutional changes. Thus a synergy was created between policy issues and institutional capacity. A further link was established between the goal of market liberalisation and the politics of redistribution. A commitment to economic and social cohesion was a necessary complement to the 1992 Programme so as to foster a favourable response from the Community's peripheral countries.

Once the Inter Governmental Conference began, the member states and the Commission entered a process of formal negotiations. The key players in the process of bargaining were France, the Federal Republic of Germany and the United Kingdom (Moravcsik, 1990). The Benelux and Italy tended to favour major political initiatives that are jointly endorsed by the Franco–Germany axis. The UK was persuaded to go along with the negotiations despite its initial hostility for fear of exclusion and because it favoured the 1992 Programme. The smaller peripheral states were content with the provisions on economic and social cohesion.

The history of the Community suggests that the building of a European Union will continue to be a gradual and evolutionary process characterised by incremental changes interspersed with periodic rounds of constitutional bargaining which establish the framework of future developments. What is striking about the current phase of integration is that formal Treaty bargaining among the member states is taking place so soon after the Single Act round of negotiations. There has never been a root and branch overhaul of the government of the Community. Each change is the outcome of tortuous negotiations leading to a package deal that is acceptable to all of the participants. Such package deals are inevitably somewhat ambiguous compromises between the competing claims and interests of the member state and Community institutions. The present negotiations on political union involve a similar process of bargaining and compromise out of which will emerge as yet another series of intergovernmental bargains moulded into a package deal, covering both the negotiations on political union and those on economic and monetary union. The resultant Treaty must at least allow the larger states to claim that their interests were protected; it is more difficult for the smaller member states to hold out in negotiations that are of major interest to the other partners.

Although there has never been a root and branch overhaul of the Community's institutional system and policy scope, disjointed incrementalism may not be sufficient to see the Community through the turbulent waters of the 1990s. Orthodox or traditional responses to institutional matters may not be sufficient to deal with the needs of a new Europe, the prospect of a succession of enlargements and the creation of an economic and monetary union. In the longer term, the question of how to provide a system of government that has sufficient capacity, political authority and legitimacy at Community level must be confronted in an overt fashion. The governance of the Union needs to be debated in a more transparent manner than is possible with terms like 'unicity' and 'subsidiarity' which are dealt with below.

(ii) Institutional Provisions of the Single Act

The Single Act made provision for a series of changes to the Community's institutional landscape and the legislative process. First, the Single Act allowed for an extension of the use of qualified majority voting in Council on matters relating to the single market. A new Article 100A provided for majority voting for the adoption of "measures for the approximation of the provisions laid down by law, regulation or administrative action in member states on matters which have as their object the establishment and functioning of the single market" (SEA, Article 100A). Article 100A has a very wide remit including the single market aspects of the free movement of goods, capital and services. A number of important areas of legislation remain, however, under the unanimity principle, notably indirect taxation, free movement of persons and the rights and interests of employed persons. Second, the Single Act altered the legislative role of the European Parliament and its powers in ratifying international agreements. A cooperation procedure was introduced to complement the existing consultation procedure. Under the cooperation procedure, which covers such fields as the single market, social policy, economic and social cohesion and technological research and development, Parliament in effect acquired a second reading of the Council's common position. Put simply, Parliament's views carry greater weight than heretofore. The Parliament was also given a role in assenting to the accession of new member states and association agreements. This significantly increased its powers concerning the Community's external policy.

Third, the Single Act made provision for an extension of the Commission's implementing or delegated powers. The Rome Treaty allowed for the delegation of implementing powers from the Council to the Commission but did not establish general principles about the process of delegation. The Single Act attempted to structure the myriad procedures and committees that characterised the Commission's role in implementation.

Fourth, the Act made provision for the establishment of a European Court of First Instance to alleviate the European Court of Justice's case load. The new court can hear cases brought by 'natural or legal persons' but cannot hear cases brought by the EC institutions, the member states and cases under Article 117 on preliminary rulings. The Court of First Instance was intended to hear staff cases and cases in the field of competition policy. Finally, the Single Act formally recognised the name 'European Parliament', mentions the European Council and codified the institutional basis of European Political Cooperation.

(iii) Impact of the Single Act in Practice

The provisions of the Single Act and its dynamic impact on the Community have had a far greater influence on the Community's institutional landscape than anticipated by commentators and academics at the outset. The Act, hailed as a "modest document" by the then British Prime Minister, Margaret Thatcher, was discounted as "an ill-fated experiment" by Pierre Pescatore, a retired judge at the European Court of Justice (Ehlermann, 1987, p. 362). In practice, the Community's institutions began to alter their approach to the policy process even before the first of July 1987 when the Act was formally ratified. The Commission adopted a provisional *vade mecum* in 1986 setting out new instructions to Commission officials for dealing with the other institutions. The two central themes in the document were the need to protect the Commission's right of initiative and to promote qualified majority voting in the Council. The Council's internal rules of procedure were formally altered in July 1987 to take account of the voting provisions of the Act. Under the new procedures, the President of the Council retains the right to call a vote on his own initiative and is obliged to do so at the request of the representative of any member states or the Commission provided there is a simple majority of the member states in favour of a vote. The European Parliament amended it rules of procedure to take account of the cooperation procedure. In an attempt to bring order to the legislative process, procedures for a legislative timetable involving the three institutions were put in place.

The Council

The greater use of majority voting has had a profound impact on the Council and, as a result, on the wider institutional system. First, the provisions on voting are being used. Even before the Single Act came into operation, the Council began to use qualified majority voting on a routine basis. Voting is now more frequent on matters relating to the single market, the Common Agricultural Policy (CAP), the Budget and the Community's external trade policy. It is difficult to get precise statistics on the number of votes taken because the Council conducts its business in secret. Moreover, formal voting statistics would not tell the whole story. A reply to a parliamentary question on voting argued that:

> The difficulty in providing statistics is related to the way in which votes are taken in the Council. On many occasions when a Member State sees that a vote will not be to its advantage, it joins the consensus rather than ask for a vote which would not alter the situation. (EP, question No. 83, Verbatim report, 13 June, 1990).

In other words, once a majority exists in the Council there may be no need to resort to a vote. Sometimes votes are taken only to enable a minister to defend himself at national level.

Second, the provisions on majority voting have led to an acceleration of decision making within the Council. Ehlermann has drawn attention to the speed of decision making in the post-Single Act environment (see Table 1). Decisions on technical standards that previously took up to 46 months are being accomplished in half that time following the Single Act. The new approach to standard setting based on 'mutual recognition' has also contributed to the acceleration of decision making (Ehlermann, 1990, p. 138). The psychological environment within which national negotiators now operate has altered 'the rules of the game' and 'norms of behaviour' in Council. Representatives of the member states must now decide at an early stage of the negotiations whether they wish to form a 'qualified majority' or alternatively be part of a 'blocking minority'. National negotiating stances must be prepared with greater speed then heretofore and with greater attention to the positions of other member states. Coalition building is even more important than before.

TABLE 1: Time Elapsed Between Referral of a Guideline to the Council and its Adoption — Before and After the Single European Act Went into Effect.

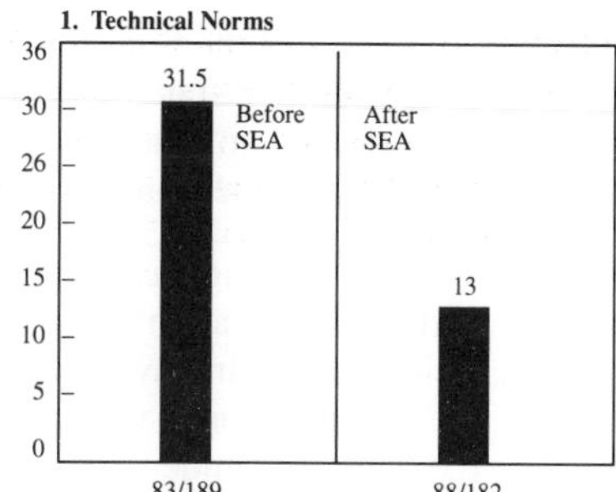

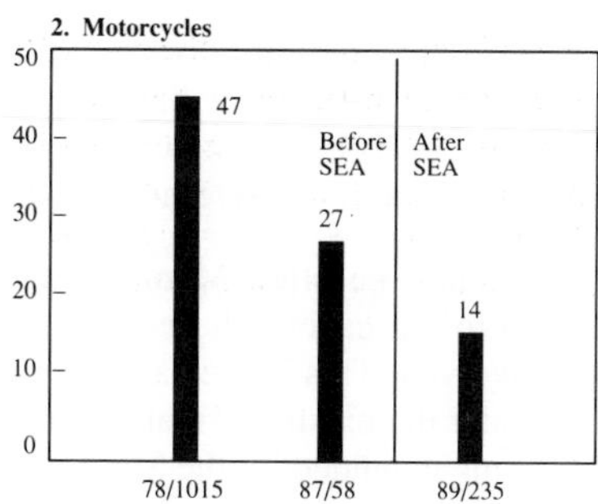

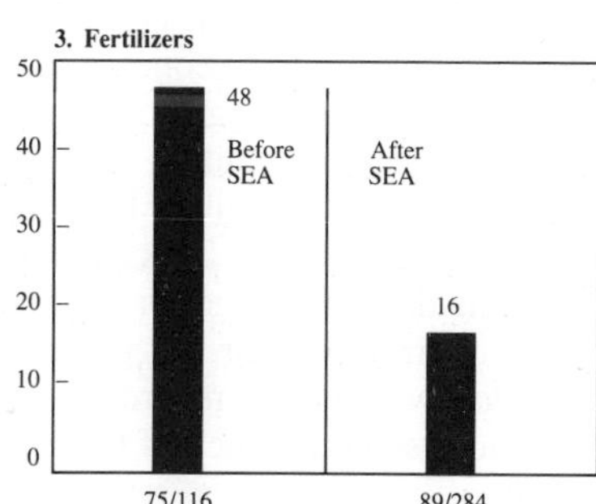

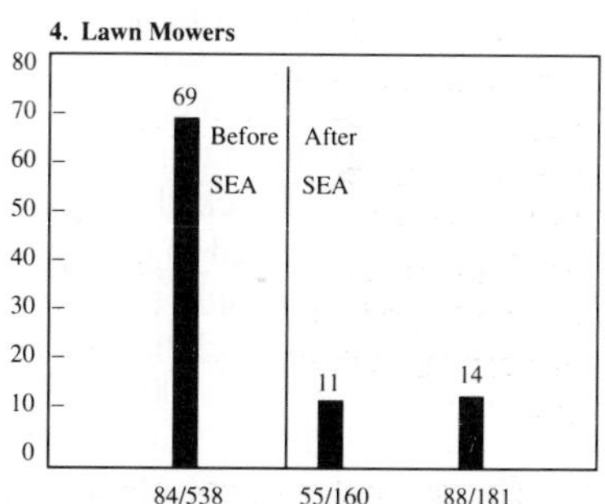

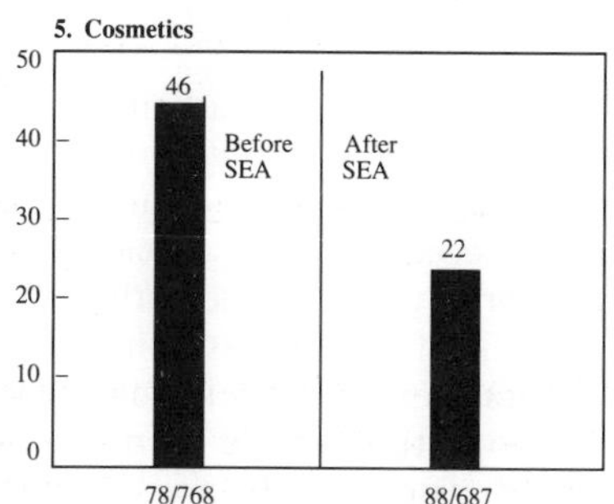

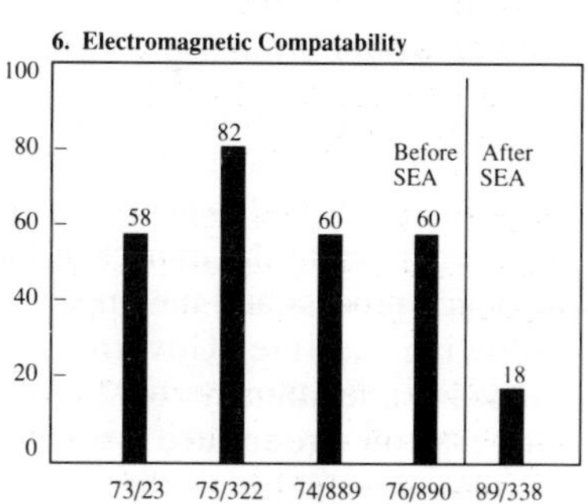

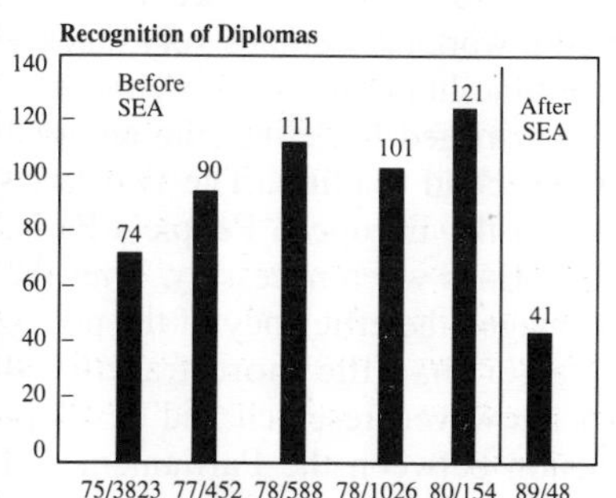

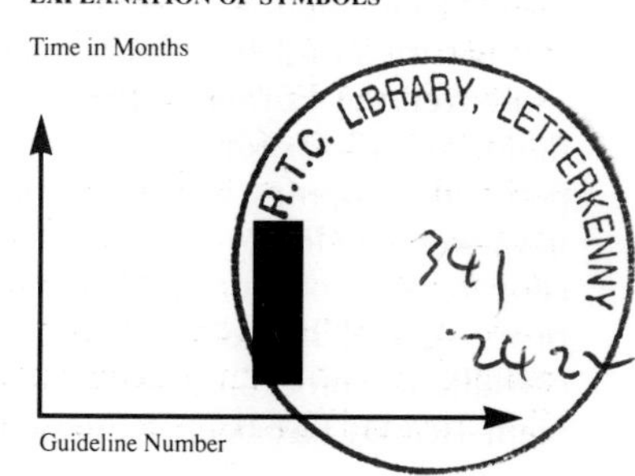

Ehlermann: *Aussenpolitik*, 11/90.

Third, the credibility of the 'veto' has been damaged. Critics of the Single Act argued that because it had not abolished the veto, the member states would continue to block Council agreement. The view that the veto had not altered was shared by the Irish government which argued in its 1986 White Paper that:

> Ireland like other Member States will continue to be entitled to invoke the 'veto' in cases where we consider that an important national interest is involved. This is the case both in areas where majority voting already applies under the existing Treaties, and in areas to which qualified majority voting is being extended by the Single Act. (The SEA: An Explanatory Guide, 1986).

In practice, the new 'rules of the game' in the Council make it difficult if not impossible for a delegation to invoke the Luxembourg compromise concerning a matter that can be taken under qualified majority voting. Negotiators are becoming accustomed to losing from time to time. To date, no qualified majority decision has been blocked because of a 'vital national interest'. Neither have the member states resorted to the 'let-out' clause under Article 100A4. This allowed a member state "to apply national provisions on grounds of major needs referred to in Article 36, or relating to protection of the environment or the working environment" (Article 100A4, SEA). This provision was widely regarded as a major loop-hole in the Single Act. All in all, the increased efficiency of Council has had an impact on the other institutions.

The European Parliament

Detailed considerations of the Single Act's provisions on the Parliament are contained in Edward Moxon-Browne's *The Legitimacy of the Union*, the following paper in this book. However, it is necessary here to make a number of points concerning the impact of the cooperation procedure on the efficiency of the policy process and the impact of Council majority voting on the Parliament. Following the Inter Governmental Conference of 1985, it was sometimes claimed that legitimacy could be enhanced only at the expense of efficiency; the cooperation procedure was regarded as a potential source of delay, a complicating factor in the search for increased efficiency. In practice, the European Parliament, although disappointed with the procedure, decided from the outset to attempt to make it work. It altered it working methods very quickly and has tried to deliver its opinions within the time limit laid down by the Act. Moreover, the European Parliament has often managed to deliver the required majorities (260) for amendments during the second reading. The two large political groupings in the EP, the Socialists and the European People's Party, have worked closely to secure the required majorities when necessary. Thus the cooperation procedure has by and large not damaged the efficiency of the policy process, and indeed it has tended to be faster than the more traditional consultation procedure of the Rome Treaties. However, research and development (R&D) has been an area of great tension between the Parliament and

Council since the Single Act; a host of specific research programmes have been blocked for a number of years in a continuing conflict about budgetary resources, the content of the programmes and the Commission's implementing powers. Such protracted negotiations colour the attitudes of the negotiators at the Inter Governmental Conference.

The 'clean car' directive on fuel emissions from small cars is however a useful example of Parliament's power under the cooperation procedure. Parliament proposed a series of amendments to Council's 'common position' for more stringent environmental protection standards. The Commission agreed with the proposed amendments and incorporated them in its proposal to Council. The Council would have required unanimity to have persisted with its original 'common position'. However, a number of member states, notably Denmark, the Netherlands and Germany supported the Parliament's amendments. The Parliament has thus greatly increased its potential influence in the policy process.

The Commission

The Single Act did not alter the Commission's powers in any way although it made provision for a streamlining of the committees that had multiplied as Council sought to supervise the Commission's exercise of its executive powers. Of more significance in fact have been the spill-over effect of changes in the Council. Given that the Council/Commission tandem is at the core of policy making in the Community, procedural and behavioural changes in the Council have a direct impact on the Commission. The Commission no longer needs to seek consensus on many policy areas, since all it requires is a majority in Council. It can thus alter its initial proposals to get the required majority. The Secretary General of the Commission works very closely with his counterpart in the Council to manage the flow of business through the Council.

The status and role of the Commission has also been transformed by the Commission President, Jacques Delors. Not since Walter Hallstein in the 1960s has the Commission played such an important role in the dynamics of integration. When Delors took over as President in 1985, he immediately looked for the 'big idea' that would relaunch the Community. Delors decided to opt for the 1992 Programme. This allowed him to build on the work of Commissioner Davignon who had identified Europe's lack of competitiveness as a major impediment to sustained industrial recovery. After the ratification of the Single Act, the Delors plan on budgetary and policy reform did much to ensure that the aspirations of the Act were credible. Not content with the completion of the single market, Delors is a major proponent of deepening the Community and, in particular, of economic and monetary union. Under Delors the Commission has reasserted its political role in the Community. It now exercises a critical role in determining the details of the legislative agenda and has begun to play an increasingly important role in international politics. The decision of the group of

24 in July 1989 to give the Commission responsibility for coordinating aid under the PHARE programme to Poland and Hungary is testimony to the growing international role of the Commission. Delors has also managed to assert the role of the Commission at the European Council, especially on matters where the Commission has a Treaty mandate.

However, the Commission's experience of 'comitology' since the Single Act has not lived up to its expectations of increased executive powers. The Council adopted a decision in July 1987 outlining the framework for committees established to oversee the Commission's executive powers. Under Article 145, the Council has the right to impose "certain requirements in respect to the exercise of these powers" (Article 10, SEA). The 1987 decision makes provision for four types of committees:

- advisory committees
- management committees
- regulatory committees
- safeguard committees

(Official Journal, L197/34, 18 July, 1987).

The main distinction between the different committees is the degree of control exercised by national civil servants. The advisory committee formula allows the Commission to consult with the representatives of the member states before taking a decision. The name of the committee is thus self-explanatory. Management committees allow national officials to block a Commission proposal by a qualified majority. In these cases the matter is referred to the Council. Regulatory committees involve even more national control. The Commission needs a qualified majority to support its position before a decision can be taken. If the Commission fails to attain sufficient support it must make a proposal to the Council. Safeguard clauses are an instrument of trade policy. The Commission favours the widest possible use of the advisory committee formula because it gives it the greatest freedom of action. The Council finds it difficult to curb its desire to control the Commission's management functions. Table 2 gives details of the different committees established since 1987.

Table 2

Comitology

Committee	Proposed by the Commission	Adopted by the Council
Advisory	22	8
Management	1	—
Regulatory	30	37
Safeguard	1	2

Source: W. Wessels, *The Institutional Debate Revisited*, College of Europe, Bruges Conference, June 1990.

Implementing committees are a source of major tension between the Council, the Commission and Parliament.

The Court of Justice

The Court of First Instance was created in July 1988 and began to hear cases in autumn 1989. The Court has twelve members who can be called to undertake the work of an advocate general in the Court of Justice. The Court of First Instance hears cases on competition policy, staff disputes and aspects of European Coal and Steel Community (ECSC) law. Decisions of the Court of First Instance are subject to appeal on points of law to the Court of Justice itself.

Summary

The Single Act has an important influence on policy making in the Community. The increased use of qualified majority voting and the cooperation procedure have altered the decision making environment and rules. Change has not been confined to the Council and the Parliament. The Commission has managed to reassert its capacity for policy initiatives and can use its position to get agreement in the Council without waiting for full consensus. The establishment of the Court of First Instance increases the efficiency of the judicial arm of the Community. However, the institutional balance is not settled once and for all. The search for political authority and legitimacy continues at the Inter Governmental Conference.

4. THE INTER GOVERNMENTAL CONFERENCES: PROPOSALS FOR CHANGE

(i) The Negotiations

The purpose of this section is to trace the debate within the IGC with a view to establishing the issues at stake in each substantive area, namely the policy scope of the Union, subsidiarity and the hierarchy of norms, and the efficiency and effectiveness of the institutions. Each national delegation and the representatives of Community institutions bring their own concerns and interests to the negotiating table. Such concerns range from matters of principle to minor technical issues. The Presidency plays a pivotal role in steering the negotiations through the weekly meetings of ambassadors, the specialist groups and the monthly ministerial meetings. The Presidency must structure the negotiations, both substantive issues and procedural matters. The political union conference, because it did not benefit from the long lead-in time accorded to EMU, is processing a flood of papers on the Community's policy scope, the institutional balance, decision making and international relations. The Commission is an active participant in the negotiations having produced a series of papers and Draft Treaty articles on all major aspects of the negotiations. The EP, although it does not have a seat at the table, has submitted a series of reports and resolutions to the conference. Submissions from the member states consist of both discussion papers and detailed Treaty revisions.

The first phase of the negotiations ended on the15th April, 1991 with the publication by the Luxembourg Presidency of a 'Non-paper' presenting detailed proposals for Treaty changes. The purpose of the paper was to provide a focus for the final rounds of the negotiations. In other words, the analytical phase of the negotiations has ended and the process of bargaining between the competing concerns of member states and the Community institutions began. The Luxembourg Presidency subsequently presented a 'Non-paper' on economic and monetary union on 6th June and a revised version of the first political union Treaty on 18th June in preparation for the European Council meeting of 28th and 29th June. The conclusions of the Council clearly indicate that the heads of government consider the Luxembourg draft as "the basis for the continuation of negotiations, both as regards most of the principle points contained in it and the state of play at the two Conferences" (European Council Communique, 28/29 June, 1991). It is the task of the Dutch Presidency to steer the negotiations to a successful outcome for the Maastricht Council in December 1991.

(ii) The Structure of the Union

Although the final Treaty may differ considerably in detail from the text of the Luxembourg 'Non-paper', the overall structure it proposes for Political Union is likely to persist. The Luxembourg text defines political union on the basis of three pillars:

- provision amending the EEC, EURATOM and ECSC Treaties
- provisions on cooperation on judicial matters
- provisions on Foreign and Security Policy

(Luxembourg Draft Treaty on the Union, 18 June, 1991).

The fourth and final pillar, economic and monetary union, completes the European Union, at this stage of its development. Defining European Union on the basis of four pillars gave rise to considerable conflict in the Community because of its implications for decision-making rules and the institutional balance. According to the Luxembourg texts, only those areas based on the original Rome and Paris Treaties would conform to the Community method of policy making (see *An Overview of the Community's Institutional System,* the last paper in this book). Policy making on the common foreign and security policy and on judicial cooperation would continue to operate on the basis of different institutional and decision rules. The Commission has argued strongly against this approach. It favours one decision-making model, the traditional Community method. Delors has made the case for 'unicity' or a uniform policy process, and has been supported by the Netherlands and Belgium. Although the second Luxembourg paper (June 1991) persisted with the four pillars approach, it included a reference to "a new stage in the process leading gradually to a Union with a federal goal" (Article A, Luxembourg, Draft Treaty on the Union, 18 June, 1991) in an attempt to satisfy those states in the Community that found fault with the fragmented and disjointed approach in the text.

The appearance of the word federal in the text immediately brought a strong reaction from the United Kingdom government. Both the Prime Minister, John Major, and the Foreign Secretary, Douglas Hurd, indicated that the UK would not sign a Treaty that included the word 'federal'. The British reaction owes much to their political culture, traditional reticience about integration, and the unease in the Conservative party about further European integration. Of all of the member states, the UK is most attached to the symbols and rhetoric of sovereignty. A political system based on a highly centralised state and on single party government sits uneasily with the diffusion of power and the sharing of sovereignty that characterises the Community. The unwillingness of the UK government to allow the word 'federal' to appear in the Treaty shows just how difficult it is to confront the question of the future government of the Community.

(iii) The Policy Scope of the Union

The original Treaties set out in broad terms the scope of economic and policy integration. Since 1958, the policy competence of the Community has widened, albeit in a halting and tardy fashion. The Rome Treaty made provision for this in Article 235 which states:

> If action by the Community should prove necessary to attain, in the course of the operation of the common market, one of the objectives of the Community, and this Treaty has not provided the necessary powers, the Council shall, acting unanimously on a proposal from the Commission and after consulting the Assembly, take the appropriate measures. (Article 235, EEC Treaty, 1957).

The drafters of the Treaty recognised that the establishment of a common market was a dynamic process and would require an extension of the Community's policy competence. This article was limited however because it is somewhat at the margins of the Treaty and relates to the common market. Consequently the Single Act was employed to give a stronger Treaty basis to a range of policy areas in which the Community has become involved during the 1970s and 1980s, notably monetary matters, regional policy, research and development, and the environment. This process is continuing at the political union conference.

To date, the Community's policy scope has tended to expand in a gradualist, incremental manner in response to changes in socio-economic conditions, the internal dynamics of market integration and the arrival of new issues on the political agenda. However, once a group of states embarks on an advanced form of economic integration such as a full common market or an economic and monetary union, more and more policy areas come within the ambit of policy integration. In the modern mixed economy, governmental intervention affects competitive conditions in a myriad of ways through direct regulation, social policy, budgetary policy, industrial policy and so on. Thus, for example, according to the NESC report, "in order to create a genuine common market it is probably necessary to create an economic and monetary union" (NESC 88, p. 43).

Nor can states pick and choose from a menu of policy areas. The strength of the Community has always been the acceptance of the *acquis communautaire* by the member states and new entrants. Notwithstanding this, the Community has been characterised by some 'variable geometry' and graduated integration: by this is meant arrangements that allow member states to have varied transition arrangements and derogations for periods of time or to be non-participants in particular developments. The EMS system is an example of 'variable geometry' at work, and the application of Community law has always allowed for some variation across the member states to take account of different national circumstances. To date, 'variable geometry' has not, however, meant different structures for different member states.

The EMU negotiations are dealing with the nature and scope of an economic and monetary union. The debate focuses on monetary policy, budgetary policy and wider issues of economic policy. The political union conference is also dealing with policy matters. The member states and Community institutions have tabled a long list of proposed policy changes. These can be categorised under three headings. First, there are proposals concerning an extension of the current Treaty basis for a number of policy areas. Second, there are proposals aimed at establishing a Treaty basis for emerging areas of policy. Third, there is discussion of how to treat policy areas presently under the rubric of intergovernmental cooperation. European Political Cooperation (EPC) is the major example of this form of cooperation. Security cooperation in what is known as the Trevi system is the other significant area of intergovernmental cooperation.

There is a long list of proposed changes to existing areas of policy. A strengthening of the Treaty basis in relation to social policy, industrial policy, and energy policy has been advocated in a number of submissions; the Commission has put forward a text on energy because although the single market and competition policy has operated in the energy sector, there is as yet no Treaty chapter in this area; a revision of the Single Act articles on economic and social cohesion including strengthened provision for the Community Budget is on the table. A number of areas that received a Treaty basis in the Single Act are under consideration. Submissions on the environment, consumer legislation and research and development seek to enhance the Community's competence. In many cases the proposals on the existing areas of policy relate to the mode of decision making and will be dealt with in the later discussion on the efficiency of EC institutions.

Economic and social cohesion has assumed a more central role than anticipated in the political union debate. The Spanish delegation in particular has insisted upon a greatly expanded Community budget with an embryo financial compensation mechanism, akin to the German *Finanzausgleich,* for interregional transfers. Moreover, it does not want to see an expansion of the Community into new policy areas unless new funds are available. Although the Commission was for long unwilling to address economic divergence at the conference, the persistence of the Spanish demands, supported by the other peripheral countries including Ireland, has forced it into submitting a series of Treaty revisions of Article 130 of the Single Act. The proposed revisions include a five-yearly report on progress towards cohesion, explicit mention of the priority of structural adjustment, the possible reform of the Structural Funds, and a possible establishment of new instruments of structural policy. (Agence Europe, 3 April, 1991). The Conclusions of the Luxembourg European Council highlights the importance of economic and social cohesion and describes cohesion as "an integral part of the general development of the Union". (Communique, 28/29 June, 1991). This amounts to a negotiating gain for those states concerned with ensuring that the benefits of integration are evenly spread.

The Commission and the member states have endorsed a revision of Article 235 so that it extends beyond the achievement of the common market to the wider domain of the Community. The Luxembourg 'Non-paper' includes a significant revision to Article 235:

> Should it prove that attainment of one of the objectives of the Community calls for action by the Community in one of the fields covered by Articles 3 (and 3a), and this Treaty has not provided the necessary powers, the Council shall, acting unanimously on a proposal from the Commission and after receiving the assent of the European Parliament, adopt the appropriate measures while taking into account the principle of subsidiarity as defined in Article 3b. (Luxembourg Draft Treaty, 18 June, 1991, p. 107).

The articles mentioned in the revised 235 allow for a significant extension of community competence. Twenty one policy areas are listed (see Table 3).

Table 3

Union Competences in Luxembourg 'Non-paper' Article 3

Elimination of customs duties and quantitative restrictions
Single Market
Common policy in the sphere of Agriculture
Common policy in the sphere of Transport
Policy on competition
Approximation of member states' laws to the extent required for the functioning of the Common Market
A Social policy
Strengthening of Economic and Social Cohesion
An Environmental policy
Strengthening of the competitiveness of industry
A Technological and Development policy
An Energy policy
Trans-European networks
High level of health protection
Education and Training, European culture
Establishment of a European Investment Bank
Development cooperation policy
Association of overseas territories
Strengthening of Consumer protection
Civil protection measures
Measures in the sphere of Tourism

Source: Luxembourg 'Non-paper', 1991

Concerning specific areas of policy, the discussions focus on education, health, consumer affairs and culture where the Community has begun to develop policy programmes without a strong legal basis. The Commission also want to provide a legal basis for the creation of a European-wide infrastructure or, in Commission parlance, trans-European networks. This stems from a realisation that the completion of the single market will not produce its potential in economic growth if bottlenecks in road and rail transport and telecommunications are not dealt with. The member states have submitted proposals, for example, on industrial policy (Belgium), tourism (Greece), civil protection (Italy), road safety (Luxembourg), animal welfare (Germany) and development cooperation (Netherlands). Some of these policy areas will be given explicit recognition in the Treaty if they are of sufficient concern to most of the member states. Others will be deemed inappropriate for the Community. The Luxembourg text also includes revisions of the existing Treaty texts concerning social policy, economic and social cohesion, R&D, and the environment. There are new titles on energy, trans-European networks, public health, education, culture and heritage conservation, consumer protection, and development cooperation: not all of which may survive the final negotiations.

Since 1976 a practice has developed of multilateral cooperation between police forces and Justice Ministries in the Community member states, known as the Trevi system. This form of cooperation is outside the Treaties but is confined to Community member states. The Commission is not associated with the work of Trevi and the system is not subject to any form of democratic control. The scope of Trevi's work, which has grown consistently since 1976, encompasses cooperation against terrorism, drug trafficking and other serious crime, problems of public order, and the policing implications of the completion of the single market.

Responsibility for Trevi business rotates among the member states in conjunction with the Presidency of the Council. The Presidency is aided in its task by a *Piatnika,* consisting of the current presidency and the two presidencies on either side. The Trevi group meets once every six months at Ministerial level. The work of the Ministers is prepared by a group of senior officials and by four working groups. The working groups include police officers as well as officials from the Justice Ministries. The essence of Trevi is its informal confidential nature.

Since April 1989, one of the Trevi working groups has been devoting its energies to assessing the implications of the free movement of goods and people for policing and security in the post-1992 Europe. This group is working in conjunction with two other intergovernmental groups, the Mutual Assistance group 1992 (customs officials) and the Ad Hoc Working group on Immigration. The three groups report to the so-called Co-ordinators group of national officials established by the Rhodes European Council to oversee all work relating to the free movement of people within the ambit of the 1992 Programme. This group submitted the Palma report which advocates extensive intergovernmental cooperation to the Madrid European Council in June 1989. The June 1990 convention on asylum-seekers, and a further convention on external borders and visa policy which is still at the negotiating stage, reflects the intergovernmental nature of cooperation in these fields. A major impetus to developments come from the Schengen process which includes some but not all of the member states.

The Schengen process, launched in 1985 by France, Belgium, Netherlands, Germany and Luxembourg, introduces a new variant to the debate on the free movement of people. These five adjacent states signed the Schengen Agreement in June 1990 with the purpose of abolishing border formalities for their nationals ahead of 1992. Italy joined the group in December 1990 and the Iberian states have also become full members. The agreement makes provision for the 'Schengen Information System' to allow the exchange of information about suspects and crime among the national police forces. There is also provision for a limited form of 'hot pursuit', cooperation on law enforcement and visa policy. The Schengen countries have been taking the lead on matters relating to the free movement of people. Cooperation in this domain of so-called 'soft security' goes to the heart of the responsibilities of the state and is thus very sensitive.

The Luxembourg Draft Treaty (June 1991) includes a separate chapter on home affairs and judicial cooperation. The first article of this chapter gives seven areas of common concern to the member states, notably, external borders, movement of third country nationals in the EC, unauthorised immigration, illegal trafficking, customs cooperation, judicial cooperation in civil and criminal matters, and the prevention and prosecution of deliquency. The chapter essentially represent a codification of existing practice with the involvement of the Commission. The Commission shares the right of initiative with the member states. Unanimity would be required in the Council for any common action. The earlier Luxembourg 'Non-paper' opened the possibility of qualified majority voting or some form of majority for implementing measures. The European Parliament is to be informed of discussions in this field and the Presidency and Commission "shall ensure that the European Parliament's views are duly taken into account". (Luxembourg Draft Treaty, June, 1991, p. 127). This formulation is, however, unlikely to satisfy the Parliament.

The German Government submitted a paper to the Luxembourg European Council on judicial policy which paid particular attention to the problems of asylum, immigration and aliens (Annex 1, Communique, Luxembourg Council, 28/29 June, 1991). The German submission also called for the establishment of a Central European Criminal Investigation Office (EuroPol) by the end of 1992 to combat serious crime. Undoubtedly the opening of borders and the revolution in the former eastern bloc have brought internal affairs and judicial cooperation into the mainstream of Community politics (see Patrick Keatinge's *The Foreign Relations of the Union,* Section 5, Security Policy: The Agenda of 'Soft Security').

The long list of policy competences listed in the Luxembourg Draft Treaty does not augur well for a highly focused approach to policy integration. There is a real possibility that the Community's policy reach will extend beyond the capacity of its institutions to deliver effective policies and beyond the capacity for effective implementation at national level. An overloaded administrative and policy-making system does little for the Community's political authority. Just how much policy competence the Community should wield is the subject of a debate on the principle of subsidiarity.

(iv) Subsidiarity

The concept of subsidiarity has become central to the debate about policy integration. Although subsidiarity has surfaced in the Community heretofore, notably in the Commission's submission to Tindemans in 1975 on European Union, it is only in the post-Single Act environment that subsidiarity has acquired such a central place in the debate about constitutional reform.

Although the notion of subsidiarity was used by Aristotle and Thomas Aquinas, amongst others, its usage this century stems from Catholic social teaching. The papal encyclical, *Quadragesimo Anno* of 1931, scripted by Pope Pius XI, endows subsidiarity with a central place in the relationship between society and public authority. A central theme in the encyclical is that the state should only assume tasks that smaller social groups such as the family or civil associations cannot carry out. The essence of the principle was to restrict the reach of the state particularly in matters of social policy. In Catholic social teaching, subsidiarity was a socio-political term rather than a constitutional principle. (Wallace and Wilke, 1990, p. 5).

Why the Constitutional Debate?

There are three related reasons for the recent interest in subsidiarity as a guide for the distribution of competences between Community level and member states. First, the Community has amassed significant policy powers as a result of the Single Act and is set to amass even greater powers in an EMU. This is therefore an appropriate time to seek guiding principles about the Community's future policy reach. The debate about subsidiarity may be seen as a response to fears of a centralising over-powerful Community. Traditionally, both Britain and Denmark have adopted a questioning stance in relation to the adoption of new powers at the Community level. There is a long tradition in British policy towards integration of attempting to maintain as much policy automony at national level as possible. This is in accordance with the priority accorded in official policy to the protection of sovereignty. The tension between integration and sovereignty surfaces also in other member states although in a less clear-cut form than in Britain and Denmark. Subsidiarity may be seen as a means of protecting the rights of states within the Union.

Second, not alone has the development of the Community affected national governments, it has had an impact on the exercise of public authority within member states, notably in Germany's federal system. The ratification of the Single Act in Germany was complicated by the opposition of the *Lander* to the encroachment of the Community into policy areas that have traditionally fallen within their exclusive competence under the Basic Law, in particular culture and education. The *Lander* used the occasion of the SEA to increase their influence on the 'European' dimension of policies that fall within their ambit, forcing the Federal Government in Bonn to concede a strengthened procedure of co-operation with them. In May 1988, the President of the Commission met with the representatives of the *Lander* and assured them that the Community would respect their interests and place in the policy process. Delors highlighted the importance of subsidiarity in this respect.

Third, the debate on subsidiarity stems from a concern about the Community's capacity to deal with an ever-widening range of policy responsibilities. Traditionally, Community institutions, notably the Commission, the Court and the European Parliament have adopted a strategy of pushing the boundaries of EC policy outwards. However, in the 1980s there is a growing realisation that an ever-expanding policy reach undermines the effectiveness of Community action. A strong theme in the single market strategy was minimal regulation and 'mutual recognition' rather than the traditional recourse to law. The Community is currently facing a very crowded internal and external agenda. It must thus be extremely careful not to undermine its activity by over-extension.

Subsidiarity therefore can be a principle that will help the Community and the member states chart the course of integration into the next century. The notion is seen as having a role in placating those who fear an overly powerful Community, in dealing with the sub-national dimension of integration, and in militating against an over-extended Community. At a minimum the debate on subsidiarity demonstrates that the *ad hoc* incremental approach to policy integration is being balanced by other considerations. The member states and Community institutions are becoming more vigilant about the vertical distribution of powers.

The Boundaries of the Concept

The discussion of subsidiarity in the context of the Community today does not relate to the relationship between individuals and the collectivity but concerns the distribution of public authority among different levels of government. As a political concept, subsidiarity is generally understood to mean that policy competence and public authority should be exercised at the lowest effective level. Put simply, policy competence should only be transferred to a higher level of government if action by the latter would be more effective than action by a lower level acting on its own. Policy problems that cross the boundaries of governmental units are more appropriately dealt with by a higher level of government. Applying the concept of subsidiarity to the distribution of power across levels of government is an essential characteristic of federalism.

So far the debate on subsidiarity in the Community has tended to focus on the inclusion of the principle in a number of texts and on references to it in a series of speeches by President Jacques Delors of the Commission. The 1984 Draft Treaty on European Union contains many references to subsidiarity, most notably in the preamble when it is stated that the member states intend to entrust common institutions, in accordance with the principle of subsidiarity, "only with those powers required to complete successfully the tasks they may carry out more satisfactorily than the States acting independently". (Preamble EP Draft Treaty on European Union, 1984). This theme is further elaborated on in Article 12.2 which reads as follows:

> The Union shall only act to carry out those tasks which may be undertaken more effectively in common than by the Member States acting separately, in particular those whose execution requires action by the Union because their dimension or effects extend beyond national frontiers (Article 12.2 EP Draft Treaty on European Union).

The insertion of subsidiarity into the Draft Treaty can be seen as a safeguard against the centralisation of policy at the highest level.

Since 1984 the principle of subsidiarity has been invoked in the Delors Report on EMU, in the Social Charter on the Fundamental Rights of Workers and in the Single Act on environmental policy. Article 25 of the Single Act referring to environmental policy states that the EC will only undertake those actions that can be better realised at Community level. (Article 130R, SEA, 1987). The EMU Report argues that:

> The attribution of competences to the Community would have to be confined specifically to those areas in which collective decision making was necessary. All policy functions which could be carried out at national (and regional and local) levels without adverse repercussions on the cohesion and functioning of the economic and monetary union would remain within the competence of the member countries. (Delors Report, 1989, p. 9).

Equally, the Social Charter states that the responsibility for the implementation of the social rights contained in the Charter lies with "the member states or their constituent parts and, within the limits of its powers, with the European

Community" (Social Charter, 1989, preamble). Subsidiarity is already being referred to as a principle governing the allocation of policy competences in the Community. However, translating the principle from an abstract formula into reality is far from simple. Subsidiarity has to answer the criticism that "it is just an empty shell devoid of any concrete substance. It is considered a fashionable term, a concept to which anyone might agree, because everybody can interpret it the way he or she wishes" (Gretschmann, 1991, p. 5). In any event, invoking a principle does not ensure that the principle will be respected. Nor does agreement on a principle solve disputes about the distribution of powers.

The Challenge for the Inter Governmental Conferences

Subsidiarity is an issue in both sets of negotiations. The Inter Governmental Conference on Political Union is grappling with a definition of the term and the manner of its inclusion in a Treaty. In deciding on the design of the EMU, the other Inter Governmental Conference will be guided by the principle as outlined in the Delors Report. Translating the principle of subsidiarity into a working formula is neither smooth nor straightforward. The Parliament's Giscard d'Estaing Report on subsidiarity drawns attention to the difficulty of delim-inating the principle because the Community is a "dynamic, constantly evolving project and, as has been seen over the last 35 years, it is continually and necessarily acquiring new powers" (EP Report, En/83354, 5 April, 1990). The main issues for the negotiators are:

- the definition of subsidiarity
- a decision on the value of listing the policy competences of national and Community authorities
- the inclusion of subsidiarity in a Treaty text-preamble, separate article or references in several articles
- rules and procedures governing the application of the principle. Use of judicial review as a mechanism.

There are many views about the application of the principle in the day to day business and politics of the Community. There are six formal proposals on the table at the conference. The negotiators are likely to agree to a definition of the principle but are finding it more difficult to take the concept further.

The Giscard d'Estaing Report, referred to above, advocates an extensive use of the principle in the Community, beginning with a new Article 3 which would allow the Community to take action in areas where it did not have exclusive powers, provided that this action met the dual requirements of transcendence of national frontiers and increased effectiveness. Furthermore, the Parliament wants to give the concept legal status by allowing the Court of Justice to rule on matters of competence, to ensure a legal guarantee of the principle of subsidiarity. The report also draws up a list of exclusive and concurrent powers although this has not found favour with the negotiators. Drawing up lists of competences may have the advantage of transparency but is inherently inflexible. Changing the lists would involve exhaustive and tedious negotiations. Involving the Court of Justice would also complicate the policy process and would require the judges to take decisions about spill-over effects, externalities, and effectiveness.

The Luxembourg Draft Treaty includes a separate article on subsidiarity which would be judiciable in its present format. The final Treaty is also likely to include such an article making judicial review of policy competence an important part of the politics of the Community.

Article 3b specified that:

> The Community shall take action, in accordance with the principle of subsidiarity, if and insofar as those objectives can be better achieved by the Community than by the Member States acting separately, because of the scale or effects of the proposed action. (Luxembourg Draft Treaty, June, 1991, p. 12).

The inclusion of a reference to the 'scale and effects of the proposed action' does establish a useful guideline. The proposers of changes in competences and in the allocation of responsibility will have to make a reasonable case for the necessity of Community action. However, the division of power and competence will remain politically charged in an evolving polity such as the Community. The balance of political forces and the perceived interests of the member states will continue to influence policy integration. The principle of subsidiarity may channel the debate and case law will over time establish guiding principles but will not take the politics out of the relationship between the Community and the national levels. In fact, the concept itself may become a resource in political conflict.

An analysis of the Delors Report on EMU which invokes the principle of subsidiarity, highlights the inherently political nature of the debate on policy competence. The Report argued that policies should only be transferred if their execution at national level would have adverse consequences on the cohesion and functioning of the EMU. Yet the Delors committee itself ignored the spill-over effects that occur in many areas of economic policy. A rigorous application of the principle would have meant a far wider sharing of policy competence, notably in relation to public finance than advocated by the Delors committee. (Keatinge, Laffan, O'Donnell, 1991, p. 290). The cautious nature of the Report concerning the public finance implications of an EMU are evidence of a sensitivity to what the net payers to the Community budget are prepared to endorse and to the desire to maintain as much macroeconomic policy making at national level as possible.

(v) Hierarchy of Norms

The debate about the Community's policy competence and subsidiarity drew attention to the instruments of Community law. This stemmed from a realisation that the Community's legislative process did not make sufficient provision for secondary legislation. The legislative system requiring a Commission proposal and one or two readings by Council and Parliament, is often required for highly technical matters that would be the prerogative of the executive at national level. Adding a single item to a list of permitted food additives requires the full legislative process (Corbett, 1990, p. 1). Domestic policy making would grind to a halt without a significant amount of secondary legislation.

Article 189 of the Rome Treaty sets out the different instruments of Community law, namely directives, regulations and decisions. The debate in the Conference about changes in this area cover three main themes. First, some consideration is being given to returning greater freedom to the member states on the means of implementation, by a greater use of framework directives. This may, in fact, be one means of translating the principle of subsidiarity into the day-to-day workings of the Community. Second, there is discussion about amending Article 189 to include a differentiated decision-making process depending on the kind of legal instrument at issue. Thus a distinction would be drawn between the legislative process for framework laws on the one hand and laws of application, on the other. Third, there is consideration of amending Article 189 to establish a new classification or a hierarchy of norms in the Community's legal order. The Commission's proposed classification is:

- constitutional or treaty
- law
- national-implementing measures or Community regulatory decisions
- administrative decisions by the Commission.

In the new hierarchy, Community law which replaces directives, would be the source of all derived or secondary legislation. It would be at the apex of the system subject to the constitutional role of the Treaty. Community laws would pass through the full legislative process and would be governed by the existing principles of direct effect, primacy and direct applicability. Regulatory and administrative acts would be undertaken by the Community or the member states within the framework of the primary law. Each law would establish the manner of implementation, namely whether or not it should be undertaken by the Commission or national authorities. The principle of subsidiarity would guide the division of executive powers between the Community level and the national level. Community law would be implemented by Commission regulation only if uniform rules were required. President Delors sees the proposed hierarchy of norms as an effective means of introducing 'daily subsidiarity' to the workings of the Community. (EIPA Conference, 28 March, 1991). The

Luxembourg draft use the concept of Community in relation to its proposals on the legislative role of the Parliament but does not incorporate the Commission's concept of a hierarchy of norms.

(vi) Efficiency and Effectiveness of the Union

Because of the Community's overcrowded agenda and the prospect of further enlargements, the capacity of the Community's institutions is under discussion at the Inter Governmental Conference. The conference is examining three facets of the decision-making process, namely the functioning of each institution, the institutional balance and the desirability of a single decision-making centre for all facts of Community policy.

The debate on the effectiveness and efficiency of Community institutions is a continuation of earlier debates on the institutions. There has been little or no attempt to debate fundamental reform of the policy process although the Community is embarking on an EMU and a heightened role in world politics.

The European Council, at the apex of the Council hierarchy, is the subject of much debate at the conference. The conclusions of the Rome summit in December 1990 indicated that it was necessary for the negotiators to assess whether or not there was a need for an accentuation of the role of the European Council. The main focus of attention here is the role of the Council in establishing guidelines and principles for a common foreign and security policy and in relation to the economic policy aspect of an EMU. Furthermore, there is some debate about elaborating on the role of the European Council in a treaty format. For example, the Stuttgart Declaration already referred to may be included in the text or appended to the final Treaty. There is some opposition from the smaller states, notably the Netherlands and Belgium, to an enhancement of the European Council's role. Traditionally, these states have expressed reservations about any perceived attempts by the larger states to create a *de facto 'directoire'*. There is also the problem of overload in the European Council; summit meetings are major diplomatic events. Whether they are appropriate to deliberation of economic policy issues except at a very general level is questionable. Furthermore, turbulence in the international environment is likely to focus the attentions of the European Council on international or Pan-European issues. The European Council may be less able to give political direction to internal Community politics and policies.

Discussion of the Council of Ministers relates almost entirely to majority voting. It is widely acknowledged that the majority voting provisions of the Single Act have had a dramatic impact on the efficiency of decision making in the Community and the quality of Community legislation. The constant search for consensus meant that Commission proposals were frequently reduced to the highest common factor. The success of the majority voting provisions of the Single Act may have introduced over inflated expectations of what the wider use of majority voting could accomplish. It is the existence of a deep-rooted consensus about the 1992 Programme that allows the majority voting provisions of the Single Act to be so effective. Without it, it is unlikely that the legislative programme would have proceeded with such speed. In agriculture, where majority voting has become the norm for price fixing, unanimity still reigns on major issues of principle.

The starting point of the Inter Governmental Conference negotiations is whether or not majority voting should become the norm, reserving unanimity for the most important constitutional issues. Majority voting would thus be extended to sensitive issues in the social domain, environmental policy, taxation, research and development. The impetus for the increased use of majority voting stems from experience since the Single Act. Items requiring unanimity take much longer to process through the Council or are blocked by one or two member states. There has also been considerable conflict in both Council and Parliament about the legal basis for Commission proposals. For example, the Commission has tried to use Article 100A on the approximation of laws for the single market to avoid the requirement for unanimity on environmental and social policy matters.

The Inter Governmental Conference is likely to treat the issue of majority voting on a case by case basis, as not all member states are willing to give it a blanket endorsement. Italy and Belgium want to see majority voting replacing unanimity in the social domain. The Commission is generally supportive of this but proposes the retention of unanimity for sensitive areas such as harmonisation of social security and access to employment for people from third countries (Agence Europe, 5 April, 1991). Some countries have suggested that a distinction should be made between the main lines of policy and detailed implementation. Unanimity would govern policy principles and majority voting would become the norm for implementation. A variation of majority voting is also mooted, namely some form of reinforced qualified majority. In other words, the present threshold of 54 votes could be raised with a stipulation that a minimum number of countries (perhaps eight) would have to agree to a proposal. The parameters of this system have not been worked out.

The issue of voting is one of major sensitivity concerning possible new competences, notably with respect to foreign and security policy and cooperation on judicial matters. One of the essential characteristics of European Political Cooperation (EPC) is the requirement of consensus. If however, EPC is to be transformed into a common foreign policy, the requirement of consensus would dilute the content of any such policy. There is some debate about retaining unanimity for major principles of policy but introducing majority voting at the implementation phase. Ambassador de Schoutheete, Belgian Permanent Representative to the Community and a long time observer of EPC, argues that "Community foreign policy should be run as far as possible by consensus but that the possibility of majority voting made consensus easier to obtain" (CEPS Conference proceedings, 26 March, 1991).

The Luxembourg Draft Treaty in fact treats majority voting on a case by case basis. It suggests the introduction of qualified majority voting for aspects of social policy, notably the work environment, consultation and information of employees and vocational training but retains unanimity on matters of social security and social protection. The proposed Treaty suggests that framework programmes for R&D and the Environment be subject to the procedure laid down for Community laws (see below) which essentially involves majority voting. Consumer protection, energy, trans-European networks, public health, education, and culture all come within the ambit of majority voting in the second Luxembourg Draft (Draft Treaty, June, 1991). For the two areas characterised by intergovernmental cooperation, foreign and security policy and judicial cooperation, unanimity is established as the norm although there is provision for qualified majority voting for the detailed implementation of joint action on foreign policy matters.

Three issues dominate discussions on the role of the Commission, namely its size, method of appointment and its implementing powers of comitology. Already in 1979 the Spierenburg Report argued for a reduction in the number of Commissioners to one per member state. The present Commission of seventeen is an unwieldy body with some Commissioners lacking a substantial portfolio. The prospect of further enlargements adds salience to this issue. The Luxembourg Draft Treaty advocates one Commissioner per member state but it is not yet clear if all of the larger states are prepared to reduce their presence in the Commission. The question of the appointment of the Commission stems from a view that as an unelected body, there should be an organic link between the appointment of the Commission and the democratically-elected parliament. The Luxembourg Draft Treaty gives the Parliament a role in the nomination of the Commission President, and a vote of approval of the entire Commission will be required by Parliament before it is finally appointed by the "common accord of the Member States" (Luxembourg Draft Treaty, p. 83).

The Commission's executive powers are a perennial issue. The Commission wants more freedom, in the execution of policy, from the constraints of regulatory committees of national civil servants imposed by Council. There is also the question of whether or not there should be more frequent resort by the Commission to executive agencies as tools of management. The abolition of regulatory committees, the most stringent form of supervisory committee is a major priority for the Commission. It is not yet clear how the member states will respond to this.

Increasing the effectiveness of the Court of Justice focuses on the division of labour between the Court itself and the Court of First Instance. It is possible that the remit of the newly-created court will be extended. The absence of sanctions for non-compliance and non-implementation of Community law is the subject of some debate. Britain in particular proposes an institutionalised system of penalties for member states refusing to accept Court judgements. The extension of the Court's remit to all aspects of the Union is a particularly delicate issue. Although the SEA codified EPC, the Courts jurisdiction does not operate in this domain.

Majority voting affects the operation of the Council, the entire institutional balance and political accountability. The supervisory role of national parliaments is eroded by majority voting because it means that no government and hence no parliament can block an unpalatable decision. With direct effect and direct applicability, Community laws would enter the national legal orders in ever greater numbers without necessarily having the consent of either government or national parliament.

Changes to the role and function of any one institution affects the wider interplay of forces among all the institutions. Political accountability rather than the imperatives of efficiency and effectiveness has greatest salience with regard to the institutional balance. There is a growing debate within the Community about the 'democratic deficit' or the perceived weakness of democratic accountability within the Community's political system. The European Parliament has consistently argued for an increased role in the legislative process. Its resolutions and reports to the Inter Governmental Conferences call for the establishment of a procedure of co-decision between Council and Parliament and the granting to Parliament of a right of initiative (see Edward Moxon-Browne's *The Legitimacy of the Union,* Section 4, 'The Democratic Deficit').

Both the first and second Luxembourg draft texts proposed a form of co-decision between Council and Parliament for what are defined as "laws". A law specifies the "fundamental principles or general rule applicable to a given matter" (Luxembourg 'Non-paper', Art. 189). The texts are vague about exactly what matters would fall under the general rubric of "laws". The proposed procedure follows the lines of the existing cooperation procedure until Council's second reading. Whereas under the existing arrangements, the Council has the final say at this stage, the proposed system of co-decision does not end with the Council's second reading. Provision is made for a conciliation committee to work out a compromise between the two institutions. If such a compromise is not forthcoming, the proposed law goes back into the Council and the EP. If at the end of this process there is no agreement, the EP can reject the text.

A number of observations can be made about the proposed system. First, it is not yet clear just what areas of EC law would fall within the terms of this system. It has been suggested that no more than four policy areas (environment, research, development cooperation and economic and social cohesion) fall within the rubric of "laws" in the proposed Treaty (Jacque, 1991, p. 2). Second, the Parliament's ultimate power is essentially the negative one of rejecting the

Council's final position which will have been arrived at after lengthy negotiations in Council, consideration by Parliament and a process of conciliation. The Parliament could not lightly resort to this power of rejection. Third, the Commission's role in the process damages its sole right of initiative. Whereas at present, the Commission is the funnel through which all Parliament's amendments flow to the Council, this would no longer be the case after the second reading. This change has implications for the standing of the Commission in the institutional balance, and also for the quality of the legislative outcome. The Commission as the policy proposer has the most intimate knowledge of the reason for a particular proposal and the conditions across the member states. A denial of the Commission's sole right of initiative right up to the end of the legislative process could affect the quality of Community legislation. The second Luxembourg Draft Treaty, in response to criticisms of the first paper, gives the Commission a slightly enhanced role in the conciliation process but does not give it the right to act as the filter for Council/Parliament debate on compromises. Fourth, the process of conciliation, already used for budgetary matters, will lead to a legislative process characterised by more conflict. There is a trade-off between legitimacy and efficiency. In any event, the debate about decision making and democratic accountability is not confined to the Inter Governmental Conference on Political Union. The parallel negotiations on Economic and Monetary Union will greatly effect the governance of western Europe.

(vii) The Political Consequences of EMU

The transformation of the present level of monetary and economic policy coordination into an economic and monetary union raises wide-ranging issues of a technical, economic and political nature. Economic management is at the heart of contemporary government and hence electoral politics. Governments are judged on their effectiveness in maintaining their citizens standard of living, in providing an adequate standard of public services and welfare and in maintaining employment. Already in 1970, the Werner Report on EMU argued that the necessary transfer of authority represented "a process of fundamental political significance which implies the progressive development of political cooperation" (Werner Report, 1970). A direct political consequence of an agreement on EMU is a further reduction in the formal sovereignty of the participating states. However, it is debatable how much domestic autonomy would be forfeited in a monetary union, given that adjustment of the exchange rate, is no longer seen as a major instrument of economic policy by many, although not all, member states. It is precisely the dominance of the Bundesbank in monetary matters that has led to pressures for a multilateral EMU. Economic union will, however, have a direct bearing on macroeconomic management and hence on the political autonomy of governments.

Economic and monetary union touches both on the substance of public policy making and the process of decision making. Whatever the final definition of the scope of the EMU, there will be a transfer of the locus of policy making on certain issues to the Community level and a strengthening of joint decision making or cooperative decision making on other matters. Because there are two distinct Inter Governmental Conferences in session, the implications of an EMU for economic management government in Western Europe is not being treated in an overt manner. In other words, there is a reticience to confront the political consequences of an EMU.

The EMU Conference is charged with designing a policy and institutional blueprint for economic and monetary union. Although the Delors Report on EMU established the principle of a parallelism between economic union, on the one hand, and monetary union, on the other, there is some separation between the two in the negotiations as agreement is being achieved more readily on monetary matters than on economic union. There is a large measure of agreement that the eventual monetary union will consist of a single currency (ecu) managed by a monetary institution consisting of the central banks of the member states and a European Central Bank (EuroFed). The European System of central banks is being endowed with the spirit of the German Bundesbank. The Bundesbank is constitutionally independent from the German Government and committed to the protection of the value of the mark and the maintenance of price stability. The ability of the Bundesbank to maintain a high degree of independence, although not absolute independence, owes much to German history. Fear of a return to the hyper-inflation of the Weimar years created a political environment that was favourable to an independent central bank, in any case, it was the preferred option of the occupying forces after the war. From the outset in the EMU negotiations, it became clear that the German government and particularly the German monetary authorities would not endorse European monetary institutions that were less independent and less committed to low inflation than the Bundesbank. The fact that low inflation is a primary goal of the EMS gives broad support to this strategy in other member states.

There remains difficult issues relating to the relationship of the European system of central banks to the Council, the Monetary Committee, the Commission and the Parliament. Furthermore, there is the related question of macroeconomic management in the EMU. These unresolved issues are critical in two major respects. First, a centre of decision making on monetary matters must be politically accountable in a democratic system of government. Second, the policies of the EuroFed must be developed in the context of wider macroeconomic considerations such as employment policy, the responsibility of elected politicians. A capacity for macroeconomic policy relies not just on institutions but on policy instruments. It appears from the negotiating documents produced so far, that apart from monetary policy, the preferred model of EMU is characterised by a high degree of decentralisation of economic policy competence and policy making (see Rory O'Donnell's paper 'Identifying the Issues' and Patrick Honohan's paper 'Monetary Union' in the series *Studies in European Union: Economic and Monetary Union,* IEA, 1991).

The Luxembourg Draft Treaty on EMU establishes:

- a system for the definition of the broad outlines of the economic policy of the Community
- a system of monitoring economic developments and compliance with the economic guidelines
- the possibility of granting financial assistance to a member state in economic difficulty caused by events beyond its control
- follow-up if a member state's economic policy proves incompatible with the guideline for the working of the economic and monetary union guidelines on budgetary policy particularly the need to avoid excessive budgetary deficits. (Luxembourg Draft Treaty on EMU, June, 1991).

How is this system to operate in practice? It is very difficult to draw up a system for economic policy making in a Treaty and even more difficult to predict how the system will operate in practice. Institutions are deeply embedded in their particular political and societal contexts; although the European system of central banks is endowed with the spirit of the Bundesbank it will not be a Bundesbank writ large because it will be operating in an evolving system, somewhat by trial and error. Moreover, the EMU will have to respond to economic shocks emanating from the international system and to the impact of an EMU on different parts of the Community. Predicting what external shocks the EMU may have to confront and their impact on different parts of the Community is an uncertain business. What is important is that the system should have the capacity to respond effectively to adverse economic developments.

The institutional blueprint in the Luxembourg Draft Treaty for the management of economic and monetary policy is largely evolutionary and based on existing institutions. The EcoFin Council after discussion in the European Council will establish the broad guidelines on economic policy by qualified majority. The Council will furthermore have responsibility for monitoring economic developments in the Community and for making recommendations to states that are pursuing economic policies incompatible with the broad thrust of Community policy, notably with respect to excessive budgetary deficits. Together with the EuroFed, the Council is responsible for determining exchange rate policy *vis-a-vis* third countries. All of these responsibilities require the EcoFin to become a *de facto* centre of economic government. Major economic issues will be dealt with in conjunction with the European Council. A Monetary Committee of national finance officials will work under the aegis of the EcoFin

Council. The Council works in all cases on the basis of a proposal from the Commission, particularly concerning economic policy guidelines and recommendations to member states on economic policy. The Commission has no independent power in the system; it cannot, for example, decide to publish recommendations to the member states. In practice, the Commission will have to work closely with the Monetary Committee, the EcoFin Council and the Monetary authority.

It is debatable whether or not the institutional blueprint in the Luxembourg Draft Treaty can be an effective centre of economic government, given the intergovernmental nature of the EcoFin. Can there be a Community economic policy or will it simply be a reflection of the policy preferences, perhaps divergent, of the member states? The path to a full EMU will involve gradual institutional development as challenges unfold. Such an evolutionary approach has many dangers. First, it will lead to an *ad hoc* reactive approach to economic policy. Second, the institutional system does not appear to amount to an authoritative executive capable of balancing the independent monetary authority with its limited but clear goal of price stability. Third, there is a clear danger that sufficient political accountability will not be built into the system. This said, the creation of an authoritative executive accountable to parliament involves nothing less than the creation of a European Government. Community member states have not in the past been prepared to openly confront the consequences of advanced integration for government.

EMU has major implications for budgetary policy and hence fiscal policy within the member states. Given the over-riding commitment of monetary policy to controlling inflation, a system of budgetary discipline is necessary to ensure that excessive deficits in a number of member states does not lead to inflationary pressures. This implies some surveillance of national budgetary policies. The principle issue in the negotiations is just how stringent the surveillance system should be. The Luxembourg Draft Treaty gives the Council the primary role in determining whether or not an excessive budgetary deficit exists and in making recommendations to the member states for corrective action. The Council is given the right to publish the recommendations if there is no effective follow-up by the member state and to decide on appropriate penalties if there is a continuous failure by a member state to take corrective action.

Budgetary discipline will have major implications for economic policy making at national level. National Finance Ministers will be less autonomous in moulding budgetary priorities and fiscal policy. This in turn will have an impact on relations within cabinet and between the social partners and government. If a member state is likely to incur an excessive budgetary deficit, by whatever criteria are established, it will have to reduce public expenditure or increase taxes, the stuff of contemporary politics. Governments will have far less room for manoeuvre in matters of budgetary policy than heretofore.

Even if the system of budgetary discipline is largely voluntary, it will over time change the nature of the domestic budgetary process. Peer group pressures will enter the 'rules of the game' and the 'norms of behaviour' at national level. The public-policy literature highlights the impact of transnational elite networks, sharing motivation, expertise and information, on policy choices within states. This process is strengthened within the Community because of its capacity for authoritative action.

The eventual timetable for the creation of an EMU may also raise fundamental political issues concerning the dynamics of integration. Germany in particular is placing considerable emphasis on convergence of economic policies and economic performance before the final fixing of exchange rates. The former President of the Bundesbank, Karl Otto Pohl, is an advocate of a multi-speed or a 'variable geometry' EMU. He argues that "it is conceivable that the Treaty will be ratified by all members but also that some who are unable or do not want to participate straightaway are invited to take part at a later stage" (Collignon, 1990, p. 65). The so-called Delors compromise whereby states could sign the EMU Treaty without committing themselves to full membership by a particular date echoes this approach. There are inevitable political consequences for states that cannot or choose not to participate in an EMU.

5. PROSPECTS AND OPTIONS

Each member state brings its own unique set of concerns to the negotiating table. Such concerns are moulded by economic, social and political conditions that together form what is regarded as the core national interests. The precise formulation of national interest in any one set of negotiations is shaped by past policies, bureaucratic preferences, influence of interest groups, external influences, and the views of the parties in power. Parliamentary influence on Ireland's European policy is marginal at best because of the weakness of the Oireachtas in this field. However, because of the inclusion of defence and security as an issue in the Inter Governmental Conference on Political Union, the government in office and civil servants are keenly aware that they are dealing with a sensitive issue of domestic politics.

Ireland's European policy has been moulded by the small size of the domestic market and a heavy reliance on external trade, by the significance of agriculture for the domestic economy, and by Ireland's lower level of economic development *vis-a-vis* the core economies. The political consequences of integration did not feature greatly in Ireland's European policy until the successful Supreme Court challenge to the constitutionality of title 3 of the Single Act on foreign policy cooperation in 1987. Since then the collapse of communism in East/Central Europe and the Gulf War have brought international politics to the fore on the Community agenda. The link between political and economic integration cannot be avoided in the Community of the 1990s. A consistent theme of Ireland's European policy as been that political integration must go in tandem with economic integration. This in turn leads to a policy that was summed up by Marie Geoghegan-Quinn, Minister for State for European Affairs, as "conditionally integrationist" (Magill Summer School, 12 August, 1990, p. 5). The Minister went on to say that Ireland favoured advanced integration provided the benefits of such integration were evenly distributed and extended to all regions of the Community.

(i) The prospects for change

Before examining a number of key questions for Ireland, it is necessary to assess the prospects for the Inter Governmental Conference on the issues raised in this paper.

Agreement is substantial on the following issues:

- an extension of the Community's policy scope to new areas of policy and a strengthening of the Treaty basis for existing policies
- the inclusion of the principle of subsidiarity in the text of the Treaty and not just in the preamble

- an extension of majority voting in the Council
- establishment of a system of budgetary discipline as part of an EMU
- the establishment of an independent monetary authority committed to price stability
- the adoption of a four pillars approach to European Union: European Community, Common Foreign and Security Policy, Judicial Cooperation and Economic and Monetary Union.

Disagreement persists in relation to a number of major issues:

- the extent of majority voting in the Council
- the legislative role of the European Parliament
- the timing of EMU
- the nature of budgetary discipline
- measures of economic and social cohesion that should accompany an EMU.

The final outcome on these issues will be determined by the balance of political forces in the Community, between those states favouring a maximalist approach to these negotiations and those that are content with incremental changes.

(ii) Issues for Ireland

The broad lines of Ireland's approach to the main issues raised in this paper are by now well established. Irish policy is characterised by:

- agreement to the extension of the Community's policy scope provided the Community is given adequate and appropriate means
- acceptance of subsidiarity although without enthusiasm for judicial review
- a desire to see the fruits of economic integration evenly distributed
- a consequent desire for Treaty change concerning economic and social cohesion
- a desire to avoid a stratified Community
- a reluctance to alter the institutional balance in any fundamental way.

For Ireland there is an underlying dilemma of what kind of Community is perceived to be in Ireland's long-term interest. This dilemma has an impact on attitudes to the policy scope of the Union, its institutional system, and speed of integration.

Ireland's policy style, characterised by excessive pragmatism and prudence, does not lend itself to a proactive and imaginative approach to change in the Community. This is reinforced by a political culture that eschews debate about institutional arrangements for government at national level. Irish policy makers tend to adopt an issue by issue, item by item approach without elaborating an overarching framework for policy. Yet choices made on one issue affect other issues on the agenda.

The Irish emphasis on economic and social cohesion is based on past policies and was endorsed by the conclusions of the NESC report on Ireland in the European Community (NESC, 88, August, 1989). The latter argues very forcibly for an advanced form of EMU, with a greatly strengthened Community budget and the transfer of major aspects of economic policy to the Union. The report advocates a system of public finance provision akin to those existing in advanced federations. Yet is this policy goal compatible with a minimalist view of political integration in the domain of foreign and security policy? And is it compatible with a conservative approach to institutional change in the Community?

Economic and Social Cohesion: Context, Issues and Proposals

Economic and social cohesion must be placed in the context of the prevailing political and economic environment in the Community and in a wider context concerning the capacity of public authorities to tackle issues of economic divergence. The O'Donnell paper on Regional Cohesion traces the need for structural policy in the Community (see Rory O'Donnell's paper 'The Regional Issue' in the series *Studies in European Union: Economic and Monetary Union*, IEA, 1991). The politics of redistribution in the Community to date suggest that the kind of economic union envisaged by the NESC report is simply not feasible in the foreseeable future. The model of EMU emerging from the Inter Governmental Conference is one without a large and flexible Community budget. Why?

Although economic and social cohesion was a central commitment in the Single Act and has again emerged as one of the main principles of the Union in the Luxembourg Communique (European Council, 28-29 June, 1991), there are widely differing views concerning the responsibility and the capacity of the Community to foster a convergence of income levels across the regions of the Community. There are simply different interests and political forces at work. The major cleavage is between the potential recipients of financial transfers and the paymasters. This is a particularly acute problem in the current environment when Germany is facing the costs of reunification and large budget deficits. Pressure on the existing Community budget is acute given the need to transfer resources to East/Central Europe, the Soviet Union, the Middle East and the Third World. National Finance Ministers from the more developed parts of the Community are constrained in the degree to which they can politically endorse a greatly strengthened Community budget. The 1980s witnessed budgetary retrenchment in all west European states as attempts were made to curb the growth of public expenditure. In addition, even the most advanced states in the Community continue to have problems of regional disparities and pockets of social deprivation. The more prosperous parts of the Community are faced with the demands of the economically weaker parts of the Community, and with the need to ensure that Western Europe as a whole remains competitive in the global economy.

The less prosperous parts of the Community have some bargaining power because their agreement is necessary to the final text that will emerge from the negotiations. The addition of Spain to the group of states highlighting the issue of cohesion strengthens this bargaining power. However, it is in the end limited because policy instruments on cohesion depend in the final resort on the willingness and the capacity of the more prosperous parts of the Community to transfer resources. The assertion in the Padoa-Schioppa Report, shared somewhat by the NESC report, that there is a "danger that imbalances in the distribution of the benefits from Community policies may become so serious as to cause mounting political dissatisfaction with the Community in some countries, leading to non-cooperativeness and ultimately the threat of secession" has limited validity (Padoa-Schioppa Report, 1987, p. 90). It is entirely possible that a country would adopt a strategy of non-cooperativeness which would make Community policy making stall; it could be argued that Spain has adopted just such a strategy in the current Political Union negotiations and in the EC/EFTA negotiations. However, the threat of secession is simply not credible. It fails to take into account the dependence of all of the less prosperous regions on the Community market.

It is necessary in an Irish context, where the expectation of financial transfers from the Community budget is so well entrenched, to probe the extent to which the more prosperous parts of the Community should burden their own economies with large scale transfers when not all the problems of the lesser developed parts of the Community stem from market integration. The conclusions of the NESC report itself on Ireland's economic performance since 1973 highlighted the extent to which the concern with short-term developments in economic policy by successive governments undermined their ability to deal with the long-term structural problems of the Irish economy (NESC 1989, p. 217). Likewise the current problems of the Greek economy cannot be laid at the door of market integration. The Community's role in redistribution must be limited to where the Community's own policies raise serious questions of equity (Padoa-Schioppa, p. 89).

It is, however, far easier to assert that the Community has a responsibility in promoting cohesion than to establish what kinds of policy instruments are likely to promote a reduction in regional disparities (see O'Donnell, *ibid.*). There are no clearcut prescriptions for reducing regional imbalances even within national economies. Wallace rightly points out that "The record of regional policies within the member states is mixed, in spite of a range of instruments and a scale of financial transfers far more extensive than the Community could hope to aspire to" (Wallace, 1981, p. 215). The SEA negotiations allowed for a strengthening of the Community's political commitment to economic and social cohesion and led to the reform of the Structural Funds. The resources of the latter were significantly increased under the terms of the 1988 budgetary agreement. However, the SEA package did not amount to a transformation of the Community's role in matters of redistribution. Rather it represented an improvement in the previous level of resource transfer and in the management of the Structural Funds. The funds are however still too small and are distributed in too restrictive a manner to become real instruments of cohesion. Paradoxically, the politics of grantmanship that characterise the Structural Funds may, in fact, lead to expenditure at national level that is simply wasteful.

For Irish policy makers the objective of economic and social cohesion remains central to their bargaining strategy and to their perception of what kind of Community is in Ireland's interest. One of the most important Irish submissions to the Political Union Inter Governmental Conference was on this topic. At the outset it did not appear as if cohesion would be the subject of much debate at the conferences. The Commission, in particular, did not want to complicate the EMU negotiations with a debate on the Community budget. However, the insistence of the peripheral states that this matter be treated has borne fruit. The Spanish government is adamant that there should be no agreement on political union without a set of arrangements for inter-regional transfers. The Irish submission seeks a revision of Articles 2 and 3 of the original Rome Treaty in addition to an extensive revision of Article 130 on economic and social cohesion. The Irish submission is based on the Conclusions of the Rome European Council (December 1990) which specified that economic and social cohesion is an essential basis for the achievement of political union.

The Irish paper calls for a periodic report to Council and Parliament on the attainment of economic and social cohesion defined as reducing "disparities in levels of development and living standards". In the absence of satisfactory progress, the Commission would be obliged to make proposals for remedial action by the Community and the member states. Decisions on appropriate measures would be subject to majority voting. Concerning policy instruments, the proposed revisions mention existing Community policies and new but unspecified Community measures. The Commission would make proposals in the context of the second stage of EMU and again no later than 1996 as the Community prepares to go into the final stage of EMU. The Irish submission is based on periodic reviews, and links cohesion to EMU.

The proposals of the Luxembourg Draft Treaty on economic and social cohesion incorporate the Irish proposal for a periodic report but do not specify that economic and social cohesion involves reducing disparities in living standards. Moreover, there is a strong focus on the existing funds and no direct link established between cohesion and EMU. The Luxembourg paper is thus considerably weaker in its formulation than the Irish submission (Luxembourg Draft Treaty, June, 1991, p. 52).

A realistic assessment of the debate about cohesion, would suggest that there will be a Treaty revision concerning this issue at the negotiations, but that there is no prospect of automatic regional transfers on a scale that characterises either unitary states or advanced federations. The European Community does not have the level of political cohesion required for such a development, nor does it need it, given its present stage of evolution. The budgetary perspective for the period 1993–1997 is likely to see an incremental increase in the size of the budget with more resources for the less prosperous parts of the Community. A further round of bargaining about the final stage of EMU will give the less prosperous regions of the Community another opportunity to press their case. It is imperative that Irish policymakers are prepared for this debate. Consequently, attention must be paid in Ireland to research not just on the causes of economic disparities but to the search for additional policy instruments, beyond the existing Structural Funds.

The Efficiency and Effectiveness of EC Institutions

Ireland has an interest in ensuring that the Community's legislative process can deliver decisions within a reasonable time period. It is not in Ireland's interest that the Community returns to the institutional inertia of the 1970s and early 1980s. That said, Irish policy makers have to assess the balance of advantages and disadvantages that would result from changes to the role of any one institution and to the wider institutional balance. In contrast to the 'maximalist' position adopted on economic and social cohesion, Irish policy makers are cautious and conservative on institutional matters.

A primary goal of Irish policy is to protect the rights of small states within the system. Although the Community is characterised by an uneven distribution of power and influence among the member states, all of the smaller states in the Community have an interest in ensuring that a *de jure* or *de facto 'directoire'* of the larger states does not dominate developments. The Dutch White Paper on political union argues that:

> The interests of small countries are best served by international cooperation based on legal structures with open decision-making processes. Large countries, on the other hand, also pursue structured negotiations but endeavour to protect their interests mainly by exploiting their position of power. (Dutch White Paper, June, 1990, p. 3).

Irish policy makers would share this view and have always placed emphasis on the importance of Community law and procedural correctness within the Community's policy process. However, whereas the Dutch argue for a strengthening of the federalist character of the Community in order to protect the interests of small states, the Irish government does not share this view. It is cautious on an extension of qualified majority voting and on increased powers for the European Parliament. Why?

While willing to extend majority voting on a case by case basis, there are a number of sensitive policy areas where the retention of unanimity is seen as a priority. Because of its implications of exchequer revenues, the approximation of indirect taxation is the most sensitive issue in the single market programme. Ireland would want to see the continuation of unanimity in this area. Equally, any attempt to include direct taxation or corporate taxation within the ambit of economic policy in an EMU would be regarded as a matter for unanimity. Social policy is another area where a selective extension of qualified majority voting would be welcomed. Areas of social policy, notably social security, that would imply costs to the exchequer or increased costs to industry, are regarded as areas where unanimity should be retained. There is also a sensitivity to policy developments that might impinge on relations between the social partners and on collective bargaining in Ireland. The conflict between increased efficiency in the Council implied by majority voting and the retention of autonomy implied by unanimity may, in fact, only have to be faced in the next round of bargaining, coinciding with the enlargement of the Community.

The major contentious institutional issue relates to the institutional balance and the powers of the European Parliament. While willing to examine new forms of cooperation, Ireland is at best lukewarm about increased powers for the European Parliament. Irish policy makers would go further than the UK and the Danes in promoting the powers of the Parliament but are far from the 'maximalist' policy positions adopted by the Italian and German governments. There are a number of reasons for this. First, Ireland has traditionally looked to the Commission rather than the Parliament as the protector of the interests of small states, because of its commitment to the general Community interest and its key role in the preparation of policy proposals. Irish policy makers would not favour any interference with the Commission's sole right of initiative because it has been one of the central features of the institutional balance from the outset. Second, there are fears that Irish interests would not be adequately protected in a legislative system characterised by co-decision.

The reserved attitude towards the European Parliament stems from two considerations. First, Irish policy makers feel more at ease in protecting and promoting Irish interests in the Council where an Irish minister is one of twelve, and even in the case of majority voting, Ireland retains 3 votes out of 76. The process of coalition building in the Council is more accessible than in the

Parliament. In contrast, Ireland has 15 MEPs from a total of 518. However, Irish MEPs are in six of the eight parliamentary political groups. See Table 4.

Table 4

Irish Representation in EP Groupings, 1989 Election

	Irish MEPs	Total
Socialist	1	180
EPP	4	121
LDR	2	50
ED	—	34
Greens	—	30
EUL	—	28
EDA	6	20
ER	—	17
CL	1	14
RBW	1	13
Ind	—	11
Total	15	518

Key to European Parliament Groups:

Socialist – Socialist Group
EPP – European People's Party (Christian Democrats)
LDR – Liberal Democratic and Reformist Group
ED – European Democratic Group
Greens – Green Group
EUL – European Unitarian Left
EDA – European Democratic Alliance
ER – Technical Group of the European Right
CL – Left Unity
RBW – Rainbow Group
IND – Non Attached

The spread of Irish MEPs across the political spectrum is useful because it ensures that Irish concerns are given a hearing in many groups. However, the Irish presence in the two largest of the groupings, the Socialists and the EPP, is very small. These groups are undoubtedly the most powerful groupings in the Parliament since the Single Act and the establishment of the cooperation procedure.

Since direct elections in 1979, only one Irish MEP, Eileen Lemass, chaired a Committee (Youth Culture, Education, Information and Sport, 1984–1989). The eighteen standing committees of the EP are at the heart of its work. Here Commission proposals and Council common positions are examined and legislative resolutions prepared for the full house. In the current parliament, five of the fifteen MEPs are Vice-Presidents of a Committee. See Table 5.

Table 5

Role of Irish MEPs on Committees and in Political Groups

	Committee/EP Group
A. Andrews	Development and Cooperation
M. Banotti	Youth, Culture, Education (VC) Environment, Public Health and Consumer Affairs
N. Blaney	Agriculture, Fisheries, Rural Development Member of Group Bureau and Treasurer
P. Cox	Economic and Monetary Affairs, Industrial Policy, Vice-President of Group
P. Cooney	Legal Affairs and Citizens Rights Institutional Affairs
J. Cushnahan	Regional Policy and Regional Planning
P. De Rossa	Regional Policy and Regional Planning (VC), Vice-President of Group, Treasurer
B. Desmond	Economic and Monetary Affairs and Industrial Policy (VC), Vice-President of Group
G. Fitzgerald	Regional Policy and Regional Planning Treasurer of Group
J. Fitzsimons	Environment, Public Health and Consumers Petitions
P. Lalor	Political Committee/Rules of Procedure One of Five Questors, Vice-President of Group
M. Killilea	Agriculture, Fisheries and Rural Development (VC) Women's Rights
P. Lane	Agriculture, Fisheries and Rural Development
J. McCartin	Agriculture, Fisheries and Rural Development Member of EPP Bureau
T. J. Maher	Regional Policy and Regional Planning (VC)

Source: IPA Diary 1990, p. 371. Note: VC = Vice Chairman

There is a heavy concentration of MEPs on the Agricultural Committee (4) and on the Regional Policy Committee (4). This leaves Ireland without full membership on six of the committees including the powerful Budgets Committee. If the European Parliament emerges from the Inter Governmental Conference with greatly enhanced powers, Irish political parties are going to have to begin to take the Parliament more seriously.

In an evolving polity like the European Community it is difficult to judge where interests are best protected and where the balance should lie between the representative branch of the polity and the executive branch. One does not find in the Parliament the clear line of political authority and responsibility one finds in the Western European tradition of liberal democracy. The absence of a clear focus of executive power at Community level means that the Parliament neither produces nor controls a government. Nor are political parties, the principal expression of political representation in the member states, found in the Parliament in quite the same way as in the national polities. An individual voter has far less chance in understanding or assessing the political or public policy consequences of casting a vote for this or that party in a European election than in a first order national election, nor can MEPs be as close to their electors as national parliamentarians.

This is not to argue against changes to the institutional balance, merely to point out that there are no simple solutions to the problem of combining integration with democracy and to combining national political systems with a Community system. There is "nothing automatic in the combination of institutions and procedures that enable government to be democratic, effective and responsible at the same time". (Coombes, 1977, p. 264). It is even less automatic in an evolving polity like the European Community which is attempting to combine democracy with traditional diplomatic negotiations between states.

Graduated Integration, Two-Speed And So On

During the long period of stagnation in the Community in the 1970s and early 1980s, there was a wide-ranging debate on the appropriateness for the Community of differentiated integration, known as 'variable geometry', two-speed Europe, or Europe *a la carte.* Close examination of the Community points to the use of such formulae, notably in the EMS, in varying transitional arrangements, and in some differentiation in the application of EC law. The debate has re-emerged in relation to two areas of critical importance in the Inter Governmental Conferences, namely, EMU and foreign and security policy. The suggestion that there could be a multi-speed approach to EMU is a central theme in the Bundesbank's thinking on EMU because of its concern for convergence. This model of EMU would involve a number of countries, whose economic performances are closely in tune, moving towards EMU at a faster pace than other EC states. The precise definition of the core or first-speed countries is not yet clear.

A 'variable geometry' approach is also maintained in relation to a common foreign and security policy. When the Italian government submitted its paper on the WEU in September 1990, it proposed an "opting-out" clause for countries like Ireland which did not want to participate in arrangements that might involve 'hard security' or defence. Clearly, if Ireland wishes to maintain a policy of military neutrality for the foreseeable future, and if the Inter Governmental Conference or the next round of bargaining includes defence, an 'opting-out' clause is one option.

Ireland's European policy has never favoured 'variable geometry' or a multi-speed Europe because of the fear that Ireland might find itself in the second tier of any such arrangement. The Taoiseach, Mr. Haughey, has underlined Ireland's intention to be a founder member of EMU. (IMI, Conference speech, *Irish Times*, 29 March, 1991). In other words, there is a strong commitment to participating in an EMU from the outset. The attitude to 'variable geometry' in the field of security policy is less clear. An opting-out clause would allow the government to respond to the sensitivity of public opinion. However, agreement to 'variable geometry' of a permanent or semi-permanent kind in any field of Community activity would alter the nature of the Community and the quality of Ireland's membership.

Heretofore, 'variable geometry', for example, the establishment of the EMS, involved all member states participating in the establishment of the ground rules, and some states being free to opt out of participation in the exchange rate mechanism. Both the UK and Spain subsequently decided to participate. A permanent opting out of any commitment to arrangements designed to give the Community a role in 'hard security', however tentative, would introduce a structured political hierarchy. The likelihood of such stratification has increased with the Austrian and Swedish applications. There is a danger that Ireland would be bound to the objective of a common foreign and security policy, but with no say about the conduct of those aspects of policy that Ireland had opted out of. 'Variable geometry' can offer a path to deeper integration while allowing individual states to deal with particularly sensitive issues, but any permanent or semi-permanent 'variable geometry' is not in Irish interest.

(iii) Looking into the Crystal Ball

The eventual Treaty to emerge from the two Inter Governmental Conferences will be the result of hard bargaining within each conference and across the broad range of issues at stake in both conferences. The final package will involve both substantive issues of policy and institutional questions. Ireland is only one of twelve states sitting at the negotiating table, and as the eventual package must be acceptable to the larger states, it is necessary to pay some attention to their policy preferences. The ingredients of a deal between France and Germany exist. Both want some movement on a foreign and security policy, and are intent in having a reference to defence in the final text. They diverge on EMU and democratic legitimacy. Germany may be persuaded to drop some of its reservations about the timing of the EuroFed, and the stringent conditions it is imposing for the final stages of EMU, in return for French concessions on the powers of the European Parliament. The UK as the third part of the large country triad is in a stronger bargaining position in these negotiations than it was in the negotiations leading to the Single Act. Because of its role in NATO and the quality of its relationship with the US, it will have an important say in the outcome on foreign and security policy. It may well go someway towards the Franco–German position in this field provided that the operational responsibility of NATO is protected, and that the US commitment to Western Europe is not undermined. Concessions on foreign policy would allow the UK to bargain on EMU.

Italy, given its 'maximalist' approach to integration, will side with the optimal package in terms of strengthening the Community. It has again lent its weight to the EP's demands for increased powers. Spain is concentrating on the issue of cohesion and the EC Budget. In this it is supported by the other less prosperous parts of the Community. There could well be a trade-off between cohesion and security in the negotiations. On institutional matters, the smaller states, particularly the Benelux and Ireland, will try to ensure that the role of the Commission is protected.

The current conferences are but a prelude to further negotiations in the 1990s. It is becoming clear that this round of negotiations is not going to provide a sufficiently tight set of policy, institutional and constitutional rules for the EC in the 1990s. Both EMU and Political Union will be revisited in 1996 or soon afterwards. The next round will be complicated by enlargement.

BIBLIOGRAPHY

Collignon, S. (1990), 'The EMU Debate: a Common or a Single Currency', *EUI Economic Trends,* No. 3.

Coombes, D. (1970), *Politics and Bureaucracy in the European Community,* London, Allen & Unwin.

Coombes, D. (1977), Part III in *Decision Making in the European Community,* Sasse, C., Poulet, E., Coombes, D., and Deprez, G., New York, Praeger.

Corbett, R. (1990), 'Efficiency and Accountability', paper delivered to a Federal Trust Conference, 4 December, 1990.

Ehlermann, C-D. (1990), 'The Institutional Development of the EC under the Single European Act, *Aussenpolitik,* pp. 135–146.

Gretschmann, K., 'The Subsidiarity Principle: Who is to do what in an Integrated Europe?' paper delivered to a conference held at the EIPA, Maastricht, March, 1991.

Jacque, J. P. (1991), 'Assessment of the Luxembourg Draft Treaty', Internal Report for EP.

Keatinge, P., and Murphy, A. (1987), 'The European Council's Ad Hoc Committee on Institutional Affairs, 1984–85', in Pryce, R. (ed.), *The Dynamics of European Union,* London, Croom Helm.

Keatinge, P. (ed.), (1991), *Ireland and EC Membership Evaluated,* London, Frances Pinter.

Moravcsik, A. (1989), 'Negotiating the Single Act: National Interests and Conventional Statecraft in the European Community', Working Paper 21, Harvard Center for European Studies.

Padoa-Schioppa, T. (1987), *Efficiency, Stability and Equity,* Oxford, Oxford University Press.

Wallace, H., Wilke, M. (1990), 'Subsidiarity: approaches to Power-Sharing in the European Community', Chatham House Paper, No. 27.

Wallace, W. (1981), 'Conclusions', in Hodges, M., and Wallace, W. (eds.), *Economic Divergence in the European Community,* London, Allan and Unwin.

Official Documents

Delors Report on EMU, April, 1989.

Ireland in the European Community, NESC Report, No. 88, August, 1989.

*Ireland: Submission to the Inter Governmental Conference, January, 1991.

*Luxembourg 'Non-paper', April, 1991.

*Luxembourg Draft Treaty, June, 1991.

Report of the Three Wise Men, 1979.

Single European Act Explanatory Guide, Dublin 1986.

Spierenburg Report on the EC Commission, 1979.

Tindemans Report on European Union, 1975.

Vedel Report on the European Parliament, 1972.

Conferences

Papers from Federal Trust Conference, London, December, 1990.

Papers from EIPA Conference, Maastricht, March, 1991.

Papers from CEPS Conference, Brussels, February, 1991.

*Deposited in the Library of the Houses of the Oireachtas

THE LEGITIMACY OF THE UNION

Edward Moxon-Browne

EXECUTIVE SUMMARY

1. Introduction

The concept of legitimacy is not easy to define, but in the context of the European Community (EC) it refers to the degree of consent that the institutions of the Community are able to attract from its citizens. This consent rests, for the most part, on the effectiveness, accountability and visibility of the Community's decision-making process.

It is generally agreed that the institutions of the Community have suffered from what might be termed a 'crisis of legitimacy' ever since they were established. Except for the European Parliament (EP), which has been directly elected since 1979, none of the other institutions is 'democratic' in that sense. Moreover, all the institutions suffer from the basic problem that they owe their existence to the governments that comprise the Community, and collectively they have not convinced the citizens of the Community that they represent a preferable alternative to the national decision-making systems based in the twelve member states. Although the European Parliament has undoubtedly gained some legitimacy by being directly elected, this has not spilled over to its relationship with the other institutions, since its role *vis-a-vis* the Council and Commission remains that of a junior partner.

The problem of the Union's legitimacy has become more serious for at least two reasons: increased powers for the Council and Commission have not been matched by commensurate power for the national parliaments; the European Parliament, although in a better position than it was before the Single European Act (SEA), remains weak, a weakness demonstrated by its inability to exert a significant influence on the current Inter Governmental Conferences (IGCs).

2. Background

Analysis of Eurobarometer opinion polls, conducted every six months throughout the Community, reveals a low degree of confidence that the European Community institutions are as 'democratic' as they ought to be. However, while most opinion regards the European Parliament as 'important', an equally large segment of opinion would like to see it becoming more important. If this reflects a wish to see the European Community decision-making system become more accountable, Irish opinion clearly has doubts about achieving this through a stronger European Parliament, and seems to prefer the Commission as a vehicle for protecting the interests of a smaller member state.

Social policy has long played a role in strengthening the Community's legitimacy. In the 1970s, the Social Fund moved from a reactive role to the more positive functions of retraining, and worker participation in industry. In the context of the Single European Market (SEM), the Social Charter provides a framework for the creation of a 'level playing field' in social security legislation across the Community.

The idea of a 'People's Europe' was conceived as a concomitant to the process of creating the Single Market and the Adonnino Report consequently laid emphasis on quality of life as well as standards of living. Proposals such as a European passport, and schemes designed to promote student and worker mobility exchanges, aimed to make the Community directly relevant to its citizens and, by the adoption of Community symbols, foster a sense of European identity.

3. European Community Citizenship

The notion of European Community citizenship reflects a series of rights and duties that are specific to, and depend upon, the existence of the Union. Three basic rights have been identified: the right of movement; the right of residence; and the right of political participation. In all three respects, progress has been slow, and patchy. Since a European Community citizen is defined as someone who is a citizen of one of the member states, national governments can determine who should be, and who should not be, entitled to the status of Community citizen. Nevertheless, Community citizenship can, in some cases, extend to the dependants of a citizen of a member state, even where these dependants are not themselves citizens of a Community country. The development of Community citizenship may be helped by recourse to the European Convention on Human Rights (ECHR), despite that Convention referring to a broader group of countries than the Twelve. At the moment, rights of political participation depend on bilateral agreements between Community governments: thus British and Irish citizens, for example, enjoy reciprocal rights that could provide a model for the rest of the Community. The proposal in front of the IGC has been that all EC citizens should have the right to take part in municipal and European Parliament elections in the member states where they reside.

Even though the legal status of Community citizenship remains rather vestigial, the 340 million inhabitants of the Community are subject to, and benefit from, the Community's own legal order. The cumulative judgements of the European Court of Justice (ECJ) not only uphold common principles in its own sphere of competence, but effectively champion the rights of individuals in cases where national laws can be shown to be at odds with Community legislation.

4. The Democratic Deficit

The introduction of majority voting under the Single European Act (SEA) has reduced the influence of national legislatures; and the European Parliament, although its involvement in decision-making has been increased, is still worse off, in relative terms, than it was before the Single European Act, since it has not gained as much power as the national parliaments have lost.

The European Parliament has been assiduous in its search for greater influence over the legislative process. Through its 'own initiative reports' it can hint at new areas for legislation. It is able to sack the entire Commission, but has only threatened to do so. It can veto the whole budget but this has proved a clumsy weapon. The cooperation procedure gives the Parliament real influence over specific areas of legislation; and the power of assent (entry of new member states and association agreements) could be, and in the case of association agreements has been, exploited very effectively.

The cooperation procedure provides for two readings (and two deadlines) and offers opportunities for Parliament to capitalise on divisions within the Council, as well as enhancing the value of close contact with the Commission. The new procedure strengthens the Parliament's position, but still does not give it the full power of co-decision.

There are various ways in which the cooperation procedure could be extended: by increasing the topics to which it applies; by giving the Parliament the right of legislative initiative in designated areas; by making the cooperation procedure and qualified majority voting the norm; and by allowing co-decision on major issues, but making the cooperation procedure the norm for everything else.

One way of alleviating the 'democratic deficit' is to strengthen the links between the national parliaments and the European Parliament. This could be achieved on a modest scale by inviting MEPs from other Community countries to attend a national parliament's 'European Committee' and by encouraging members of national legislatures to attend European Parliament committees. A more far-reaching change would be to create a European Senate in which delegations from national parliaments would constitute a second chamber alongside the present European Parliament. The European Parliament is not in favour of this latter suggestion.

The relationship between the Commission and the Parliament has become characterised by more extensive consultation of an informal kind, something that is seen as beneficial by both sides. The Parliament could be given a greater role in the appointment of the members of the Commission, or the President, and this would enhance the latter's legitimacy. Likewise, a blocking role for the Parliament could be envisaged in cases where a national government decided not to renew a Commissioner's term of office.

Among the more radical revisions that might be made to the Community's decision-making process, a parliamentary model and a presidential system have been suggested. The parliamentary model assumes that the Parliament would become much more important as a lower chamber operating a co-legislative system with a Council of Ministers as the upper chamber. These two chambers would then bargain with the Commission as the 'government' subject to votes of confidence in the Parliament.

The presidential system makes the Parliament either marginal or superfluous, as the Commission becomes directly elected and thereby assumes legitimacy as the Community's sole legislature. The Council of Ministers, as the representative of discrete national interests, would then bargain directly with the Commission.

The two models highlight the distinct but related concepts of legitimacy and efficiency. While the latter system might appear more efficient, it is clearly less legitimate in terms of popular participation, and with the former it is the other way round. Nevertheless, efficiency is part of legitimacy and vice versa: the problem is finding the right balance between the two.

5. Options for Ireland

In the light of the preceding discussion it is possible to suggest a number of policy options for Ireland in the hope that they will provide a focus for the wide-ranging debate that should precede a referendum.

Firstly, there is the question of Community citizenship: how far should rights of movement, residence and political participation be extended to all EC citizens on a universally reciprocal basis? Given that there are more Irish nationals living in other EC countries than other EC nationals living in Ireland, the maximum extension of these rights would appear to be in Ireland's interest.

Secondly, the IGC is faced with the proposal that an ombudsman acts as the interlocutor between the citizens of the EC and the Community institutions. Is it in Ireland's interests to support this proposal, and indeed to advocate its extension to a network of ombudsmen in all Community countries?

Thirdly, there are at least two ways in which links between the Community and national legislatures might be strengthened: national influence over the Community's legislative system can be increased at the centre (e.g. by creating a Senate); and the quality of Community information in national parliaments could be enhanced by, for example, creating a powerful European Affairs Committee which MEPs from other member states might be invited to attend. Fourthly, to what extent is it in Ireland's interest to see the role of the European Parliament enhanced? There must be some doubt, given Ireland's numerically small representation in the Parliament, whether this is the road to follow; and Irish public opinion appears to favour a stronger Commission. Thus there would seem to be a strong case in favour of giving the Commission greater legitimacy by making it more accountable to Parliament. The whole decision-making system would then be perceived as more legitimate.

1. INTRODUCTION

The theme of 'legitimacy' and the ways in which it affects the evolving Community institutions are as old as the EC itself. In the 1970s, the prospect of direct elections was seen as not only giving the European Parliament "a new political authority" but also reinforcing "the democratic legitimacy of the whole European institutional apparatus" (Tindemans, 1976). The European Parliament is best thought of as part of a system, comprising several discrete but linked institutions. Although the Parliament is the natural focus for any discussion of legitimacy, it is in the relationship between the Parliament and other institutions that legitimacy more accurately resides.

Legitimacy involves the capacity to "engender and maintain the belief that the existing political institutions are the most appropriate ones for the society" (Lipset, 1960) or, in the context of the European Community:

> Europe's institutions will be legitimate insofar as individual citizens are prepared to accept decisions made by them even when their own lives and livelihoods are affected and insofar as there is (consequently) a transfer of loyalties and expectations to those institutions . . . It is desirable, of course, that the European institutions receive the accolade of legitimacy only if they are organised in accordance with certain democratic principles, but the critical condition for integration is legitimacy rather than democracy (Henig, 1974 : 397).

A less stringent view, and one that better reflects the reality of the Community in the 1990s, considers mere acquiescence in Community rule-making as a sufficient basis for legitimacy (Lindberg and Scheingold, 1970). What this means in practice is that institutions and power-holders are able to exercise authority to the extent that power is based on consent rather than coercion. In a liberal-democratic milieu, this consent is the product of several factors: the effectiveness of institutions; their accountability; and their visibility. Thus, to achieve legitimacy, institutions have to be seen to achieve objectives expected of them. They have to be accountable in the sense that they can be changed or abolished if they do not meet the needs of those who establish them; and they have to be visible by being recognisable, open to public scrutiny, and possessing a remit that is clearly defined and easily comprehensible (Herman and Lodge, 1978 : 82).

The institutions of the European Community (EC) have generally suffered from what might be termed a 'crisis of legitimacy' throughout their existence. At least three reasons can be adduced to account for this. Firstly, the institutions have owed their existence to the national governments that comprise the Community itself. The institutions have not been directly elected (except for the Parliament since 1979) and therefore have no authority except that attributed to them by national governments and, indirectly therefore, by the people of the EC.

Secondly, the institutions have not generally been able to convince the peoples of the EC that they make decisions more efficiently, or more wisely, than do the national governments.

Consequently, there has not been a significant expansion of loyalty to EC institutions that would form the bedrock of legitimacy. Finally, the institutions lack the tangibility and intelligibility that would enable them to capture the imagination, and therefore gain the voluntary support of public opinion. Widespread ignorance of even the existence of EC institutions, let alone of what they do, has made it difficult for them to compete with national governments in the affections of their publics. This problem has, perhaps, been compounded by the propensity of national governments to pin the blame for policy failures on Community institutions. Unemployment, high food prices, and unpalatable economic measures, can be conveniently blamed on Community policies.

The direct election of the European Parliament from 1979 onwards was seen as an attempt to accord the Parliament greater legitimacy. However, it is disputable how far this has been accomplished. Firstly, the differences between national parliaments and the European Parliament make it difficult for citizens of the EC to apprehend the true nature of the European Parliament. Secondly, low turnout figures in some member states have simply confirmed their inhabitants' scepticism towards the role of the European Parliament. Thirdly, and most crucially, the legitimacy of the Parliament cannot exist in a vacuum: it is dependent on the Parliament's functions in the EC's overall legislative processes and, since the Parliament's powers have remained marginal as compared with those of the Council and Commission, any legitimacy that has been gained by the Parliament through direct elections does not transfer automatically to other EC institutions. An electoral basis is clearly a necessary condition for legitimacy, but it is not sufficient. Efficacy in making decisions that matter is equally important.

(i) The significance of legitimacy for the EC in the 1990s

In the 1990s, the question of the Community's legitimacy is likely to become more pressing, for at least two reasons. On the one hand, the extension and acceleration of decision-making by the EC institutions suggests that these institutions will impinge more directly on the consciousness of the Community's citizens. On the other hand, if the Community is enlarged to encompass new member states, the efficacy (and, therefore, the legitimacy) of its institutions may be challenged afresh; and there will, in any case, be a dilution of the Community's 'identity' in the sense that new member states, some accustomed to very different political patterns of decision-taking in the past, may thwart the current consensus of the Twelve on how the EC should evolve in the future.

(ii) The wider competence of EC institutions

The Single European Act came into force in 1987 and among its many consequences, some of them unforeseen, has been an extension of the Community's concerns, and an acceleration in the speed with which decisions have been taken (Ehlermann, 1990). The Single European Act represents both a formal extension, and a formal amendment, of the Treaty of Rome. It achieves, also, the formal recognition of practices and institutions that had become customary, but had hitherto remained unofficial. For our purposes, it suffices to mention only that the Single European Act extends the competence of the Community more clearly into areas such as the environment, regional policy, social policy, technological collaboration and transport; and to add that, on some of these issues, weighted majority voting in the Council of Ministers would henceforth suffice.

Although one does not have to subscribe to the view that 80 per cent of all economic and social legislation after 1993 will be enacted by the EC rather than the national governments, it is obvious that increasing segments of economic legislation will be subject to the constraints of norms set in Brussels. For the citizens of the EC, this entails an enlargement of power for institutions of which many remain ignorant, and towards which no great affinity is felt. Increased efficacy, unmatched by commensurate accountability, threatens legitimacy.

(iii) Enlargement of the EC

The legitimacy of the Community's institutions may also be threatened by the enlargement of the Community. Although the prospects for East European countries joining as full members in the near future, look rather bleak at the moment, even the addition of Austria, Sweden or Turkey would place some strain on the perceived legitimacy of the EC institutions. This is partly for reasons referred to above, namely that new political traditions could weaken the Community's solidarity as a focus of decision making; but equally important is the blurred conception of 'Europe' that the entry of new members might signify.

A Community that included Sweden, but not Norway, Austria but not Switzerland, Turkey but not Malta or Cyprus, could look 'ragged at the edges'. If it is true that legitimacy must be grounded in the tangibility and intelligibility of the Community's institutions, and if this is to be underpinned by a real 'sense of community', the heterogeneity of an enlarged Community (and especially its 'incompleteness') could weaken perceptions of its legitimacy.

(iv) The scope and purpose of the paper

The ensuing discussion falls into three parts. As the European Parliament represents the only EC institution subject to popular election, a consideration of its role in relation to other institutions constitutes the final and central part of this discussion. The principal issue addressed is the gap between the powers of the EC institutions and their accountability (the so-called 'democratic deficit'). Although the European Parliament is the focus of this part of the discussion, it is clear that the broader legitimacy of the Community rests on the interplay between the Commission, the Council, the Parliament and, indeed, the national legislatures. Therefore, the role of the Parliament can be enhanced only in the context of a broader readjustment of the Community's decision-making processes.

That discussion is preceded by a consideration of the separate but linked concept of 'EC citizenship'. Here it will be argued that any enhancement of the Community's legitimacy ought to be complemented by, and should itself reinforce, a politico-legal relationship between the Community and its citizens, a relationship that would, in albeit restricted spheres, supersede the relationship between a national government and its own citizens.

However, to set both these main themes in a proper perspective, the Community's efforts in the past to present a 'human face' are discussed in relation to the evolving Social Policy, the 'People's Europe' initiative, and popular attitudes towards the Community's policies and institutions. These three themes provide the essential background for any discussion of the Community's efforts to develop its own legitimacy in the 1990s. It is to this background that we now turn.

2. BACKGROUND

(i) The evolution of public opinion

Eurobarometer surveys, carried out every six months in the EC, make it possible to measure public support for, and belief in, the Community and its institutions. Only one EC citizen in eight (13 per cent) thinks that the way the Community functions is "completely democratic" (Eurobarometer 32 : 57) and the figure for Ireland is even lower at 8 per cent. Nevertheless, there seems to be widespread satisfaction, and especially in Ireland, with the impact of the Community's policies. Asked whether they think that, on balance, their country's membership of the European Community has been beneficial, 58 per cent of EC respondents reply in the affirmative while Ireland's figure of 84 per cent is the highest in the EC.

When asked to judge the EC Commission, 51 per cent of EC respondents regard it favourably as do 68 per cent in Ireland — again the highest figure in the EC. On the issue of extending the competence of the Community (see Appendix 1) to create a single currency, or a central bank, support in Ireland matches that of the EC generally (about 55 per cent in favour in both cases). However, on the more political issues of a common foreign policy and a common security/defence policy, the level of Irish support (43 per cent and 49 per cent respectively) is markedly, and unsurprisingly, less than for the EC generally (51 per cent and 66 per cent respectively).

Since the passing of the Single European Act, the European Parliament has been regarded as increasingly important. Today, 58 per cent see it as important in the "life of the European Community" (Ireland 70 per cent) and 37 per cent see it as important in the "everyday life of citizens" (Ireland 53 per cent). Clearly, there is some disillusionment with the European Parliament's role since although many regard it as important, many also feel that its role should be enhanced. 53 per cent of EC citizens feel that the European Parliament "should play a more important role than it does now" (44 per cent in Ireland). In Ireland, 65 per cent of respondents have a favourable impression of the Parliament (compared with the 68 per cent regarding the Commission favourably) but this represents a fall of 11 per cent over the previous six months (Eurobarometer 34).

Except in Denmark and the United Kingdom, there is generally strong support for giving the European Parliament extra powers that would go some way towards remedying the Community's 'democratic deficit'. On five specific proposals to strengthen the European Parliament, there is majority support across the EC as a whole with the Italians being particularly enthusiastic. In Ireland, however, support for strengthening the European Parliament seems rather muted (see Appendix 2) especially in the light of the high approval rating that EC membership currently enjoys in Ireland. This apparent paradox may be explained by concern that Ireland's representation in the Parliament is numerically insufficient to protect threats to national interests that might arise there. Confidence in the Commission, already noted, may therefore be based in the belief that its integrationist and redistributive priorities are in Ireland's best interests.

(ii) Social policy as a reinforcer of EC legitimacy

The regular monitoring of public opinion in the EC has revealed a persistent disinclination on the part of EC citizens to identify strongly with the EC institutions and a consistent reluctance to extend loyalties from national to Community symbols. Since the early 1970s, it can be argued that Social Policy has been used, in part, as a vehicle through which a greater affinity with the Community can be fostered.

Although the roots of EC social policy can be traced back to the Rome Treaty and, indeed, to the European Coal and Steel Community (ECSC), it was not until the 1970s that a broader interpretation of the Community's role was perceived as desirable. Inflation and unemployment throughout the EC in the early 1970s, a more vocal opposition to EC membership evident in Denmark and the United Kingdom, the latter's 'renegotiation' of its membership in 1974–5, the rejection of EC membership by the Norwegians in 1972, and a growing belief among West Europeans that "quality of life" was as important as "standard of living", all contributed to the need to foster a more'positive' image of the Community.

Thus the Social Fund, for example, no longer claimed simply to tackle the negative effects of unemployment but took on more positive goals such as the setting up of vocational training centres, and helping workers to adapt to new working environments. Phrases such as 'European Social Union', and 'European Human Union' (used by British Regional Affairs Commissioner Thompson in 1975) reflected the new thinking, as did the establishment of the European Foundation for the Improvement of Living and Working Conditions in Dublin in the same year. During the 1970's steps were taken to improve the Commission's information services when it became clear that increased knowledge of the Community was reflected in more supportive attitudes. By the late 1970s, one writer saw the Community's social policy as:

> . . . no longer concerned with rectifying and redressing negative effects of integration. Instead, it provides the context in which a new image of the EEC may be articulated and projected. The awareness-creating and image-building tactics associated with the social policy may well be more important than the actual 'goods' disbursed to relatively small numbers of EEC citizens under this policy; and may well be a way of promoting transnational socio-psychological community formation and increasing public support for — or at least lessening public disaffection from — the EEC (Lodge, 1978 : 132).

In the 1980s, social policy continued to be important although for slightly different reasons. The anticipated impact of the Single European Market is leading to a new emphasis on 'economic and social cohesion' among the widely disparate regions of the Community; and a renewed concern to bridge the gap between employers and employees. In 1985, the so-called 'Val Duchesse' dialogue between the 'social partners' was established by Delors; and a mild commitment to social policy in the Single European Act was strengthened by the detailed provisions of the 'Social Charter' (1989). This latter document, although not itself binding on EC governments, is providing the legislative guidelines for a whole range of directives aimed at creating a 'European social area'.

Within the single market, it is intended that a 'level playing field' in the realm of social policy will make it impossible for multinational firms, for example, to exploit workers in countries with inferior social legislation. To avoid what is sometimes called 'social dumping', the Social Charter covers issues such as: trade union membership; child labour; maternity leave; equal pay for men and women; health and safety in the workplace; nightwork; and part-time work. The thrust behind this programme is clear enough: it is to create a Europe-wide work area where the conditions are broadly similar so that the free movement of workers becomes a realistic prospect.

During the 1980s, this preoccupation with 'cohesion' in the realm of social policy has been paralleled by a continuing campaign to create a 'People's Europe'. Since a narrow emphasis on 'workers' unrelated to broader human rights concerns would be unlikely to enhance the Community's legitimacy in the eyes of its citizens, there has been a sustained attempt to offer tangible benefits that are clearly associated with, but clearly additional to, the purely economic purposes of the single market. Symbols of 'European identity' have been increasingly deployed to nurture a transnational sense of community although the value of these, in the absence of tangible evidence that the single market provides benefits and opportunities, is questionable. Programmes like ERASMUS and COMETT, that aim to promote transnational contacts in higher education and industry sow the seeds for a more Europeanised workforce; but this harvest will be reaped only if the single market itself is a success.

(iii) 'People's Europe' and the Adonnino Report (1985)

Speaking in Strasbourg in January 1988, Jacques Delors argued that the completion of the single market would become meaningful only if it brought balanced economic and social progress within a large frontier-free area. "Each and every Community citizen needs to feel bound by the links which unite European society".

What distinguishes current Community social policy in this area from the past is the comprehensive scope of its objectives, and its multifaceted approach. The concept of a People's Europe is deliberately intended to move well beyond a preoccupation with rather mundane issues such as unemployment, training and worker participation, towards a more positive vision of Community rights, and a better quality of life incorporating not simply the obvious economic components but also important educational, cultural, and legal dimensions.

The project of a People's Europe was given its formal launching at the Fontainebleau Summit in 1984. There, a committee, that became known as the Adonnino Committee, was charged with making recommendations whereby the Community would 'strengthen and promote its image both for its citizens and for the rest of the world'. In particular, the Committee was asked to look at matters such as frontier formalities, EC symbols, youth exchanges, the minting of EC coinage, and the mutual recognition of university diplomas. The Committee actually presented two reports whose contents ranged rather more widely than the original remit.

In the first report, some specific recommendations relating to the freedom of movement for people and goods across national frontiers were made. For example, it was suggested that vehicles crossing an internal land frontier should be observed 'travelling at low speed' and should carry 'a green label showing a white E' to indicate that the vehicle and its occupants were in conformity with all Community regulations (European Commission 1985 : 10). For tax-paid goods, it was recommended that the personal allowance should be raised to 350 ecus from 1 July 1985, and that the tax exemption limit on small parcels should be raised to 100 ecus from the same date.

Attention was also drawn to the problems of people living in one country but employed in another since many countries tax non-residents on a different basis from residents. On rights of establishment, the Committee called for the mutual recognition of diplomas and professional qualifications to avoid the lengthy delays involved in achieving harmonisation. On the related issue of the right of EC citizens to reside in any part of the EC, the Committee said it was convinced that this right was 'an essential element of the right to freedom of movement' (EC Commission 1985 : 14) but it was clearly aware of the need to ensure that migrants within the EC had sufficient funds at their disposal to prevent them being a burden to the social security system of the host country.

In the second report, the Committee moved into areas that overlap, to some extent, with the concept of 'EC citizenship' (see below). Suffice to say that here the Committee was primarily concerned with citizens of the EC as political actors in a variety of contexts. The Committee called for a common electoral procedure for European Parliament elections; for common rules regarding voting by EC citizens in local elections; for common procedures to ensure that EC law is applied uniformly throughout the Community; and to speed up consular cooperation in third countries so that EC nationals can avail of any EC consulate when their own government is not represented in a specific country.

The remaining recommendations were all designed to enhance the 'European identity' and the Community's 'image' in the minds of EC citizens. Among such measures were: a common television area with more co-production between EC networks, a Euro-lottery, youth exchanges, an increased European dimension in education, the twinning of towns across the Community, and the adoption of two important unifying symbols: the circle of gold stars on a blue background as the Community emblem and flag, and the theme of the fourth movement of Beethoven's Ninth Symphony as the Community's 'anthem'.

In commending the two reports to the European Council, the Committee expressed the hope that the proposals contained in them would 'give the individual citizen a clearer perception of the dimension and existence of the Community' (European Commission 1985 : 30). Although the implementation of these proposals has been patchy, their influence has been apparent in various developments that have followed the ratification of the Single European Act, such as the ERASMUS, COMETT, and LINGUA programmes and the impulses that lie behind the Social Charter.

In trying to match the expanding competences that flow from the Single European Act (see below) with enhanced perceptions of legitimacy in the hearts and minds of its 340 million citizens, the Commission is openly challenging the member states' exclusivity in this regard. However, in this competition, the Commission is caught in something of a bind. In seeking to redirect the loyalties of its citizens away from national governments, the EC has to demonstrate that it can deliver as effectively, if not more effectively, the services rendered by national administrations. At the same time, however, there will be a built-in reluctance to hand over areas of competence to the EC until the transfer of loyalty has taken place.

Symbols of European unity are, in themselves, unlikely to create new reservoirs of popular support for Community institutions before those institutions have proved their worth in a number of practical ways; but, equally, these institutions are unlikely to be given the chance to prove their efficacy until support for national institutions has been gradually eroded by a manifest inability to cope with the tasks placed on them. In elaborating a concept of 'EC citizenship', the Community is seeking to develop a category that complements rather than replaces the traditional notion of national citizenship. Nevertheless, it is clear that EC citizenship, could erode the exclusive claims of national citizenship.

3. EUROPEAN COMMUNITY CITIZENSHIP

(i) The origins and meaning of EC citizenship

The progress being made towards the Single European Market, the prospects of Political Union and Monetary Union, and the pressure for greater coordination in foreign policy, all imply a more central role for citizens of the EC. The transformation of the 'Community' to a 'Union' should be reflected in a transformation of the status of those who inhabit the Union. EC citizenship thus reflects a series of rights and duties that are specific to the nature of the Union and are exercised and safeguarded within its boundaries, without excluding the possibility that such citizenship may also extend beyond the borders of the Community.

Needless to say, and as we have hinted above, the concept of EC citizenship will evolve *pari passu* with the Community's own evolution. The scope of EC citizenship will reflect the dimensions of political union as it takes shape so that it will become increasingly immaterial in which part of the Community its citizens reside: their rights and duties in respect of their Community citizenship will become progressively more uniform.

The concept of EC citizenship presupposes a third sphere of rights and duties in addition to the two which currently exist, i.e. the national sphere which derives from the citizenship of the member states, and the Community sphere which results from the treaties for nationals of any member state. This third sphere results from transforming the Community into a Union and involves the transformation of EC citizens from being merely 'privileged aliens' into citizens of the new Union.

(ii) The scope of EC citizenship

The 'core' of EC citizenship should be seen to comprise three basic rights: full freedom of movement; freedom to choose one's place of residence; and the right to political participation at the place of residence. Progress towards these goals has, so far, been rather fragmentary; and almost always the result of either European Court of Justice judgements on specific issues, or bilateral arrangements between two or more member states and often, therefore, beyond the Community's purview.

In all cases, these rights and freedoms are tied to the possession of the nationality of one of the member states, not simply to being a citizen of the EC. This basic prerequisite is enshrined in the European Parliament's recent Declaration of Fundamental Human Rights (adopted in 1989) where a Community citizen is defined as "any person possessing the nationality of one of the member states". The definition of nationality is left to the governments of the member states, and no suggestion is being made that this intimate area of national competence should be transferred to the Community itself. Thus, insofar as EC citizens' rights are dependent on the holding of a nationality of one of the member states, it is the member states themselves who define who will benefit from EC citizenship and who will not.

However, not all benefits of EC citizenship are restricted to the nationals of the twelve member states. Some categories of persons, the dependants of EC nationals for example, who are not themselves EC nationals, may receive the same benefits, and exercise the same rights, as EC citizens *stricto sensu.* What this distinction suggests, therefore, is that we are witnessing an embryonic development of EC citizenship that is substantially, but not exclusively, coterminous with the nationalities of the member states and which depends, in fact, on the extent to which Community legal provisions succeed in replacing national provisions in matters essential to the concept of citizenship.

The future evolution of EC citizenship is made more complicated, but may in fact be facilitated, by norms flowing from the European Convention on Human Rights (ECHR). This Convention, although it applies to a broader group of countries than the EC, contains basic principles that could be usefully exploited in any future development of EC citizenship. The European Court of Justice has already established precedents for the incorporation of the Convention's articles into EC law.

The right to participate in free elections in the European Convention on Human Rights might well conflict with the denial of such a right to EC nationals to vote in European Parliament elections if they happen to be living in a country other than their own. Likewise the expulsion of a non-EC national related to someone living in a member state might be construed as violating the right to respect for family life (Article 8 of the ECHR). These examples are not in themselves an argument for the Community's signature of the ECHR, although other arguments might be so deployed, but rather suggest that the current propensity of the European Court of Justice to recognise 'rights' (outside the Rome Treaty and the Single European Act) may be helpful in constructing a definition of EC citizenship in the future.

One of the most basic rights attaching to EC citizenship is freedom of movement and freedom of residence, but so far this freedom has been granted in a rather restricted matter. Until the social welfare provision of member states becomes virtually uniform across the Community, governments will worry about the propensity of migrants from poorer countries with high unemployment moving to take up residence in the more prosperous regions, thus becoming a burden to the social security system.

The 1989 proposal on freedom of movement (see Official Journal, 1989, C191/5) requires only that EC nationals not enjoying the right of free movement under existing EC law, should be covered by sickness insurance and provide proof that they will not become a financial burden on the host country. Residence permits are still required by some governments, implying that the right of residence is not equally available to all EC nationals. Ideally, proof of citizenship of one member state should be sufficient to permit entry and residence in another member state.

Possession of Community nationality ought, in the future, to have greater significance outside the territory of the EC. With the development of European Political Cooperation (EPC), and trade agreements concluded between the Community *per se* and third countries, the diplomatic protection of EC nationals in third countries would seem to be a natural corollary. Ideally, this would evolve alongside a network of EC diplomatic missions whose functions would be to subsume effectively the previous functions of individual national missions in third countries. Such an eventuality was, as we have seen, anticipated in the Adonnino Report.

Political participation is another important area where EC citizenship ought to be taking shape but where agreements between national governments have so far been patchy, at best. In 1982, the European Parliament proposed that EC nationals living in a country other than their own should be allowed to participate in Direct Elections: nearly ten years later the Council of Ministers has still not agreed to this proposal. Such rights as do exist stem from initiatives taken by individual national governments; but the inequities that this involves may eventually be challenged in the European Court of Justice.

Local elections have provided another arena for Community action. In 1988, the Commission issued a draft directive (COM [88] 371) on local elections where people who have been resident in a country for a minimum period (to be fixed by the government of that country) may take part in local elections. When a person has resided for twice the minimum period, (s)he would be entitled to stand for election. This proposal does not provide for the harmonisation of the rules of eligibility for local elections but simply a system of mutual recognition of national criteria. More seriously, however, it excludes national elections which are, arguably, more conducive to the integration of migrants into host countries and therefore more likely to enhance the concept of EC citizenship.

However, even the Commission's 1988 proposal awaits Council action; and for the relatively large number of Irish citizens living in other member states the matter is one of some importance (except in the United Kingdom and Ireland where reciprocal voting rights could well provide a model for the entire Community).

In the absence of anything more robust than rather vestigial notions of Community citizenship, it is worth emphasising that Community law, and the cumulative rulings of the European Court of Justice provide a legal framework of protection for individuals on an increasingly wide range of matters that fall under Community competence. This is worth noting not only because it has long provided, at the Community level, one of the attributes of citizenship, namely access to legal redress, but also because its efficacy constitutes an important source of legitimacy for the Community generally.

In 1977, a pig farmer in Co. Armagh was prosecuted for moving pigs without proper documentation but the case against him was dropped because the legislation under which he had been charged was found by the Luxembourg Court to be incompatible with the provisions of the Common Agricultural Policy. Likewise, in 1990, a French national, Danielle Roux, had her expulsion from Belgium on the grounds that her profession (the oldest) was a 'threat to public order', overturned by the European Court of Justice. In its judgement, the Court ruled that possession of an ID card, and proof of 'the exercise of some kind of economic activity' were sufficient for an EC national to reside in another member state, and that the 'public order' argument could not be sustained in view of the numerous others engaged in the same profession (EP News, 1991b).

European Community law provides part of the infrastructure on which the legitimacy of Community institutions increasingly rests. Community law creates rights and obligations, attaching to both governments and individual citizens, even in those cases where a government may have improperly or only partially fulfilled the purposes of a directive. Community law takes precedence over national law; and national courts must therefore set aside national legislation found to be incompatible with Community legislation. What this means, also, is that individuals can sometimes have their rights protected or upheld against the effects of national law.

4. THE DEMOCRATIC DEFICIT

(i) The Single European Act and the 'democratic deficit'

The introduction of majority voting in the Single European Act has reduced the influence of both the national parliaments and the European Parliament. On matters relating to the completion of the single market, governments can be outvoted in the Council of Ministers and no matter how effective national parliamentary control may have been previously, it will be rendered superfluous in such circumstances. If this loss of control at the national level had been compensated for by increased supervision in the European Parliament, a 'democratic deficit' might not exist or, at least, not be so pronounced. However, the pooling of sovereignty in the Council of Ministers has not been matched by commensurate increases in the role of the European Parliament.

In its own Resolution on the 'democratic deficit' in the European Community (Official Journal, C187/229–231, 17 June, 1988) the European Parliament spelt out the dimensions of the problem: "the limitations on the powers of national parliaments may involve either a loss of power to pass laws or an obligation to adopt certain implementing or contingency measures or to refrain from using the powers reserved to them, without those powers being transferred to the European Parliament, in a way which compromises the democratic legitimacy of its decisions . . . the loss of these democratic powers by the national parliaments is not counter-balanced by any increase in democratic control at European Community level . . . the danger of bureaucratisation and estrangement from the popular will is compounded in the case of questions withdrawn from the scope of national parliaments, and therefore from national debate, since citizens feel alienated from large areas of Community decision-making" and the fact that legislation is adopted (by the Council of Ministers) behind closed doors is "responsible not only for a democratic shortfall but also for a low level of effectiveness in the Community's work" and since most people in the Community are "unaware of the democratic deficit . . . there is a danger that this deficit will seriously mislead the peoples of Europe as to accountability and the decision-making process in the European Community".

These sentiments express the disappointment that inevitably flows from the realisation by the Parliament that it has been sold short by the Single European Act. This disappointment is, perhaps, all the greater in view of the fact that the roots of the Single European Act lie in Parliament's own efforts to adopt a new Draft Treaty for the Community in 1984.

(ii) The European Parliament

The foregoing comments by the Parliament reflect the frustration experienced by an institution whose supposed *raison d'etre* has always been to act as the Community's democratic conscience within a decision-making process that is, by any reasonable standards, arcane, byzantine and cumbersome. Although calling itself a 'parliament', the two essential functions of a parliament — legislating and raising taxes — have so far eluded it. Nevertheless, and especially since it became directly elected in 1979, the Parliament has left few stones unturned in its search for greater influence and greater powers.

Through the use of 'own initiative' reports, the Parliament has been able to send a signal to the Commission indicating the outlines of desirable new legislation. Through oral and written questions tabled by individual MEPs, the Parliament has persuaded members of the Council of Ministers to respond in person, although they are not obliged to do so. The right to sack the entire Commission, although threatened on a number of occasions, has proved too unwieldy to put into practice, not least because the Parliament could not prevent the reappointment of those sacked.

In the budgetary arena, the Parliament has been given, and has successfully exploited, limited powers. It can veto the whole budget, and can alter expenditure (within limits) on its non-compulsory sections. The prospects of using the budget weapon successfully depend on the attitudes of national governments towards specific items in the budget, as well as the Parliament's own determination effectively to freeze the Community's development pending the successful resolution of a budgetary impasse. The Parliament has also used articles of the Rome Treaty as a lever to assert its own powers: in 1982, for example, it took the Council to the European Court of Justice for failing to act on transport policy; and in 1979 the Court struck down a piece of draft legislation as illegal because the Council had passed it without awaiting the Parliament's opinion.

An important link between the people of the Community and the European Parliament is the right of petition. Any EC citizen with a grievance against either an EC institution or concerning EC law can petition Parliament directly. During the parliamentary year 1990–91, 785 petitions were submitted and among notable achievements were forcing the French authorities to allow job applications for physiotherapists' posts from other EC nationals, and obliging the Greek authorities to charge EC citizens the same entry fee to museums as Greek nationals (EP News, 1991a).

One of the proposals being considered by the governments in the IGCs is the appointment of an ombudsman, to take over the role of the Petitions Committee in the Parliament. The Parliament would be responsible for appointing the ombudsman, for receiving his annual report, and requesting his dismissal in cases of neglect of his duties. Otherwise the ombudsman would serve the same term of office as the Parliament. The ombudsman would be entirely independent in the performance of his duties. Despite being an apparently reasonable proposal, and one which would help to make the EC institutions more responsive to public concerns, the Petitions Committee of the European Parliament was reported (in June 1991) as being opposed to the suggestion on the grounds that it would be more 'bureaucratic' than the present system.

Impressive though many of the Parliament's attributes may be, they do not add up to anything like legislative power on a par with that exercised by the Council of Ministers. The Single European Act gives the Parliament little except for the new cooperation procedure, although the possibilities inherent in Parliament's new right to veto the entry of new member states (Article 237) and associated agreements (Article 238) have, perhaps, been underestimated.

However, it is possible that the Parliament could use these veto powers to extract new institutional reforms from the Council (Lodge, 1989 : 69; Ehlermann, 1990 : 142). In the short term, the best chance for the European Parliament to make any progress towards being a 'real' legislature will be by exploiting, and possibly expanding, the new 'cooperation procedure'. Already, the experience of that procedure has caused the Parliament to streamline the management of its own business, and enhance the effectiveness of its contacts with the Commission. At the end of the day, however, there can be no substitute for formal legislative powers: the new cooperation procedure opens the door only a little in that direction.

(iii) The cooperation procedure: problems and prospects

The cooperation procedure applies to only ten articles of the Rome Treaty but it has been estimated that two-thirds of the single market programme falls under these ten articles. Among the issues covered by the cooperation procedure are: freedom of movement; freedom of establishment; mutual recognition of qualifications; provisions relating to the establishment and functioning of the internal market; social policy; economic and social cohesion; and technological collaboration. How exactly does the cooperation procedure work?

The cooperation procedure establishes a system of two readings (and two deadlines) designed to speed up what has been a rather drawn out process in the past. During the first reading, the European Parliament may reject, amend, withhold, or issue an opinion. It may persuade the Commission to amend or withhold its proposal but even if the Commission is unwilling to do so, the Parliament can delay things by referring the proposal back to its own committee.

Even if the Council has a 'common position' ready, it cannot announce it until Parliament's own opinion is made public. When it is made public, it goes with the Commission's reactions to the opinion to the Council. The Council reaches its 'common position' by a qualified majority. The Parliament has three months to approve the 'common position' and if it does, or if it fails to express a view, the Council adopts the proposal. If, however, the Parliament decides to reject the common position (which it must do by an absolute majority) the Council may still adopt the proposal, provided it can do so unanimously.

At this stage the Parliament can obstruct progress by persuading one member government to prevent unanimity by withholding its consent or, more constructively, the Parliament can amend the common position by an absolute majority. If it chooses this latter course, the Commission has a month to revise the proposal before sending it to the Council for the second reading. A three month period then ensues during which the Council may (a) adopt (but only if unanimous) Parliament's amendments which the Commission has not put into the proposal or (b) adopt the Commission proposal (by qualified majority) or amend it (if unanimous) or (c) delay a decision for a month (but only with Parliament's agreement) or (d) it may fail to act at all in which case the proposal falls.

This new procedure thus requires the Council, the Commission and the Parliament to cooperate with each other in a way that they have never done before. It is more difficult now for either the Commission or the Council to ignore the views of Parliament and, perhaps more significantly, the new procedures have encouraged informal contacts between the three institutions on a scale that was not necessary hitherto.

The natural alliance between the Commission and the Parliament has been reinforced: the two bodies quickly agreed that cooperation should start during the first reading, so as to avoid nasty surprises during the second; and both bodies benefit from majority voting in the Council since the amendments to the Directive (in 1990) on car emissions would certainly not have been achieved had the Council not been able to accept the Commission's amended proposal with a qualified majority (Ehlermann, 1990 : 141). The new procedure gives the Parliament influence, but not a veto; it makes it a more effective participant in the legislative process, but it does not make Parliament a 'co-legislator' as the European Union Treaty (EUT), for example, would have done.

Among possible ways of extending the cooperation procedure are the following: (a) the issues to which it applies could be extended; (b) the cooperation procedure could be extended to all issues on which the Council votes by a qualified majority and (c) the Parliament could be granted the formal right to initiate legislation in designated areas, and a modified form of the cooperation procedure could then apply.

(iv) The European Parliament and the national parliaments

Since the 'democratic deficit' is correctly perceived as involving a loss of power on the part of both the national parliaments *and* the European Parliament, many suggestions for remedying the 'deficit' advocate closer links between the national parliaments and the European Parliament.

In the Final Declaration, following the Conference of Parliaments of the European Community (held in Rome, 27–30 November, 1990), "enhanced cooperation between the national parliaments and the European Parliaments" is called for "through regular meetings of specialised committees, exchanges of information and by organising Conferences of Parliaments of the European Community" (para. 13); and the principle that "each national parliament must be able to bring its influence to bear on the shaping of its government's policy stances on Europe" is asserted (para. 14) although no specific mechanisms for achieving this are suggested.

The Commission is not directly involved in the enhancement of relations between the European Parliament and the national parliaments but supports, in broad terms, what the Parliament is trying to achieve: "the Commission believes that it is first and foremost for the European Parliament, in consultation with national parliaments, to consider what is the best way to improve relations between the elected representatives of the people" (EC Commission, 1990 : 19). However, the Commission rather grudgingly concedes that "should new arrangements prove to be essential", delegations from national parliaments could be given an explanation from the Council Presidency and the Commission before major decisions are taken; but this is preceded by the rather naive assertion that since "national governments are accountable to national parliaments, it is for them to involve elected representatives in Community affairs in a manner which respects national traditions"! (EC Commission, 1990 : 18).

It has, therefore, been left to national parliaments to react to these broad *desiderata*. In the Irish case, the dwindling significance of the dual mandate has concentrated attention on how to maintain effective contact between the Oireachtas and the European Parliament. When Ireland joined the EC in 1973, the appointment of ten MEPs by the Oireachtas meant that the dual mandate was automatically exercised by all. By 1991, only two of the country's fifteen MEPs serve in both parliaments and, in view of the increasing workload in the European Parliament, it is unlikely that the dual mandate will be sustained by Irish MEPs in the future.

In its seventh Report (February, 1991), the Joint Committee (on the Secondary legislation of the European Communities) ruled out two possible linkages between the MEPs and the Oireachtas: (a) ex officio membership and (b) a right of audience for MEPs in the Dail and Seanad. Instead, it has recommended "a liaison body, comprising members of the Joint Committee" which would "act as a delegation for relations with the European Parliament and other Community institutions" (para. 35). In addition, it is suggested that all MEPs (from *any* member country) should have a right of audience in the Joint Committee and, if this principle was established on a mutually agreed basis across the Community, it could provide "a degree of cohesion and common identity at the level of national parliaments" (para. 36).

Even these modest reforms would require a revision of the Joint Committee's terms of reference; and its broader concerns would be accurately reflected in its suggestion for a new title: Joint Committee on European Community Affairs. As the Committee itself argues, a broader remit will only be realistic if the resources provided to the Committee are adequate, and its Reports are promptly debated (para. 31).

The foregoing proposals, and analogous suggestions in other member states, represent the minimalist option for linking the national parliaments to the European Parliament. The maximalist option is represented by a much more far-reaching institutional reform involving the creation of a 'European Senate'. This idea, recommended by the Oireachtas Joint Committee for serious consideration (Joint Committee, 1990, Appendix iii), is not supported by the European Parliament itself. A 'European Senate' would consist of delegations from the twelve national parliaments and would constitute a second chamber alongside the present European Parliament.

Within this model, there are variations: it can be seen either (a) as a body that would meet two or three times yearly to fulfil the vital function of bridging the gap between the national and EC legislative processes or (b) it could be a permanent institution through which the Community's draft legislation could pass with a view to ensuring, firstly, that it conforms with national parliamentary opinion in the member states and, secondly, that the principle of subsidiarity is observed (see vii below). In the run-up to the Assizes (in November, 1990) the European Parliament did not recommend the creation of a European Senate because (i) it felt that the experience of the Parliament before 1979 did not augur well for such a body; (ii) the Council of Ministers already represents the member states and (iii) decision-making would become more cumbersome (European Parliament, 1990 : 165–6); and the new body might well detract from the Parliament's own authority. Thus, as we have seen, the Parliament decided to focus on achieving 'enhanced cooperation between the national parliaments and the European Parliament'.

(v) Parliament's relations with the Commission and the Council

The Parliament and the Commission are often regarded as 'natural allies' within the institutional framework of the EC. Both purport to represent the interests of the Community *qua* Community; both have traditionally viewed the Council of Ministers as the villain of the piece when it comes to advancing the broad goals of the European Community. In fact, neither the Parliament nor the Commission is as *communautaire* as this simple dichotomy implies. The Commission is in theory autonomous, and Commissioners undertake not to be swayed by national loyalties or national pressure. In reality, the right of governments not to renew a Commissioner's term of office can act as a powerful brake on a Commissioner's independence.

Nevertheless, governments rarely obtain unswerving loyalty from their appointees even if they hope, sometimes, to win short-term concessions from them. The Parliament, although dominated by political groups that are, by definition, multinational, is not immune to national influences especially in those groups that are dominated by one member state (e.g. the European Democrats tend to be largely a British grouping).

The relationship between the Commission and the Parliament has normally been cooperative: and has become more so since the Single European Act. Except for the rather draconian power to sack the entire Commission, the Parliament's other contacts within the Commission tend to be mutually constructive. Firstly, the Commission is often represented in the Parliament's committees, enabling an exchange of views to take place prior to what is often a common battle with the Council of Ministers. Secondly, the Commission answers questions (oral and written) in the Parliament, a process that hints at the Commission's accountability to the Parliament although falling far short of making the Commission a true 'government' for the Community. Thirdly, the Commission presents its annual programme to the Parliament for debate, an event that has tended more to symbolise than reinforce the Parliament's legitimacy. Fourthly, since the inception of the cooperation procedure in 1987, there has been much more intensive consultation between the Commission and the Parliament to ascertain the legal basis on which draft proposals are going to be based.

This is critical for deciding whether a proposal progresses according to the cooperation procedure or through the traditional channels where the Parliament obviously has much less influence. Since the Single European Act came into effect, committees responsible for dealing with Commission proposals also consider their legal basis, something that the Commission has supported. It has, accordingly, been in the interests of the Parliament to ensure that as many proposals as possible are interpreted as being related to the completion of the single market (Single European Act, Article 100a and b) and hence subject to the cooperation procedure.

The Single European Act has also improved the atmosphere in which Parliament's relations with the Council operate. Under the Rome Treaty, the only formal provision linking the two institutions was the requirement that the Council should obtain an Opinion from the Parliament before adopting new legislative proposals, a requirement that was tested in the European Court of Justice in the isoglucose case (1980) where the Council had attempted to legislate before the Parliament had emitted an Opinion.

With the advent of the Single European Act, the Parliament and the Council have been forced into a more collaborative pattern of interaction, at least on proposals subject to the cooperation procedure. Nevertheless, the Parliament is far from having achieved real legislative power in its relations with the Council. Once its Opinions have been given, the Parliament has little control over what happens to them: at any given time 400–500 proposals, on which the Parliament has given an Opinion, are awaiting a Council decision. However, Parliament's monitoring of Opinions has improved: conciliation meetings, at which Parliament and Council representatives try to iron out differences, often find the Council more conciliatory than hitherto.

Other problems facing the Parliament in dealing with the Council are that the Council may adopt (at least unofficially) an attitude on a proposal before the Parliament (through no fault of its own) has produced an Opinion; and on external trade matters the Council has no obligation to consult the Parliament at all, although for proposals to admit a new member to the EC, or to conclude an association agreement, Parliament's assent (by absolute majority) is required under the Single European Act (Articles 8 and 9).

(vi) The Commission's accountability to Parliament

In redressing the imbalance between the Parliament's role and that, respectively, of the Council and Commission, much more hope attaches to enhancing the accountability of the Commission to the Parliament. It is in this direction, rather than in any real realignment of the Council–Parliament relationship that progress is likely to be achieved. As a starting point, we can note that since 1983 it has been customary, although not mandatory, for the governments of the EC to consult the Parliament on the appointment of the Commission President; and the Parliament has started giving a 'vote of confidence' to a new Commission at the time it is sworn in, but the significance of this is little more than symbolic.

In its submission to the Inter Governmental Conference in 1991, the Parliament takes the view that:

> the President of the Commission must be elected by the European Parliament on a proposal from the European Council, by an absolute majority; that the President of the Commission, in agreement with Council, should appoint the members of the Commission, and that the incoming Commission as a whole should present itself and its programme to the European Parliament for a vote of confidence; the Commission's term of office will start at the same time as that of the European Parliament (para. 18).

Although even these modest changes are unlikely to be accepted in full by the IGC, they represent a step in the direction of making the Commission, as an executive, more fully accountable to the Parliament and thereby enhancing the latter's legitimacy. However, it is not clear what would happen if the Parliament rejected either the European Council's nominee for the Commission Presidency or the Commission's programme.

There are, however, two other variations of these proposals that ought, at least, to be open for discussion:

(a) that the President of the Commission, once selected, would choose his own Commission from among MEPs whose vacancies would then be filled according to procedures already agreed for that country's MEPs; and these Commissioners would then present themselves and their programme before the European Parliament for a vote of confidence. This proposal would emphasise more clearly the responsibility of the Commission to Parliament

and a more modest suggestion:

(b) that the present system should continue but that when a government decided not to renew a Commissioner's appointment, such a decision could be overridden by an absolute majority in the European Parliament.

(vii) The European Parliament and the impact of 'subsidiarity'

Subsidiarity can be defined as the notion that the Community will only act to carry out tasks which can be undertaken more effectively by the member states acting in common rather than separately. The principle was implicit in the Rome Treaty, endorsed in the Parliament's Draft Treaty on European Union and is now made quite explicit in the Single European Act. Its importance in the present discussion arises because any delineation of the interface between powers to be discharged by EC institutions and powers to be left with national governments, touches on the relationship between the European Parliament and, respectively, the Council of Ministers and the national parliaments and, hence, on the 'democratic deficit'.

In its Special Report for the Conference of the Parliaments of the European Community (November, 1990) the Joint Committee raised the question of whether subsidiarity might be used to 'limit the development of the Community' (para. 14) but this underlines the importance of how subsidiarity is defined in any Treaty revision, and how disputes between the national and Community levels of competence are resolved. Any suspicion of subsidiarity being deployed by national governments simply to preserve some freedom of manoeuvre in the wake of the Single European Act, is best countered by strengthening links between national parliaments and the European Parliament.

The European Parliament's submission to the IGC combines two rationales for subsidiarity: objectives requiring intervention because (a) "their scope or their implications transcend member state frontiers" or (b) they are likely to be carried out "more effectively by the Union than by member states acting alone" (para. 23). These categories are not, of course, mutually exclusive: in the Single European Act (Article 130R) the environment is specified as a subject on which joint action might be more effective than individual national actions, but clearly there could be trans-frontier implications in some EC legislation on the environment.

The Parliament favours incorporating the principle of subsidiarity into the preamble of the Treaties and establishing mechanisms for *a priori* evaluation and *a posteriori* adjudication on the extent of the powers to be exercised by the Community institutions. The European Court of Justice is envisaged for the latter role. The question is left open as to whether specific powers should be enumerated as belonging to either the national governments or the Union (a practice followed in many national federal systems), but in preliminary discussion of these issues (European Parliament, 1990) powers 'which the Community envisages acquiring' (but many of which would effectively be shared with national governments) the parliament suggested European Monetary Union (EMU), foreign policy, development aid, and EC citizenship. Among powers which should not be removed from national control are: national and local taxation; education; sport; civil law; criminal law; police forces (except for TREVI).

The Parliament's Final Declaration (to the IGCs) does not make recommendations on how subsidiarity should be evaluated politically or guaranteed judicially beyond saying that the European Court of Justice should play the latter role. In the Giscard d'Estaing Report cited above (European Parliament, 1990) a number of possibilities are raised that might stimulate discussion in Ireland.

One of these is that a European Senate, drawn from the members of national parliaments, and in one version (Heseltine, 1989) consisting of 152 members, should reverse the current tendency for power to drift away from national legislatures. Representation from national parliaments could either be distributed unequally to reflect qualified majority voting strengths in the Council of Ministers (and follow the model of the German Bundesrat) or be distributed equally to reflect the equal representation of member states in the Council (and follow the model of the United States Senate).

Likewise, there are various ways in which representatives from national parliaments could be selected or elected: the Bundesrat model would imply that only the governing party from each member state would be represented in the European Senate, while the United States Senate model permits representation from opposition parties as well. The former model would appeal to national governments; the latter to national legislatures. The creation of a European Senate would mean "a shift of power from national governments to national parliaments but, since power has been shifting steadily in the other direction for a long time, this would be no bad thing" (Heseltine, 1989 : 35). More importantly:

> . . . such a change would being European affairs into the mainstream of national political life. The debates in the senate would be open. European political decision-making would . . . begin to attract the fuller attention of the media and would be much more widely understood. Public opinion would be given a better chance to form its own views on what was going on and would

be better able to judge the wisdom of political decisions (Heseltine, 1989 : 36–7).

An alternative suggestion is that the Council of Ministers, reconstituted as a Chamber of States, could be responsible for delineating exactly how the principle of subsidiarity would be applied in practice. An associated suggestion is that these essentially political decisions could then be subjected to judicial scrutiny by a European Court of Justice revamped as a Constitutional Court:

> It could have matters referred to it *a priori* and *a posteriori* by the Community institutions, i.e. the Council, the Commission and the Parliament (at the request of a third of its members, for example), possibly by the European Senate, the Member States and possibly, under certain conditions, the supreme courts of the Member States. Its tasks would be to ensure compliance with the federal pact. In this context, one might also imagine that the new treaty would contain a number of guarantees concerning the inadmissibility of proposals to revise the Treaty which would infringe the federal nature of the European Union or which would lead to infringements of the principle of subsidiarity (European Parliament, 1990 : 12).

(viii) Reforms involving major changes

The changes discussed so far involve gradual and piecemeal tinkering with the present institutions. However, this is not to argue that even these changes will be acceptable to national governments in the current discussions, but rather that they do not involve wholesale redistribution of power between the Parliament, the Council and the Commission. A discussion of such major changes lies outside the remit of this paper, but is discussed elsewhere (see Brigid Laffan's *The Governance of the Union,* the preceding paper in this book). However, if only to provoke discussion in the context of our concern with enhanced legitimacy for the Community, it is worth mentioning two 'models' on which a future reorganisation of the Community's institutions might be based (Bogdanor, 1986):

> (a) a parliamentary model: here the role of the European Parliament would be greatly enhanced by becoming the lower chamber of a bicameral system where the Council would constitute the upper chamber. The two chambers would operate a co-legislative system whereby the Council defended the interests of the nation-states (based on the principle of subsidiarity), and the European Parliament those of the Union. The Commission becomes the 'government' of the Union losing its sole right of legislative initiative, and being subject to votes of confidence in the European Parliament. Individual Commissioners could be sacked by the European Council which would become the 'board', laying down general principles for the Council of

Ministers, enforcing the principle of subsidiarity, and electing the Commission President (subject to European Parliament endorsement). The immediate advantages of this model are that it would legitimise 'Community government' by tying the Commission more closely to the directly-elected European Parliament, and stimulating a more vigorous system of European political parties.

(b) a presidential system: here the role of the European Parliament becomes marginal or even superfluous as the Commission becomes directly elected (Bogdanor, 1990) and thereby gains the necessary legitimacy to act as the legislative authority of the Community. In this task, it would be counter-balanced, but not outweighed, by the Council of Ministers which, legitimised itself by representing the discrete national interests, would bargain with the Commission on an equal footing as does Congress with the Executive in the United States. Each party group would put up a team of Commissioners including at least one from each member state led by a candidate for the Presidency. The number of parties involved would require a two-ballot system (as used in France for the President) and its effect would be to realign the present multiparty system along more bipolar lines so that the electoral choice would become simpler and more comprehensible.

Such an election would:

> . . . enable the electors both to choose the government of the Community and also to indicate its conception of what the future public policy of the Community should be. It would therefore give the Commission both a democratic base and a legitimacy which it at present lacks . . . Direct election of the Commission would focus popular excitement and interest on Community issues, giving them glamour and excitement, qualities sadly lacking in the Community at present (Bogdanor, 1990 : 12).

These two models highlight the contrast between legitimacy and efficiency that also lies at the heart of the debate on institutional reform in the EC. On the face of it, the second model might produce greater decision-making efficiency, if only because it represents a simpler structure than the one that currently exists in the Community. On the other hand, the first model might be less efficient — one could imagine stalemates between the Council and Commission, and between either and the Parliament, but the system appears more democratic because it places a large, directly-elected parliament at the heart of the system.

In any reorganisation of the Community's decision-making process, a balance has to be struck between efficiency and legitimacy. They are not synonomous but they are mutually reinforcing in the sense that truly legitimate institutions are likely to be effective because they command widespread support; and truly effective institutions are likely to be legitimised when they are seen to serve the interests of those they represent.

The evolution of EC citizenship is part of the same process. As individuals begin to identify more and more with the Community, and come to rely on it rather than nation-states for the protection of certain rights and the defence of certain interests, the legitimacy of the Union will grow commensurately. It is important that the notion of EC citizenship should move from largely rhetorical statements to a "framework that will allow for practical measures to be adopted" (Joint Committee, 1990 : 10). The areas where this is most desirable and most likely have already been discussed.

5. OPTIONS FOR IRELAND

The following options are put forward simply to provide a basis for discussion. None are singled out as being preferable, although some of the more obvious advantages and disadvantages of specific options are spelt out. The options are not, for the most part, mutually exclusive, although alternatives are indicated where appropriate. These options also cover a spectrum of possible reforms ranging from modest adaptations of the present system to a major (and, therefore, unlikely) overhaul of the whole relationship between the present institutions.

For a fully informed debate to take place, it seems desirable that not only modest proposals, but also more radical suggestions, should be presented side by side as a context for discussion in the political parties, interest groups, and the public at large. The results of the IGC will touch everyone in Ireland; the 'democratic deficit' is, by definition, a matter for all the citizens of the European Community, and it is therefore appropriate that everyone should be involved in the debate.

(i) European Community citizenship?

In view of the relatively large number of Irish nationals living in other EC countries, it would appear to be in Ireland's interest to advocate rights of movement, residence and political participation for all EC citizens on a universally reciprocal basis. The voting rights enjoyed by Irish and British nationals in each other's jurisdictions could provide a model for the rest of the Community. Indeed, it is conceivable that if Irish and British voting privileges in each other's countries remained more generous than those accorded to other EC citizens, they might be challenged as discriminatory under EC law, but only if it was argued that voting rights *per se* were within the Community's competence.

Another way of approaching the objectives of Community citizenship would be for EC governments to make it easier for the nationals of other EC countries to become nationals of the country in which they reside (for example, by requiring a much shorter period of residence). This obviates governments having to surrender the control over the sensitive issue of citizenship while, at the same time, promoting the idea of Community reciprocity on the matter of citizenship.

(ii) A Community ombudsman?

In the IGC, the governments are faced with a proposal that there should be a Community ombudsman who would act as an interlocutor between the citizens of the Community and the Community's institutions. Anything that is likely to bridge the gap between the people of the Community and its institutions ought to command support. On the other hand, it might be argued that such an office would be insufficient to tackle the widely perceived 'democratic deficit' in the Community.

The Petitions Committee of the European Parliament has recently opposed such an ombudsman apparently on the grounds that it would be 'more complicated and more bureaucratic' (EP News, 1991a) but probably because it would challenge the role of the Petitions Committee itself. If the ombudsman system were adopted, serious thought should, perhaps, be given to establishing a network of ombudsmen across the Community, preferably of a nationality other than that of the country in which they are appointed, so as to emphasise both their impartiality and *communautaire* character.

(iii) A European Senate? A European Affairs Committee?

Two ways of creating a stronger link between the Oireachtas and the European Parliament are: (a) strengthening the national influence over the Community's legislative system at the centre (e.g. by creating a European Senate) and (b) enhancing the quantity and quality of Community information in the national parliaments (e.g. by creating a powerful European Affairs Committee). The former proposal is not supported by the European Parliament allegedly on the grounds that it would introduce another layer of bureaucracy to the decision-making process, but more probably because it would detract from the Parliament's own status. The latter proposal is supported in the parliaments of most member states, although less so by their governments.

There are various forms that such a committee could take but clearly its powers, support, and access to information would be crucial. The proposal that MEPs from other member states might be invited to attend the meetings of all 'European Committees' has much to commend it, but would not, in itself, be sufficient to redress the imbalance between the national parliaments and the European Parliament that lies at the heart of the 'democratic deficit'. Ways may need to be found to involve the members of national 'European committees' more effectively in the committees of the European Parliament.

(iv) Wider powers for the European Parliament?

The most realistic way forward may lie in granting wider powers to the European Parliament. In the discussion above we have alluded to the various ways in which this can be done. Firstly, it is possible to extend the scope of the cooperation procedure. Secondly, co-decision on some issues, or all issues, would make the Parliament a real actor in the legislative process for the first time. Thirdly, the Parliament could have the right of legislative initiative — either on all topics or on some. Any real extension of the Parliament's legislative powers is likely to be resisted by some national governments; but it is clear that if the ‘democratic deficit’ in the Community is going to be seriously addressed, progress will have to be made in this area.

Given Ireland’s representation in the European parliament (15 out of 518 seats), a stronger Parliament may not necessarily be in the national interest. Suggestions for enhancing the legitimacy of the Commission and, indeed, strengthening its hand against the Council might be as much in Ireland’s interest.

APPENDIX 1

ATTITUDES TOWARDS ROME INTER GOVERNMENTAL CONFERENCES PROPOSALS / Attitudes à l'égard des propositions des conférences intergouvernementales de Rome (%, by country, par pays).

QUESTION: The Council of Heads of State and Governments of the European Community has called for Inter Governmental Conferences this December to discuss details of a European Economic and Monetary Union and of a Political Union. I am going to read you a number of statements. For each one, please tell me whether you are IN FAVOUR / NOT IN FAVOUR, of . . . / Le Conseil des Chefs d'Etats et de Gouvernements de la Communauté Européenne a demandé des conférences intergouvernementales en décembre pour discuter des détails d'une Union économique et monétaire et d'une Union politique. Je vais vous lire quelques phrases. Pour chacune, pourriez-vous me dire si vous êtes FAVORABLE / DEFAVORABLE à ce que . . .

As an Economic and Monetary Union, the European Community having a common European Central Bank, with the heads of national central banks on its board of Directors / En tant qu'Union Economique et Monétaire, la Communauté Européenne ait une Banque Centrale commune Européenne, avec les directeurs des banques centrales nationales faisant partie de sa direction (EUROPEAN CENTRAL BANK)

Within this European Economic and Monetary Union, a single common currency replacing the different currencies of the Member States in five or six years' time / Dans une Union Economique et Monétaire Européenne, une seule monnaie commune remplace dans cinq ou six ans les différentes monnaies des Etats Membres (SINGLE CURRENCY)

As a Political Union, the European Community being responsible for foreign policy towards countries outside the EC / En tant qu'Union Politique, la Communauté Européenne soit responsable de la politique étrangère *vis-à-vis* des pays hors de la CEE (EC RESPONSIBLE FOR FOREIGN POLICY)

As a Political Union, the European Community being responsible for a common policy in matters of security and defence / En tant qu'Union Politique, la Communauté Européenne soit responsable d'une politique commune en matière de sécurité et de défense (EC RESPONSIBLE FOR SECURITY/DEFENCE)

1st column: % in favour 2nd column: % not in favour	B		DK		D WEST		D		D EAST		GR		E		F	
	+	–	+	–	+	–	+	–	+	–	+	–	+	–	+	–
European Central Bank	55	16	44	38	55	20	57	19	64	13	62	9	52	9	63	15
Single Currency	61	16	35	50	50	27	50	27	53	26	64	10	53	10	62	19
EC responsible for foreign policy	53	20	40	45	52	25	51	27	44	34	54	18	39	21	48	30
EC responsible for security/defence	66	10	50	37	66	16	68	14	76	10	67	11	52	11	69	14

1ère colonne: % "favorable" 2e colonne: % "défavorable"	IRL		I		L		NL		P		UK		EC 12		EC 12+	
	+	–	+	–	+	–	+	–	+	–	+	–	+	–	+	–
European Central Bank	53	18	64	13	47	18	62	19	54	13	45	30	56	18	56	18
Single Currency	58	17	72	11	47	26	61	25	55	16	38	43	55	23	55	23
EC responsible for foreign policy	43	31	71	12	50	20	55	25	48	21	40	38	51	25	51	26
EC responsible for security/defence	49	27	82	6	55	17	70	16	65	9	57	25	66	15	66	15

Note: EC 12 results exclude former DDR; EC 12+ results include former DDR / Les résultats CE 12 excluent l'ex-RDA; les résultats CE 12+ l'incluent.

APPENDIX 2

ATTITUDES TOWARDS INCREASING THE POWERS OF THE EUROPEAN PARLIAMENT / Attitudes à l'égard de l'elargissement des pouvoirs du Parlement Européen (%, by country, par pays).

The Council of Heads of State and Governments of the European Community has called for Inter Governmental Conferences this December to discuss details of a European Economic and Monetary Union and of a Political Union. I am going to read you a number of statements. For each one, please tell me whether you are IN FAVOUR/NOT IN FAVOUR, of . . . / Le Conseil des Chefs d'Etats et de Gouvernements de la Communauté Européenne a demandé des conférences intergouvernementales en décembre pour discuter des détails d'une Union économique et monétaire et d'une Union politique. Je vais vous lire quelques phrases. Pour chacune, pourriez-vous me dire si vous êtes FAVORABLE/DEFAVORABLE à ce que . . .

The European Parliament having the right to decide together with the Council of Ministers representing the national governments, on the legislation of the European Community / Le Parlement Européen ait l droit de décider avec le Conseil des Minstres représentant les gouvernements nationaux, de la législation de la Communauté Européenne (CO-LEGISLATION)

The European Parliament having the right to put forward draft laws for the European Community on its own initiative / Le Parlement Européen ait le droit de proposer des projets de lois pour la Communauté Européenne sur sa propre initiative (EP TO INITIATE LEGISLATION)

The European Parliament having the right to approve the nomination of the members of the Commission of the European Community / Le Parlement Européen ait le droit d'approuver la nomination des membres de la Commission de la Communauté Européenne (EP COMMISSIONER APPROVAL)

The European Parliament having power to ratify all international agreements and conventions of the European Community before they come into action / Le Parlement Européen ait le pouvoir de ratifier tous les accords et conventions de la Communauté Européenne avant qu'ils prennent cours (EP TO RATIFY INTERNATIONAL AGREEMENTS)

The European Parliament having control over a European Central Bank's management of the Economic and Monetary Union / Le Parlement Européen contrôle la gestion de l'Union Economique et Monétaire par une Banque Centrale Européenne (EP TO CONTROL EURO-BANK)

1st column: % in favour 2nd column: % not in favour	B		DK		D WEST		D		D EAST		GR		E		F	
	+	–	+	–	+	–	+	–	+	–	+	–	+	–	+	–
Co-legislation	67	10	49	36	59	18	60	18	65	15	68	7	56	7	68	13
EP to initiate legislation	63	14	51	35	57	23	56	24	54	27	51	23	49	15	62	21
EP Commissioner approval	60	13	43	38	59	17	60	16	62	14	48	18	45	13	58	16
EP to ratify international agreements	52	19	28	53	47	26	46	28	42	33	44	22	46	12	47	25
EP to control Euro-Bank	55	16	33	48	50	25	52	23	59	18	58	11	47	12	57	19

1ère colonne: % "favorable" 2e colonne: % "défavorable"	IRL		I		L		NL		P		UK		EC 12		EC 12+	
	+	–	+	–	+	–	+	–	+	–	+	–	+	–	+	–
Co-legislation	62	12	80	6	49	19	66	20	65	7	54	22	64	14	64	14
EP to initiate legislation	39	34	73	14	52	21	58	26	60	13	41	38	57	23	57	23
EP Commissioner approval	49	23	69	11	44	20	63	18	53	16	45	30	56	18	56	18
EP to ratify international agreements	43	28	66	13	46	23	52	28	54	15	44	30	50	23	49	23
EP to control Euro-bank	47	24	63	12	43	25	65	17	50	16	34	39	51	22	52	21

Note: EC 12 results exclude former DDR; EC 12+ results include former DDR / Les résultats CE 12 excluent l'ex-RDA; les résultats CE 12+ l'incluent.

BIBLIOGRAPHY

Bogdanor, V. (1990). *Democratising the Community.* London: Federal Trust.

Ehlermann, C.-D. (1990). 'The Institutional Development of the EC under the Single European Act', *Aussenpolitik,* pp. 135–146.

EP News (1991a). 'Residence Rights'. Brussels: European Parliament DG for Information and Public Relations. March 1991.

EP News (1991b). 'Plan for a Euro "Watchdog" opposed'. Brussels: European Parliament DG for Information and Public Relations. June 1991.

Eurobarometer 32 (1989). *Public Opinion in the European Community.* Brussels: EC Commission DG for Information, Communication, Culture.

Eurobarometer 34 (1990). *Public Opinion in the European Community.* Brussels: EC Commission DG for Information, Communication, Culture.

European Commission (1985). *A People's Europe: Reports from the ad hoc Committee,* Bulletin of the European Communities, Supplement 7/85.

European Commission (1990). *Commission Opinion of 21 October 1990 on the proposal for Amendment of the Treaty Establishing the European Economic Community with a view to Political Union.* Luxembourg: Office for Official Publications of the EC.

European Parliament (1990). *Interim Report drawn up on behalf of the Committee on Institutional Affairs on the principle of subsidiarity,* (Rapporteur G. d'Estaing), Session Documents, Series A, A3–163/90/Part B, 4 July.

Henig, S. (1974). 'The Institutional Structure of the European Communities', *Journal of Common Market Studies,* XII, pp. 373–409.

Herman, V. and Lodge, J. (1978). *The European Parliament and the European Community.* London: Macmillan.

Heseltine, M. (1989). *The Challenge of Europe: Can Britain Win?* London: Pan Books.

Joint Committee (1990). *Special Report for the Conference of the Parliaments of the European Community, 27–30 November 1990,* 21 November.

Joint Committee (1991). *Review of the Functions of the Joint Committee on the Secondary Legislation of the European Communities,* Report No. 7 of the Sixth Joint Committee on the Secondary Legislation of the European Communities, 13 February.

Lindberg, L. and Scheingold, S. (1970). *Europe's Would-be Polity,* Englewood Cliffs: Prentice Hall.

Lipset, S. (1960). *Political Man.* New York: Doubleday.

Lodge, J. (1978). 'Towards a Human Union: EEC Social Policy and European Integration', *British Journal of International Studies*, 4, pp. 107–134.

Lodge, J. (1989). *The European Community and the Challenge of the Future*. London: Pinter.

Tindemans, L. (1976). *Report on European Union*, Bulletin of the European Communities, Supplement 1/76.

THE FOREIGN RELATIONS OF THE UNION

Patrick Keatinge

EXECUTIVE SUMMARY

The Inter Governmental Conference (IGC) on Political Union is taking place at a time of fundamental change in world politics. The decline in Soviet power since the end of 1989 has marked the end of the bipolar system which has been a major force in the shaping of the European Community. In spite of negative characteristics, the stability of East-West relations allowed west European states to overcome destructive antagonisms and develop a unique system of economic inter-dependence. Now the European Community is faced with the challenge of redefining its relations with the rest of the world, in order to provide a centre of stability for the new broader European system.

The paper examines the issues arising from this redefinition, the consequent changes being proposed in the negotiations for a new Union Treaty, and the implications for Ireland. A description of the Community's existing role as an *international actor* provides the background for the subsequent analysis. Three policy frameworks have been employed: trade policy under the original EEC Treaty; development policy; and foreign policy consultations in the European Political Cooperation (EPC) process. All three embody varying degrees of dualism, involving the Community as such alongside the member states, with different policy making arrangements. This dualism is particularily marked in political cooperation, demonstrating a tension between the Community's evolving diplomatic persona and the national foreign policies of its member states.

EPC is based on the general aim to 'speak with one voice'. In practice it amounts to routine sharing of information, the gradual evolution of common views, and different forms of common action, from joint statements to economic leverage. Decision making is intergovernmental, requiring a consensus of participating governments, and remaining outside the jurisdiction of the European Court of Justice (ECJ); however, the Irish Supreme Court has interpreted the legal base of EPC with differing emphases.

Since that legal base was agreed, in Title III of the Single European Act (SEA) which was implemented in 1987, a significant expansion has occured in the activities of political cooperation. Superpower detente, the collapse of the eastern bloc, and the moderation of several regional conflicts all contributed to a wider agenda and more joint positions being agreed. However, diplomatic solidarity is far from being guaranteed, even though the rest of the world has increasingly come to see 'EC Europe' as a unitary actor, with which to engage in political dialogues. The Commission's role in ensuring consistency between political cooperation and trade and development policies has become more critical in these circumstances. The small EPC secretariat established by the Single Act is seen as a useful administrative innovation.The European Parliament's new powers of assent to association agreements have given it some influence, but in general political cooperation has escaped close parliamentary supervision.

The *proposals for change*, as seen during the first six months of the Inter Governmental Conference, place a considerable emphasis on the need for a 'common foreign and security policy'. In the negotiating text, the Draft Treaty presented to the European Council in Luxembourg on 28–29 June, 1991, the relevant provisions are placed in a separate 'pillar,' apart from those for trade and development policies. Although the latter may be subject to incremental modification, and there are also foreign policy implications in the new section on cooperation on home affairs and judicial cooperation, the central focus of the negotiations is in effect, on the revision of Title III of the Single Act.

The *institutional framework* is amended in several respects. The European Council remains at the apex, but Council procedures are streamlined. The EPC Secretariat is absorbed into the Council's General Secretariat, and the Commission may acquire a non-exclusive right of initiative. There is little change to the Parliament's position, and the Presidency of the Council retains its managerial role. The implications of this structural reform for Ireland are positive, insofar as more efficient multilateral procedures protect the interests of small states with limited administrative resources.

The proposals on *decision making* are more controversial. There is a distinction between 'cooperation', which is a continuation of the inter-governmental procedures of EPC, and 'joint action', in which an element of majority voting is being considered for the first time, albeit in a limited way. This raises the question whether foreign policy issues are different in kind, and whether special provisions should be made for states to opt out of a joint action. So far a clear divergence of views has prevented progress on this key aspect of the negotiations. Ireland is in a minority of member states which adopts a minimalist position on the issue.

One reason for the sensitivity concerning the introduction of majority voting lies in the emphasis placed on *security policy* in the Inter Governmental Conference. This rather ambiguous term requires further elaboration. Security relates to a broad range of threats and policy instruments to deal with them. The latter include coercive measures ('hard security') as well as preventive action ('soft security'), and defence policy — with its specialised military institutions — forms a part of security policy as a whole.

Since 1945, all modern states have undertaken some form of multilateral security obligation, and in the current transition in the international system it is not surprising that these commitments are being subjected to an intensive reappraisal. Three types of multilateral organisation are relevant to the debate on the European Community's possible role in this field. All member states apart from Ireland are in a military alliance, NATO, and nine of them are in the

Western European Union(WEU).They are all members of the United Nations, in which security obligations may be more salient in the future, if Security Council consensus becomes more frequent, and they are all in the Conference on Security and Cooperation in Europe (CSCE), which faces the challenge of a more heterogeneous Europe.

The most distinctive aspect of Ireland's security policy has long been a refusal to enter into military alliance commitments — the stance of 'military neutrality'. Neutrality is not by or of itself the whole of the state's security policy. In recent years it has not led to any clear formulation of national defence policy, and in the public mind it is often associated with broad political values which in some cases go beyond the realm of security. These values include independence of decision, minimal resort to force,the state's credibility as peacemaker and peacekeeper, and its role in development cooperation. Taken together they are sometimes seen as the necessary elements of a policy of 'positive' or 'active' neutrality which is deeply embedded in Irish political culture. This general image of neutrality is reflected in Irish attitudes to the issues raised in the Inter Governmental Conference, and for many people may be a yardstick against which proposals may be measured.

As yet the *European Community's involvement in security policy* has been tentative. Title III of the Single Act distinguishes the 'political and economic aspects of security', which can be discussed in political cooperation, from the main business of the military alliances. In practice, this distinction was operable in the generally benign context of the late nineteen eighties, but the the Gulf crisis of 1990–1991 demonstrated the limitations of EPC when military issues arose.

The participants in the Political Union negotiations have already accepted that they are working gradually towards an approach which may 'extend to all areas of foreign and security policy'. In practice what they are talking about is joint action of a preventive nature. The emphasis is on cooperative measures to do with the limitation, rather than the threat or use of force; this is *the agenda of 'soft security*'.

Industrial and technological cooperation in the armaments field, and an attempt to control arms exports may involve bringing the arms industry within the scope of general industrial policy, as well as trying to curb the temptation to compensate for declining European arms stocks by increasing exports to the third world. The development of non-proliferation regimes for nuclear, chemical and biological weapons, and for missile technology, has an obvious priority in the aftermath of the Gulf war. In the two multilateral organisations where the member states have already developed a high degree of solidarity, the CSCE and the United Nations, more concerted joint action is being considered. Peace-keeping, for long practised in the latter context, could be adapted to the former, with the Yugoslav crisis demonstrating both the need and the difficulties involved. Similarily, the plight of the Kurds in northern Iraq put 'humanitarian intervention' on the agenda.

Involvement in activities of this kind does not in principle pose problems for neutral states. The opportunity directly to influence such policies within a group of states is not incompatible with a stance of neutrality, so long as the neutral state is not bound to alter its own position by the vote of a majority of its partners.

The question of defence has a more ambiguous place in the Inter Governmental Conference. The Draft Treaty refers to the 'eventual framing of a defence policy', reflecting considerable differences about the inclusion of defence in the Union at present. The adoption of a commitment to mutual assistance was put forward in the early stages of the negotiations. For Ireland, this would represent a major change: independence of decision would obviously be constrained; and by implication existing alliance military doctrines and costs might have to be accepted. Even if it is arguable whether the state's credibility as peacekeeper or developer would necessarily be significantly affected, the overall consequences would be considerable.

However, the issue of an alliance commitment is on the Political Union agenda as a marker for the medium rather than the short term; the immediate issue concerns the merits of an incremental approach by establishing links between the new Union and the WEU. The most likely model for such a connection is to make the European Council the source of general policy 'guidelines' for both organisations, but even though a majority of member states and the Commission appear to favour this line it has met with determined opposition from the supporters of a traditional 'Atlanticist' orientation. The United States may be trying to limit its foreign policy commitments, but it became clear in the spring of 1991 that it wished to retain its influence in Europe through the NATO framework. This position is also adopted within the Inter Governmental Conference by the United Kingdom and the Netherlands, with the result that the question of developing links with the WEU has so far made little headway. The Irish position is similar, though for reasons which have little to do with the defence debate between 'Atlanticists' and 'Europeans'. However, Irish governments have in the past conceded that they would consider participating in a Community defence arrangement in the event of one being agreed, and recent government statements repeat this proposition.

What are *the prospects for change* in the external aspects of a Union Treaty? There appears to be substantial agreement on: (i) the consolidation and amplification of existing arrangements for trade and development policies; (ii) a rationalisation of the institutional framework for foreign policy; (iii) and a focus on the agenda of 'soft security'. However, disagreement persists on: (i) majority voting; (ii) commitment to an eventual defence role; (iii) and links with the

WEU. 'Gradualism' is the order of the day; the overall prospect is for a Single European Act Mark II.

When considering *the options for Ireland* two broad questions are relevant. First, do the proposed changes meet Ireland's interests within the scope of the Union's external action as such? Secondly, how do the proposed changes in the Union's external action, and Ireland's choices in that respect, affect Ireland's interests with regard to the *internal* development of the Union? In particular, is there a possibility of a two-tier system of integration arising in this context? Four broad options are examined. The first, to insist on no change, would in effect be a renationalisation of foreign policy, and would invite pressures for two-tier integration. The second consists of the minimalist position as represented in the Inter Governmental Conference so far, in which the Union remains a confederation of limited scope. This is close to the government's existing approach, but may be vulnerable to threats of a two-tier system. A third option reflects the maximalist elements in the Draft Treaty, amounting to a comprehensive confederation. This would increase ambiguity about neutrality, but would reduce two-tier pressures. The final option, proactive federalism, eliminates such pressures, but, given that the Union Treaty is unlikely to go this far, may be regarded as a premature concession of existing foreign policy positions.

It is already clear that the political context in which the Political Union negotiations are taking place is *a moving target*. The major transition in international politics continues to raise questions which are likely to remain unresolved well beyond the time frame of the conference. The Union Treaty will probably have to be reviewed within the next five years, in the context of a significantly larger Union.

1. INTRODUCTION

The European Council, in establishing guidelines for the Political Union Inter Governmental Conference at Rome on 14-15 December 1990, agreed that the Union would be based, inter alia, on the "coherence of the overall external action of the Community in the framework of its foreign, security, economic and development policies . . ." (Presidency Conclusions 14-15 December, 1990). This statement not only presupposes that the Union will be a distinctive actor in the international political system — it suggests the existing Community already is. Yet while the recent history of west European integration bears out this claim, it also reveals tensions between the Community's evolving diplomatic persona and the persistence of the national foreign policies of its member states. External sovereignty is a basic attribute of statehood, and foreign and security policies are among the most politically sensitive symbols of national identity; that such topics now enjoy an enhanced place on the agenda of integration is a reflection of very considerable change over the last five years.

In part this change has arisen within the Community. The expectations about the completion of the single market and the push for Economic and Monetary Union (EMU) reinforce the weight of what is already the world's largest trading bloc. However, to this evolutionary economic change has been added a revolution in the world political system. The unexpectedly swift and far-reaching collapse of Soviet power in 1989 marked the end of a predominantly bipolar system, and a significant reduction in the credibility of 'international communism' as the major ideological challenge to free market democracies. The East-West conflict had hitherto been a constant element in the history of west European integration, and a major force in the shaping of the EC system. It helped determine the Community's territorial scope and political values, and provided a stability which, in spite of negative characteristics, allowed west European states to overcome their destructive historical antagonisms. It is not surprising, therefore, that the end of this stability has given rise to apprehension as well as celebration. Now the European Community itself has to serve as a major centre of stability in the new European system — hence the pressing need to redefine the way in which it conducts its relations with the rest of the world.

This paper examines the issues arising out of this redefinition, and assesses the implications for Ireland. The starting point is a description of the basic characteristics of the Community's 'external action', with particular emphasis on the process of foreign policy coordination between member states, or European Political Cooperation (EPC) as it is generally known. The development of this process since it was incorporated into the legal base of the Community through the Single European Act forms the background to an analysis of current proposals for changes in the institutional framework and decision-making procedures, aiming at a Common Foreign and Security Policy (CFSP). The following section introduces the rather amorphous concept of 'security policy', identifying its major manifestations in the post-1945 world system before commenting on Ireland's security policy, and the tentative inclusion of security in EPC. This lays the basis for a detailed examination of the relevant proposals on security and defence at the Inter Governmental Conference, and their implications for this country. The final section looks at the prospects for agreement in this part of the negotiations, and summarises the options facing Ireland.

2. THE EUROPEAN COMMUNITY AS AN INTERNATIONAL ACTOR

(i) The European Community's 'external action'

Given its economic weight and status in international law, the European Community is an important but also unusual type of actor in international relations. In practice it operates through three policy frameworks:

(i) The original EEC Treaty, in establishing a common market with its corresponding customs union, ensured that trade policy lies within the Community's competence. Under Article 113, a Common Commercial Policy was established, in which the Commission, on the basis of a Council mandate, is responsible for negotiating trade agreements. More generally, the external aspects of the Community's internal competences fall within the treaty framework. In addition the economic influence of the Community is exerted by the sponsorship of, and participation in, a wide range of multilateral networks involved in scientific cooperation and environmental regulation.

(ii) An EC development policy has also evolved, more pragmatically, mainly on the basis of the former colonial links of most of the member states.

(iii) Finally, since 1970 foreign policy consultations between the member states have taken place in the European Political Cooperation (EPC) process.

In all these spheres of action there are varying degrees of dualism in both policy substance and policy making procedures, involving Community action alongside that of the member states. Even with regard to trade policy, which comes most clearly within the scope of the Community, commercial competition is still often perceived in national terms. The Community's development policy exists alongside the national development policies of the member states. But nowhere is this dualism more marked than in political cooperation. The attempt to forge a single diplomatic persona rests on the coordination of twelve national foreign policies, and the policy process, even after twenty years, retains distinctive features which set it apart from the rest of the Community's political system. A major question in the Inter Governmental Conference (IGC) is how far this dualism can be reduced, thereby creating the basis of a common foreign policy. The Commission is seeking to integrate all three types of external action within a common legal base and *communautaire* policy making procedures. The strongest resistance to this approach can be seen in the negotiations on EPC, which has proved to be the dominant aspect of the Inter Governmental Conference so far as the Union's foreign relations are concerned. Although this emphasis is necessarily reflected in the analysis of institutional reform which follows, this is not to deny the significance of the substance of either commercial or development policy in the future evolution of the Union.

(ii) European Political Cooperation

There has long been agreement on the main goals to be followed in political cooperation, but at such a degree of generalisation (e.g. 'international peace and security') as to make it unexceptionable. The preamble to the Single European Act refers to "the responsibility incumbent on Europe to aim at speaking ever increasingly with one voice and to act with consistency and solidarity in order more effectively to protect its common interests and independence". This exhortation is reflected in Title III of the act, which provides the legal base for political cooperation in the commitment to "endeavour jointly to formulate and implement a European foreign policy". (SEA: 30.1).

In practice, the output of political cooperation is more appropriately described in more mundane terms. It starts with the governments' commitment to "inform and consult each other on any foreign policy matters of general interest" (SEA: 30.2). This routine sharing of information can form the basis for the gradual evolution of common views, though there is nothing automatic in this process and interpretations of what constitutes 'a matter of general interest' may vary. Where common views do emerge, common action may be undertaken, using different types of policy instrument. The most usual is a joint statement of the Twelve's position ('declaratory policy'). Joint representations may be made, mainly in the *troika* format where the government holding the Presidency, together with its immediate predecessor and successor, acts on behalf of the Twelve. The most concerted form of action involves deploying the Community's economic influence; the granting or withholding of material favours through the operation of EC trade policy — within the constraints of GATT rules — represents a form of economic leverage, which may be used in conjunction with diplomatic rewards or sanctions.

Precisely how these policy instruments are used, and with what effect, varies from case to case. Political cooperation is a long way from achieving a consistent and uniform Community foreign policy; national policies persist, and may often diverge. For example, in recent years the Twelve attempted to follow a policy of economic and diplomatic sanctions against South Africa, but the content of the sanctions was limited by internal disagreements as to their utility. In spite of this the member states still pursued a collective role through troika missions to South Africa. In the early stages of the Gulf crisis in 1990, the Community states acted together with regard to economic sanctions and diplomatic consultations, though when military action was contemplated the Community as such had no role. In the Yugoslav crisis at the end of June 1991, the Twelve assumed the role of mediator, operating through emergency meetings of the foreign ministers and *troika* missions to the disputants; that they felt able to do so, and were expected by others to do so, was largely attributable to the economic leverage they could bring to bear through the Community's existing economic relations with Yugoslavia. The economic weight of the Community is also the central element in response to the Soviet Union's worsening crisis, but there is nothing automatic about the extent to which the Twelve might reach agreement or how it is brought to bear.

The institutional framework of political cooperation was developed on the basis of an intergovernmental model of decision making rather than the supranational method associated with the original treaties. Indeed, prior to the Single Act it had no legal basis, and even when it acquired one the legal language employed in Title III implies a subtly different level of integration than that achieved elsewhere. It refers to "high contracting parties" rather than 'member states', and the collectivity it represents is generally referred to as "the Twelve" rather than 'the Community'.

The method of decision making in EPC is one of the most important aspects of the dualism in the Community's 'external action'. Decisions to take any common action require a consensus of all the governments. Although the signatories of the Single Act are obliged "as far as possible [to] refrain from impeding the formation of a consensus" (SEA, 30.3c), the inclusion of the phrase "as far as possible" introduces a subjective element into the obligation. Together with the fact that political cooperation remains outside the jurisdiction of the European Court of Justice (SEA, 31), this suggests that the individual government retains its formal sovereignty in arriving at foreign policy decisions.

The judgement of the Irish Supreme Court on the constitutionality of the Single Act (Crotty v. An Taoiseach, 1987) appeared to cast doubt on this view, if for no other reason than the fact that the five judges produced two contrasting interpretations (Hogan, 1987; McCutcheon, 1991; Temple-Lang, 1987). The majority saw the obligations undertaken in Title III as representing "a fundamental transformation in the relations between the member states" and "the threshold leading from what has hitherto been an essentially economic Community to what will now also be a political Community". But the two dissenting judges did not see Title III as the end of national foreign policy, the Chief Justice arguing that political cooperation "did not impose any obligations to cede any national interest in the sphere of foreign policy . . . they impose an obligation to listen and consult and grant a right to be heard and consulted". The experience of EPC since the Single Act was adopted suggests the latter view was the more plausible.

(iii) European Political Cooperation after the Act

The gradual evolution of political cooperation cannot be understood without reference to the political context, and the particular context of the late nineteen eighties goes a long way to explaining the increased activity it experienced.

The increasing confidence about the Community's internal development — the "1992 Programme" — was no doubt a contributory factor, but the external context, which bears most directly on political cooperation, also changed quite dramatically. Three features were particularly significant:

(a) The superpower detente, expressed in the Intermediate Nuclear Forces Treaty in December 1987, reinforced the general east-west detente in Europe as well as leading to agreement on substantial conventional arms cuts in 1990. Although the Community states did not always share the same view on the substance of arms control, their disagreements arose mainly in NATO. As on previous occasions, EPC was a viable framework in which to formulate positions on the more general issues of detente.

(b) When the 'new detente' was overtaken by the collapse of the eastern bloc in 1989–1990, a qualitatively different international system was created. With the unification of Germany in 1990, and the collapse of a centralised Soviet Union the following year, this represents the most significant change in the distribution of power in Europe since 1945.

(c) The 'new detente' was accompanied by the moderation of several regional conflicts outside Europe (Iran–Iraq, Afghanistan, Central America, Southern Africa), in which the Twelve's diplomacy could expect to play a more emphatic role. The larger Community states already had considerable interests at stake, and the decline of Soviet influence gave new opportunities for new initiatives. However, the greater instability of the post-cold war system also demonstrated the limits of such a role. When the Gulf crisis of 1990–1991 raised the question of the military enforcement of UN Security Council resolutions, the influence of political cooperation was slight indeed. Although several member states were very closely involved, it was in the context of the *ad hoc* coalition led by the United States.

The pace and extent of these changes in the external environment account for the widely-felt need to anticipate the planned review of Title III of the Single Act (SEA, 30.12). Even by the middle of 1990 it was clear that there had been a remarkable increase in the output of the political cooperation process, at least in quantitative terms (Regelsberger, 1990). The number of joint declarations, which had been as low as 25 in the difficult year of 1983, rose to 52 in 1985 and to 99 in 1989. There was also an increased level of activity in the United Nations; in 1987, for example, the Twelve produced 92 statements or explanations of vote, often on issues which had hitherto not been covered in this way. Indeed, the agenda of political cooperation seems to have become more comprehensive, with subjects which had previously been deliberately avoided ('*domaines résérvés*') being included in what was understood to be the 'general interest'. While the reforms adopted in the Single Act no doubt accommodated this expansion of activity, the main stimulus was external pressure rather than procedural change.

Does an increase in activity necessarily represent an improvement in the quality of the Twelve's diplomatic solidarity? Evaluations of this sort must at best be impressionistic; the issues are not equally important, and it is often impossible to gauge the impact of the Twelve's positions as compared with other sources of influence. Yet it may be possible to identify some suggestive trends. Referring to data of voting behaviour at the UN between 1973 and 1989, "unanimity is achieved in almost 50% of those UN resolutions put to a vote compared to previous years when the Ten/Twelve managed to agree only in 30 to 40% of the votes" (Regelsberger, 1990, 8). Where unanimity is not possible it seems that delegations have made more strenuous efforts to soften the edges of their disagreement.

Nevertheless, the basic dualism remains. The United Nations data indicates a number of 'non-conformists', including the two permanent members of the Security Council — France and the United Kingdom — and Greece, Spain and Ireland (Regelsberger, 1990, 9–10). If in general, governments are reluctant to block an emerging consensus or to subvert an agreed position — the *'acquis politique'* — there have been some noticeable departures from the Twelve's solidarity in recent years. British support for the US attack on Libya in 1986 and French diplomacy on the eve of the Gulf War in 1991 were perhaps the most dramatic instances of the absence of the most basic obligation of political cooperation. In neither case did a major member state consult its partners before adopting a unilateral position on what was clearly a general interest. Although such blatant neglect of the rules of political cooperation is exceptional, it reflects the persistent differences between well-established national foreign policy traditions.

It might be expected that the credibility of any form of collective diplomacy is most vulnerable at times of crisis, and it is not fair to judge political cooperation solely in that context. Indeed, it can be argued that over time the influence of the Twelve is most likely to be effective where the economic weight of the Community is deployed in conjunction with agreed political positions. The Single Act emphasises the need for consistency in this regard (SEA, 30.5), and much the same point is conveyed in the guidelines of the current Inter Governmental Conference where they refer to the 'coherence' of external action (Presidency Conclusions, 14–15 December, 1990). Circumstances in recent years have often favoured such a 'global' approach, for example in East-West relations and with regard to Central America. The rest of the world increasingly has come to see 'EC Europe' as a unitary actor, and the development of political dialogues with other groups of states (e.g. ASEAN, the ACP Group, the Gulf states etc.) has been a remarkable feature of modern diplomacy (Edwards and Regelsberger, 1990). An important consequence of this has been to bring the Commission closer to the centre of the political cooperation process. Originally kept at arms length by the national governments, the Commission's representatives have increasingly been accepted as a *de facto* 'thirteenth member' of the EPC 'club'.

The principal institutional innovation in the Single Act, so far as political cooperation was concerned, was the provision of a small secretariat in Brussels (SEA, 30.10g). Headed by a Secretary-General, a senior professional diplomat appointed for a fixed term by the member governments, the secretariat is staffed on a rotating basis by the Presidency government plus its two predecessors and its two successors. For the first time there was an administrative centre in the 'Community capital' for a process which had hitherto been managed solely by the government holding the Presidency. The secretariat acts as the institutional 'memory' of political cooperation and also has the capacity to assist in drafting texts. However, with its personnel numbered in single figures, there are limits to what it can do. Moreover it operates under the authority of the Presidency, and although it appears to be regarded as a useful addition to the institutional framework, any evolution towards a more political role (e.g. as spokesman of the Twelve) has so far been resisted.

The Single Act gave the European Parliament the power of assent both to Accession Agreements (i.e. a veto on new membership) and to Association Agreements (SEA 8 and 9). The former power has not yet been exercised, but may prove to be important in the next decade, when many states are anxious to join the Community (see Tony Brown's *The Extension of the Union*, the following paper in this book). When the protocols of Association Agreements come up for renewal the Parliament has already demonstrated the capacity to exert influence by delaying its assent. However, while it is supposed to be 'closely associated' with EPC (SEA, 30.4), the interpretation of 'closely' is more ambitious in the Parliament than in the foreign ministries. The number of parliamentary questions increased from 208 in 1985 to 330 in 1988, but the response of the Presidency has been perfunctory on occasion, and the Parliament's role therefore remains a consultative one (Regelsberger, 1990, 21–23). That said, the European Parliament has instruments and procedures for the oversight of political cooperation which go beyond those enjoyed by some member state national parliaments with regard to their own foreign policies (Millar, 1991, 156). Where national parliaments are also remote from foreign policy — and this is arguably the case in Ireland — the 'democratic deficit' may therefore be considerable (see Edward Moxon-Browne's *The Legitimacy of the Union*, the preceding paper in this book).

3. FOREIGN POLICY: PROPOSALS FOR CHANGE

(i) From 'EPC' to 'CFSP'

The guidelines laid down for the Inter Governmental Conference at the European Council in Rome directed the participants to "address the Union's objectives", and included a standard list of general policy goals: "maintaining peace and international stability; developing friendly relations with all countries; promoting democracy, the rule of law and respect for human rights; encouraging the economic development of all nations". A reminder that such goals are expressed at a very high level of generalisation can be seen in the rider that the participants "should also bear in mind the special relations of individual Member States" (Presidency Conclusions 14–15 December, 1990). Nevertheless, the European Council's guidelines do have the force of political agreement at the highest level. That cannot be said for the first negotiating text produced by the Luxembourg Presidency. Described as a 'Non-paper', it was published in April 1991 and represented the Presidency's initial ordering of the proposals on the table (Agence Europe Documents, No. 1709/10). An amended version, the 'Draft Treaty on the Union', likewise commits no one to a particular position (Agence Europe Documents, No. 1722/23). It was accepted by the European Council in Luxembourg on 28–29 June as the basis for further negotiation. Both documents place these broad aims, inherited from political cooperation, under a new label —'common foreign and security policy' (CFSP).

'CFSP' is not just another addition to the prolific menagerie of Euro-acronyms.In the Luxembourg texts it is introduced in more forthright language than the Single Act employed,with its rather tentative commitment to 'endeavour' to formulate and implement policy (SEA 30.1). The proposed scope of the common foreign and security policy is comprehensive: "the policy of the Union may extend to all areas of foreign and security policy", and one objective is to "strengthen the security of the Union and its Member States in all ways" (Draft Treaty, CFSP–A). Although the explicit inclusion of 'defence' remains a contentious matter (see Section 6, below), both the broader scope and confident tone of such formulations suggest at least an incremental change since the mid-eighties.

Nevertheless, the common foreign and security policy — like political cooperation in the Single European Act — retains its own place in the overall structure envisaged for the Political Union, which consists of separate 'pillars' for the original treaties, judicial cooperation, EMU and the CFSP itself (see Brigid Laffan's *The Governance of the Union,* Section 4, The Structure of the Union, the first paper in this book). In the Draft Treaty its relationship to the other aspects of "external action" (trade and development policies) thus remains one of cohabitation rather than seamless union. The need for the "coherence" of the overall external action, emphasised in the Rome guidelines and a major preoccupation of the Commission, has to be met through specific procedures; there is no sign in the negotiating text of a serious attempt to create a truly uniform system of policy making under a single central authority. This is in contrast to the Commission's own proposed Draft Treaty, which insists on a closely integrated legal base, allowing for the gradual 'communitarisation' of policy making procedures (Agence Europe, Documents No. 1697/98). Following the publication of the 'Non-paper', the Commission, with the support of Belgium, Germany, Greece, Italy, the Netherlands, Portugal and Spain, criticised its structure of separate 'pillars', on the grounds that it fragmented political authority and weakened the Commission's central position in the Community's overall legal structure. The Luxembourg Presidency responded by an amended introductory section for the Draft Treaty which put the 'pillars' in a more explicit 'federal' context but which nevertheless retained a confusing legal base with different modes of decision making for common foreign and security policy on the one hand and trade and development policies on the other.

The first six months of the Inter Governmental Conference saw little public debate on changes to the latter aspects of the Community's external action. However, there are signs that the existing provisions in the EEC Treaty may be consolidated and even extended. The Luxembourg non-paper, for example, referred to "external economic policy" rather than 'commercial policy', allowed for the inclusion of external relations arising from any new EMU provisions, and redefined Article 113 (EEC) to include services in the Community's trade competences ('Non-paper' Title VI, chapter IV). Although the Draft Treaty subsequently reverted to the previous terminology, it paid attention to the inclusion of trade in services.

The possible broadening of existing economic competences will probably be supplemented by a more clearly defined development cooperation policy, although this topic received little attention during the first stage of the Inter Governmental Conference. The Draft Treaty places development policy in a separate title, which restates the relevant policy means and objectives more fully than previously (Draft Treaty, Title XX). The common foreign and security policy section also refers to both development cooperation and external economic policies under the heading of objectives, even though their legal basis and policy-making process remain in the 'Community pillar'. The Draft Treaty also includes a new pillar providing for an intergovernmental approach (similar to that which was enjoyed by political cooperation in the Single Act) with regard to "cooperation on home affairs and judicial cooperation". The term 'home' (or 'internal') should not be taken too literally, for many of the issues arising under this heading concern the access of nationals of third countries to the territory of member states, with important implications for external policy (see Section 5, below and also Brigid Laffan's *The Governance of the Union,* Section 4, The Policy Scope of the Union).

(ii) The institutional framework

The institutional framework which evolved with the practice of political cooperation and which was formalised in Title III of the Single Act is intergovernmental in character. The European Council gives general direction, but the foreign ministers represent the centre of decision, in close association with their senior officials, the Political Directors, who meet regularly and frequently in the Political Committee. The system is managed by the Presidency, supported by the separate EPC secretariat. The only supranational organ to be closely involved is the Commission,which has established a presence albeit with rather limited formal powers. The European Parliament is much further removed, while the European Court of Justice barely features. The significance of this framework hinges on the nature of the method of decision-making, but before examining the proposals to change the latter it is necessary to consider amendments which have been put forward with regard to the framework as such.

Although the role of the European Council is a matter of contention in the context of the overall balance between the institutions (see Brigid Laffan's *The Governance of the Union,* Section 4, Efficiency and Effectiveness of the Union), its position at the apex of the CFSP pillar reflects continuity rather than innovation. The ministerial level, on the other hand, has been the object of attention in the Inter Governmental Conference. The Draft Treaty refers simply to 'the Council' as the body responsible for conducting policy (Draft Treaty CFSP–C.2). This represents the end of the formal distinction between the General Affairs Council and the foreign ministers meeting as the Twelve, in which the same group of people was supposed to defer to a division of labour which in practice was often meaningless. In fact the Irish Presidency during the first semester of 1990 experimented successfully by including both types of business in two 'special meetings of foreign ministers' (20 January, 21 April), a precedent repeated by the Italian Presidency. It is not yet clear how senior officials are to relate to this change, in so far as there are two quite separate channels at present — the Political Directors via the Political Committee, and the heads of economic divisions in conjunction with the Permanent Representatives via Coreper. Be that as it may, what used to be seen as a definite boundary between intergovernmental and supranational policy making is now viewed primarily as a streamlining of administrative procedures.

The EPC Secretariat — the major institutional innovation in Title III of the Single Act — may also be absorbed into the General Secretariat of the Council. This, too, can be seen as a rationalisation of bureaucratic structures, though it will not necessarily lead to the effacement of a specialised body of expertise. Indeed there is a case for expanding the number of officials in such a unit, both to cover the increasing workload and to maintain contacts with national foreign ministries (Regelsberger, 1990, 28). The secondment of officials from each foreign ministry might serve both these purposes, though possibly at the risk of replicating national positions too faithfully.

A more overtly 'political' innovation which seems to have attracted a high level of support has been the attribution of the right of initiative to the

Commission. This must be distinguished from the exclusive right of initiativ which has underpinned the Commission's central role in the Communit framework; here the Commission is being treated as the thirteenth participant i the policy process, on an equal basis with each member state. Justification fo such a change rests largely on the need to maintain consistency between th common foreign and security policy and the matters arising under th Community's competences;experience suggests that the need is genuine and i the recent practice of political cooperation there has been an informal acceptanc of the Commission's role. Granting the non-exclusive right of initiative to th Commission can thus be seen as a formalising of this practice.

It may be expected that the Commission for its part will review the existin division of labour between Commissioners' portfolios bearing on relations wit the outside world, and will reconsider the structure of Directorates General. rationalisation of Commission structures might reinforce the coherence betwee the disparate elements of external action, perhaps with the explicit inclusion o CFSP matters. Changes of this nature are, however, a matter for the Commissio itself rather than for the Inter Governmental Conference.

There appears to be little inclination in the Inter Governmental Conference t involve the European Parliament more closely with the common foreign an security policy than it was with political cooperation. The Draft Treaty refers t the obligation to keep it informed of "the basic choices made" — hardly formulation to indicate that serious *prior* consultation is envisaged (Draft Treat CFSP–E). The Parliament retains its right of assent to Association Agreements a not inconsiderable power at a time of unusual flux in international politics, bu in general it would appear that any increase in the Parliament's influence on th Union's external action will depend primarily on its own capacity to monito events in a purposeful way.

The persistence of the intergovernmental character of the institutiona framework can be seen in the continuing role of the rotating Presidency in the management of the proposed common foreign and security policy. In the Draf Treaty as in the Single Act, it is responsible for the preparation and implementation of policy, and for convening emergency meetings. The problem of sustaining continuity between Presidencies is resolved as before by the device of the *troika,* where the preceding and succeeding Presidencies buttress the President-in-office. The Presidency also looks set to remain the primary externa representative of the Union, with the qualification that where a Presidency state has no diplomatic representation of its own it can be assisted by another member of the *troika.* That is already normal practice, along with regular consultations between the embassies of member states in third countries. However, there seems to be little likelihood of any attempt to merge existing national embassies, even on a limited experimental basis, for example to a relatively 'non-political' international organisation. The Franco-German experiment on these lines, a joint representation in Mongolia (Regelsberger, 1990, 32), remains isolated (in every sense of the word) as a model of administrative rationalisation. Still less likely is a merger of national foreign services and the Community's own quite extensive diplomatic representation.

An initial assessment of the institutional proposals described above suggests that what is being envisaged under this heading is appropriately seen as incremental structural reform, with a view to increasing the managerial efficiency of the policy process. The changes outlined do not appear to have been contentious in the early stages of the Inter Governmental Conference, with national positions converging either explicitly or implicitly. So far the Commission has consolidated its position, and the ire of the Parliament has been directed at more general issues.

The implications for Ireland are generally positive. It can be argued that the smaller member states, with much more restricted diplomatic representation and fewer administrative resources than the larger countries, have a particular interest in access to clear and efficient procedures at the multilateral level. Most of the institutional innovations represented in the Draft Treaty meet these criteria, with the possible exception of a cryptic reference to a "crisis mechanism" (Draft Treaty CFSP–D.5). Procedures for emergency meetings of foreign ministers already exist, and it is not clear what purpose would be served by an additional arrangement. The reinforcement of the Commission's role can also be seen as an element which more often than not will serve to reassure smaller states that they are not being unduly ignored or manipulated by their larger partners. However, from the point of view of political accountability, the conference's consideration of the institutional framework offers little to date. The European Parliament's position has already been referred to, but the remedy for this aspect of the democratic deficit may be found equally if not more so in improved procedures at the national level.

(iii) Decision Making

A full evaluation of the proposals requires more than the static analysis of institutional structures. The way in which decisions are made, and the extent to which they bind the participants, are at the core of the deliberations in the Inter Governmental Conference. On this point, a clear divergence of views between advocates of maximal and minimal change is evident, with the former attempting to move towards majority voting and the latter insisting that foreign and security policy still requires consensus.

However, even the Commission's Draft Treaty, to date the most detailed expression of the maximalist stance, distinguishes between the Union's "vital common interests," which are then subject to a regime involving majority voting, and other questions which are dealt with by a continuation of the political cooperation procedure (Commission Draft Treaty, Articles Y3 and Y4). The implication that it is possible, both intellectually and politically, to prioritise ends in this way is not so emphatic in the Luxembourg negotiating text though there is a broadly similar distinction between two different procedures, for "joint action" and "cooperation."

In both cases 'cooperation' is in effect the continuation of existing intergovernmental policy making. It involves a commitment to consult, with the possibility of the Council defining common positions on the basis of unanimity. The Single Act's exhortation to voluntary restraint by those member states not wholly convinced of possible consensus is retained in rather different but equally general wording in the Draft Treaty (Draft Treaty CFSP–H). There is as yet no more specific codification of procedures of non-participation or abstention, as suggested in the original guidelines (Presidency Conclusions 14–15 December, 1990). Probably the most significant change in the Draft Treaty is a stronger form of wording concerning the obligation to consult on issues arising in international organisations in which not all member states are represented (Draft Treaty CFSP–I.2). This applies above all to the United Nations Security Council, where only France and the United Kingdom are permanent members and where the presence of other Community states depends on the accident of infrequent election. Given the recent re-emergence of the Security Council as a potentially significant political forum after its routine negation during the cold war, this explicit obligation could be increasingly important in allowing member states to influence their more privileged partners.

The real attempt to innovate in the negotiating text, however, is contained in the concept of "joint action", in which for the first time an element of majority voting is at least being considered (Draft Treaty CFSP–J, K). In this mode of decision making, the European Council's guidelines may provide the basis for a decision by the Council of Ministers that an issue should be the subject of joint action. The Council, on taking this decision in principle, is also required in the Draft Treaty to define the objectives, means, and procedures which must be followed. Now up to that point the decisions which have been taken (in the European Council's guidelines and by the foreign ministers) have been taken on the basis of consensus, thus preserving the formal sovereignty of the member states. However, the Council is then empowered to decide "detailed arrangements" for implementing joint action by some as yet undefined form of majority voting (Draft Treaty CFSP–J).

The Draft Treaty then retreats somewhat from this tentative departure by reverting to consensus for "changes in the situation". This experiment is framed in a more hesitant way than that in the Commission proposals which envisage an earlier resort to majority voting, but it nevertheless represents a move away from the prevailing principle and practice of consensus decision making.

Advocates of change in this direction argue that in general decisions in common foreign and security policy have less impact on the autonomy of member states and the lives of their citizens than directives relating to the single market, which are now routinely decided by majority vote. They also point to the anomaly whereby decisions concerning an important instrument of foreign policy, trade sanctions, are already subject to majority voting under Article 113 of the EEC Treaty. If this particular implementing measure can be decided by a majority, why should other such decisions be subject to consensus? The counter-argument is based on the view that foreign policy issues are characteristically difficult to define in a concrete or programmatic fashion; by definition, they relate to an environment over which the political authority has no control, unlike the single market environment which is its own creation. Hence such issues are less predictable in their evolution than the more readily quantifiable issues of economic and social policy covered by the Community method of decision-making. Also, in practice it may prove impossible to distinguish strategic decisions on ends (subject to consensus) from tactical or implementing decisions on means (subject to majority vote). At the best of times choosing issues for joint action would be something of a gamble; in the inherently chaotic arena of international diplomacy even "detailed arrangements" could have unforeseen and possibly dangerous consequences. Indeed, it is argued, they may prove more rather than less susceptible to national sensitivities than do the very general decisions or guidelines at the level of the European Council.

Some of the dilemmas raised by the question of majority voting are reflected in the Draft Treaty. There is an emphasis on the requirement of prior information to be given by member states when they are taking national action as the agents of joint action (Draft Treaty CFSP–K.2). Presumably this is designed to curb the temptation to resort to the sort of solo diplomacy which has been possible under political cooperation. There is also an attempt to deal with the possibility of a member state's national interests being compromised in some way in the implementation of joint action. In this case the problem is referred back to the Council for "an appropriate solution", which must not, however, have the effect of countering the joint action (Draft Treaty CFSP–K.4). Beyond that there is as yet no explicit indication of the circumstances in which it is permissible for a member state in effect to abstain from or opt out of a joint action. If the general Community ethos concerning derogation were to apply, however, both the scale and duration of any such departure from a common policy would be limited.

It is noticeable that even though majority voting has been raised in the Inter Governmental Conference there has been no serious attempt to bring decision-making on the common foreign and security policy within the jurisdiction of the European Court of Justice. In the Draft Treaty it is explicitly excluded (Draft Treaty general provisions – O.2), as it has been in Article 31 of the Single Act,with one exception. This concerns the procedure for imposing economic sanctions, which has hitherto been a mixture of consensus (in political cooperation) and majority voting under Article 113. The possibility of a member state withdrawing from a consensus but at the same time being in breach of a Community regulation — a possibility realised by Ireland and Italy during the Falklands conflict in 1982 (Kuyper, 1982) — was provided for in the Luxembourg 'Non-paper' by a specific clause bringing it wholly within the Court's purview (Non-paper N). However, the Draft Treaty adopts a different solution by including the contingency in a new Article 228a in the "Community pillar".

Any assessment of the situation regarding decision making must start with the recognition that the proposals tabled during the first phase of the conference demonstrate a clear divergence of views. The advocates of change — the 'maximalists' — include the Commission and a majority of member states. The Commission Opinion of 21 October, 1990 had already stated a preference for augmented qualified majority voting requiring the votes of eight member states, to apply to common policy with the exception of security policy (Political Union, 15). At the same time the Italian Presidency was explicit in its advocacy of some degree of majority voting, a position it has subsequently maintained in the Inter Governmental Conference. The 'integrationist axis', France and Germany, as well as Belgium, the Netherlands, Spain, and Greece would appear — with varying degrees of enthusiasm — to be in the maximalist camp.

The minimalist position has been tabled by the United Kingdom and Denmark, and may also be held by Portugal (Agence Europe, 17 April, 1991). The British formulation is a rather more emphatic version of Article 30.3(c) of the Single European Act; member states are enjoined to "make every effort to form a consensus", but majority voting is nowhere to be seen. The Danish draft simply says that the common foreign and security policy shall "in principle cover all aspects on which unanimity is arrived at among the Member States" (Agence Europe, 5 April, 1991).

No narrowing of the gap between maximalists and minimalists on decision making was evident by the European Council's meeting in Luxembourg at the end of June. The Irish government has not tabled any paper on this issue (or indeed on any aspect of the common foreign and security policy), but throughout the early stages of the Inter Governmental Conference it has been clear that it pursues the minimalist approach. As the Taoiseach reported to the Dáil, "our view is that foreign and security policy is a very sensitive area for all states, and where it is made the subject of joint action or common policy for the first time, it is simply not realistic to think that states will allow themselves to be bound by the votes of others if interests which they consider vital are at stake" (Dáil Debates, 9 July, 1991). This can be represented as a restatement of the orthodox view that an acceptance of majority voting is in principle a diminution of formal sovereignty. It is arguable that in legal terms such a diminution has already been accepted on joining the United Nations Organisation,where Ireland, like all members apart from the permanent members of the Security Council, must defer to the direction of that body, in which it is rarely represented. However, the insistence on maintaining consensus in the more close-knit and more directly and continuously relevant Community forum may indeed reflect a genuine apprehension that foreign policy issues cannot be satisfactorily managed in any other way. In the UN context, formal sovereignty has been conceded, but the political autonomy of the state has rarely been affected; among the Twelve, questions concerning political autonomy may arise quite frequently. The government's reticence must also be understood in the context of the Inter Governmental Conference's emphasis on extending the scope of a particular aspect of foreign policy, in which sensitivities about sovereignty and autonomy are often acute, the controversial field of 'security policy'.

4. SECURITY POLICY: A SUITABLE CASE FOR DEFINITION

(i) What is 'security policy'?

One of the most controversial and least clearly defined set of issues in the Inter Governmental Conference is encapsulated as "security policy". The usage of the term is often imprecise and sometimes confusing. "Security policy" can appear by itself, but is often also twinned with 'foreign policy' or 'defence'; in the first case the impression is given that it is a distinct sector of public policy, in the second that it is an aspect of other sectors. These different usages are not merely semantic curiosities, and the confusion they engender may not always be accidental; thus before examining the specific questions about security as they arise in the Inter Governmental Conference it is necessary to provide a general clarification of the relevant terms and their application to the international system.

At its simplest 'security' may be seen as a fundamental goal, which involves "the pursuit of freedom from threat" (Buzan, 1983, 11). In the interdependent international system of the late twentieth century the range of potential threats is broad indeed. A conventional categorisation (Buzan, 1983, 75–83) starts with the classical military threat, where force is deployed or actually used in order to influence the policy of a state, or even to eliminate it altogether. But other types of threat are also encountered: political threats, in the form of ideological competition through propaganda or even subversion; economic threats — beyond the bounds of fair competition — in which access to supplies or markets is denied; and even ecological threats arising from the side-effects of destructive technologies.

If the range of threats is diverse, so too are the means to counter them. The policy instruments which can be deployed may be placed on a continuum between coercive and preventive measures, or 'hard' and 'soft' security. At the 'hard' end of this continuum lies the actual use of military force, and especially weapons of mass destruction, while the more common threat of force, through policies of deterrence, is placed nearer the centre, along with diplomatic and economic sanctions. Measures of arms limitation, peacekeeping, diplomatic persuasion and mediation are found towards the 'soft' end of the spectrum, which can also encompass material and political rewards for non-threatening behaviour.

A state's security policy, then, may be seen as the application of any, or more usually a complex mix, of these means to security as an end. It may impinge on foreign and economic policies, and — given the prevalence of social movements across state borders — even on policing and judicial arrangements traditionally described as 'internal'. It is not a clearly defined policy sector with its own set of institutions; rather, depending on the nature of the threat, many governmental institutions may have a 'security dimension'. However, so far as military instruments of policy are concerned there is an obvious policy sector in its own right. Defence policy — the provision for and deployment of armed forces — is the responsibility of specialised government agencies and the military establishment. Nevertheless, defence policy remains only a part of the broader and more heterogeneous activities which compose 'security policy'.

(ii) Multilateral security frameworks

Thinking about security policy in purely national terms is, of course, a gross distortion of reality. Quite apart from the fact that policy makes no sense if unrelated to external threats, no modern state in the post-1945 international system forms policy outside the obligations incurred through membership of some form of multilateral organisation. Three different types of such organisation are particularly important in the context of the European Community's tentative role in security, and it is necessary to be aware of the different tasks they perform, as well as the demands they impose on their members.

The first such type of security framework is the classical military alliance, based on a guarantee of mutual assistance. Article 5 of the North Atlantic Treaty of 1949 provides just such a guarantee, in the event of an armed attack on any of its members by a third party. However, the member's commitment is qualified in two respects; it is obliged to take "such action as it deems necessary" (thereby giving each member some formal freedom of decision), and Article 6 of the treaty defines a specific geographical zone of application. Thus NATO cannot operate "out of area". Like its now defunct opposite number, the Warsaw Pact, it went beyond traditional alliances in establishing an integrated command structure, together with an elaborate deployment of forces in peacetime as an instrument of deterrence.

The purely west European predecessor of the North Atlantic Treaty, the Brussels Treaty of 1948, is also relevant to current considerations of European security. Amended by the Paris Agreements of 1954, it served as a political device to legitimise the rearmament and incorporation into NATO of the Federal Republic of Germany. The organisation thus formed, the Western European Union (WEU), acquired no significant operational capacity — that was the prerogative of NATO — but it rests on a guarantee of mutual assistance which in legal terms is more automatic than that of the North Atlantic Treaty, and is not bound by the latter's geographical limitation. In 1984 the WEU was 'reactivated', its goals were updated in a 'Platform' in 1987, and its membership was increased with the accession of Portugal and Spain in 1988 (Cahen, 1990). The WEU's European rather than Atlantic composition — its membership consists of the Community states minus Denmark, Greece and Ireland — makes it an important element in the current debate about the changing role of alliances in the post-cold war era.

A quite different type of multilateral security system is contained in the provisions for collective security in the United Nations Charter. Whereas an alliance consists of like-minded states combining against a perceived enemy, collective security under the United Nations may be seen as a form of 'self-regulation' within the universal UN 'family' (Dorr, 1986, 23). Given the loose usage of the term 'collective security' to encompass all types of multilateral security systems, the provisions of Chapter VII of the Charter will be referred to below as 'universal collective security'. This concept is based on a simple proposition — "that aggressive and unlawful use of force by any nation against any nation will be met with the combined force of all other nations" (Claude, 1964, 224) — but in practice it is inherently demanding.

Never properly implemented during the cold war, because of 'automatic' disagreement among the permanent members of the Security Council, even during the Gulf crisis of 1990–1991 its most rigorous obligations remained a dead letter. The requirement to become directly involved in military enforcement measures at the direction of the Security Council (implied in Article 43 of the Charter) was not applied, thus permitting member states considerable latitude in defining the extent of their involvement. The price of ensuring more direct United Nations control over the enforcement of universal collective security might well include a more far-reaching commitment than the limited and essentially voluntary contribution to UN peacekeeping which Ireland has made for more than thirty years.

A theoretically less demanding type of security system, but one of direct relevance to the current changes in Europe, is the Conference on Security and Cooperation in Europe (CSCE). Created in the early nineteen seventies on the basis of the membership of all European states (less isolationist Albania) and the United States and Canada, it evolved into a framework of East-West contact, which was simultaneously part of the discourse of inter-bloc antagonism and a means of sustaining and developing European detente. By including non-alliance states and being based on consensus, the CSCE presented a more inclusive and less deterministic image than the rigid confrontation between the two alliances; with the dissolution of the Warsaw Pact, expectations were aroused that it would form the centre of the 'new European security architecture'.

However, such expectations presume a degree of stability which is proving to be elusive with the disappearence of the bleak discipline of the cold war. The CSCE is a framework for developing cooperative preventive measures, and for reinforcing arms control agreements and verification, but it is hard to see how crises involving political violence within or even between member states can be resolved in a system where each government has a formal veto on its application. The new issues of European security are as likely to be internal as inter-state in character (as, for example, in the Soviet Union and Yugoslavia), and in these circumstances the role of the CSCE may be circumscribed. The first test of new emergency procedures, in the Yugoslav crisis at the end of June 1991, demonstrated that while the Yugoslav federal government could not prevent the CSCE as a whole discussing the issues, the influence the latter could bring to bear was tentative and indirect. External mediation was legitimised by the CSCE, but it was the Community which had the operational structure and capacity to act.

The radical changes in the international system since the middle of 1989 — only barely captured in the phrase "end of the cold war" — pose basic challenges to the existing concepts and organisations of international security described above. Changing threat perceptions require the reassessment of the utility of familiar policy instruments and of the role of existing multilateral frameworks. The 'victorious' cold war alliances are in search of a rationale, universal collective security is struggling to rise from the ashes of the Gulf War, and the cooperative security system of the CSCE is faced with major problems. Thus the context in which Community governments are deciding their own security policies and their view on a common security policy is one of considerable uncertainty.

(iii) Ireland: security and neutrality

The most distinctive aspect of Ireland's security policy has long been the state's deliberate abstention from one of the three types of security framework described above; by not participating in any military alliances the stance of 'military neutrality' has been adopted. In that respect, Ireland is similar to Austria, Finland, Sweden, and Switzerland, the generally recognised "European neutrals" (Hakovirta, 1988; Keatinge, 1984; Kruzel, 1989; Sundelius, 1987). However, it has been argued that when set against objective criteria for an ideal type policy for neutrality, or even if compared to the actual practice of other European neutrals, Ireland's use of the label 'neutrality' is not justified (Salmon, 1989). Be that as it may, the refusal to undertake alliance commitments is the starting point for any analysis of Ireland's security policy. Yet it is only the starting point — neutrality is not by or of itself the whole of security policy.

Indeed it is all too easy to forget that neutrality, like membership of an alliance, is not an end of policy in itself but is rather one possible means to security as a necessary end (Murphy, 1990).

Ireland's 'military neutrality' is also less than the sum of the state's security policy in a more concrete sense because, having rejected participation in alliances, Irish governments have been less than clear as to what, if any, alternative military posture was being adopted. Elements of defence policy do exist — the military establishment provides aid to the civil power against terrorist violence, it deals with fishery protection, and has a very considerable tradition of contribution to UN peacekeeping. The latter mission is clearly relevant to international security, but does not represent the defence of the national territory against external threat. Official statements rarely advert to this supposedly primary mission of the defence forces, and there is no systematic public process of relating explicit threat assessments to defence expenditure. Ireland's 'military neutrality' is, therefore, somewhat devoid of military content, in contrast not only to alliance states but even more to other European neutrals, where military credibility has long been regarded as a *sine qua non* of neutrality policy in peacetime.

Although the lacuna concerning defence policy begs questions about Ireland's security policy, in public debates neutrality is often associated with political values which are relevant to security, but which also in some respects go beyond it. Like most political values these may be imperfectly realised in the actual behaviour of governments, but that does not detract from their validity as guidelines for policy. It is therefore worth examining these values in more detail since they point to some of the political criteria which are likely to be applied to any proposals which seem to indicate a move away from neutrality.

Independence of decision: This may arise simply from the view that the exclusive power to use force is the basis of national sovereignty. It is often accompanied by the proposition that small states can only suffer from entanglement in great power wars. An attachment to these beliefs can be observed in various forms in all neutral countries, and is particularly evident in the origins and evolution of Irish neutrality. Neutrality became synonymous with national independence — especially during and after World War II — and since independence meant *independence from British rule* the main bone of contention in Anglo-Irish relations, Northern Ireland, also became closely entwined in the rationale for neutrality.

Minimal resort to force: Neutrality is not to be equated with pacifism — in time of war the neutral is legally obliged to defend itself — but the political culture of neutrality at the very least emphasises a strict interpretation of the principle of proportionality in the use of force. Two corollaries may be observed in Irish attitudes to force in international politics. The first is a rejection of the legitimacy of weapons of mass-destruction, and of doctrines of nuclear deterrence; such views became particularly pronounced in the 'new cold war' of the early nineteen eighties, and have received the endorsement of the Catholic church's interpretation of just war doctrine. A second theme is the distaste for the projection of force outside the territory to be defended. For a small state with a colonial past such a policy suggests a form of neo-imperialism. In this context, in recent years neutrality has been associated with a critique of American foreign policy as well as with the action of the larger European states. In short, 'neutrality' is often regarded as being an appropriate antidote to the militarism which is assumed to be an inherent attribute of military alliances.

Credibility as 'peacemaker': The neutral is often seen as an international mediator, being able to provide 'good offices' for contacts between disputants.

However, the rigid bloc system which evolved after 1945 tended to reduce the opportunities to perform such a role with regard to the large issues of East-West relations.

Credibility as 'peacekeeper': It is sometimes assumed that neutrality is a *sine qua non* of the state's capacity to play the role of UN peacekeeper. Though experience does not support such a claim, as alliance states can and do play this role, there may be apprehensions that membership of an alliance would reduce the state's capacity in this regard.

Credibility as 'third world developer': Similar assumptions may be espoused in this context, reflecting a belief that the identity of 'neutral' gives access to, and displays greater sensitivity towards, developing states.

It may sometimes be possible to demonstrate that the assumptions underlying these values are ill-founded, that their relationship to security policy can be tenuous, or that the values themselves are not the exclusive property of neutral countries. Indeed, debates on many of these issues are features of the foreign and security policies in alliance countries; the latter in practice may dilute the principles of alliance just as neutral governments fail to live up to the more severe interpretations of their stance. Nevertheless, taken together the values described above are sometimes seen as the necessary elements of a policy of 'positive' or 'active' neutrality. There is evidence that an attachment to such an image of neutrality is deeply embedded in Irish political culture. The values associated with it are therefore an important part of the political base of Irish positions in the Inter Governmental Conference.

(iv) Security in European Political Cooperation

The European Community's involvement in the politics of security has always been tentative. The early attempt to establish a European Defence Community (EDC) collapsed in 1954, a failure which brought in its train that of a more ambitious 'European Political Community' (Cardozo, 1987). Defence integration provoked divisive political sensitivities, and in any case the main purpose of the Defence Community — the rearmament of the Federal Republic of Germany — was met by the formation of the Western European Union within the broader NATO framework. From that time on, most supporters of west European integration thought it prudent to adopt a "defence last" strategy (Rummel and Schmidt, 1990, 261). However, when East-West detente developed during the nineteen seventies, the broader concept of 'security' led to the enhancement of a cooperative approach to measures which did not impinge directly on the military core of alliance business — hence the 'S' in CSCE. This even included "confidence building measures" to lower the risk of war by miscalculation, but the main emphasis was on non-military issues. Thus the sensitivities, whether of alliance commitments or of neutrality, were not at stake, and the fledgling EPC process could be employed to coordinate positions on issues which lay towards the 'soft' end of the security spectrum. Indeed, this experience is generally regarded as one of the major formative influences on political cooperation.

It was against this background that security was included in Title III of the Single European Act. The signatories agreed to a general and rather loosely worded proposition that "closer cooperation on questions of European security would contribute in an essential way to the development of a European identity in external policy matters". Questions may be begged in the words 'closer' (how close?); 'questions' (what questions — all of them?); 'would contribute' (provided what?); 'identity' (in what institutional form?); and so on. The following sentence provided a more concrete commitment: "they [the signatories] are ready to coordinate their positions more closely on the political and economic aspects of security" (SEA, 30.6a). There is also a commitment to maintain "the technological and industrial conditions necessary for their security" (SEA, 30.6b), and a clause which seems designed to separate security cooperation in EPC from that which "certain" of the signatories are committed to in NATO and the WEU (SEA, 30.6c).

Much of this carefully-chosen language was taken from the London Report of 1981, which reflected agreement on a subtle division of labour between the political cooperation and alliance spheres of action. This formula was designed not merely to accommodate Ireland's 'military neutrality'; for most Community states it avoided cutting across the difficulty which the United States and the other non-Community members of NATO (currently Canada, Iceland, Norway, and Turkey) might have about being excluded from security consultations. In particular, the phrase "political and economic aspects of security" was devised in order to define political cooperation as the business of foreign ministries, but not defence ministries. Insofar as this question was referred to in the Irish Supreme Court's judgements on the Single Act, different interpretations emerged. Mr. Justice Walsh wondered whether the reference to NATO and the WEU might not in some (undefined) way impinge on the defence policy of a Community state which remained outside either alliance. However, a more confident view can be seen in Mr. Justice Griffin's assertion that since "military and defence aspects are not included [they] should accordingly be considered to be excluded" (Crotty v. An Taoiseach, 1987: 458, 465).

Experience since the Single Act was implemented in 1987 has borne this out. The general foreign policy orientations related to international security are covered in political cooperation, where, according to one study of this period, "Irish representatives are said to show a remarkable flexibility particularly as long as the EPC debate remains informal" (Regelsberger, 1990, 5). But the same author points out that when a formal military commitment was envisaged — in this case "policing" the Persian Gulf during the latter stages of the Iran–Iraq War

— consultation and some coordination of action took place in the WEU, not among the Twelve.

The compatibility of security and political cooperation in the late nineteen eighties probably owed a good deal to the generally benign international context which prevailed up to the middle of 1990. The peaceful reunification of Germany represented an extraordinary achievement for the ethos and methods of multilateral diplomacy, of which the Twelve's political cooperation is probably the most advanced form. However, the Iraqi invasion of Kuwait — leading to the second Gulf War — demonstrated the limitations of political cooperation when military issues or 'hard security' become more evident. EPC was the forum for considering diplomatic and economic responses, but the coordination of the actual blockade authorised by the UN Security Council — with which all Community states concurred — took place elsewhere, including the WEU. The participation of some Community states in the enforcement phase, the war of January–February 1991, was under the aegis of the *ad hoc* American-led coalition. In the final week of the war the Twelve declared that they were "at the side" of the coalition, thus underlining the reactive and marginal nature of political cooperation so far as hard security is concerned. This experience could hardly be ignored by the Inter Governmental Conference, which by this time was in the third month of its deliberations, but different conclusions were drawn by the various participants. As we shall see in the following sections the issues of security and defence proved to be among the most difficult it has had to face.

5. SECURITY POLICY: THE AGENDA OF 'SOFT SECURITY'

(i) Towards a new formulation of 'security policy'

It is hardly surprising that the guidelines for the Inter Governmental Conference emphasised security. The international context in which they were formulated was characterised by momentous change and great uncertainty. German unification had just been formally celebrated in the Charter of Paris,but the prospects for an orderly reform of the Soviet Union had deteriorated; the Gulf crisis seemed increasingly set for war. Thus, in addition to the inclusion of the term 'security' in the statement of general goals and in the label 'common foreign and security policy,' the guidelines listed specific objectives related to "issues debated in international organizations: arms control, disarmament and related issues; CSCE matters; certain questions debated in the United Nations, including peace-keeping operations; economic and technological cooperation in the armaments field; coordination of armaments export policy; and non-proliferation" (Presidency Conclusions, 14–15 December, 1990).

This is a different formulation of security policy from that employed in the Single European Act. Instead of the very general division of labour between the Twelve dealing with 'the political and economic aspects of security' in political cooperation and the alliances covering the other (i.e. military) aspects, the list just cited clearly includes issues which have a direct bearing on military or defence policy. Yet this change does not imply an abrupt or wholesale embrace of the military sphere. 'Defence' as such is treated separately (see Section 6, below). Moreover, the topics referred to are raised in the restricted context of "issues debated in international organizations", which does not reach wholly into either the national domain or that of bilateral arrangements. The wording of the guidelines stresses the "gradual extension" of the Community's role in this field.

The Draft Treaty maintains this approach. Its general statement of objectives eschews the Single Act's division of labour in favour of a policy which "may extend to all areas of foreign and security policy" (Draft Treaty CFSP–A). However, an explicit reference to defence is both tentative and contested. The specific items listed at Rome appear in an annex of topics susceptible to joint action. It is clear that they do not in fact cover 'all areas' of security policy, but rather relate to the preventive end of the spectrum of policy instruments. The emphasis is on the limitation,rather than the threat or use, of force; this is the agenda of 'soft security'.

(ii) The agenda of 'soft security' in 1991

Industrial and technological cooperation in the armaments field is not a new objective. Article 30.6(b) of the Single Act refers to it with some circumspection

— the taboo word 'armaments' is not employed — and the coy reference to working towards it "at the national level and, where appropriate,within the framework of the competent institutions and bodies" (SEA 30.6(b)) hardly suggests a determined common policy. The key indicator of any move in that direction would be the amendment of Article 223 of the EEC Treaty, which gives member states the right to restrict information concerning their national arms industries. As yet there appears to be no serious attempt in the Inter Governmental Conference to go down this path. Nevertheless, there is an incentive to at least try to bring the arms industry within the scope of general industrial policy, particularly at a time of arms reductions and the consequent difficulties of reconversion to non-military production.

The transfer of military technology to third countries and the control of arms exports is obviously a serious issue in the light of some of the Community states' involvement in the arming of Iraq prior to the Gulf crisis of 1990, though the ramifications of the problem go well beyond this particular case. Even where the official policy of national governments was to restrict the export of certain items which might contribute towards an Iraqi nuclear or chemical capability, there is evidence that national controls did not work effectively. Here too the retention of Article 223 (EEC) in its present form would seem to inhibit a fully-fledged multilateral regime; joint action under the common foreign and security policy heading is only a beginning.

Non-proliferation issues are closely connected to the items described above. The best known non-proliferation regime, covering nuclear weapons, was set up by the Non-Proliferation Treaty of 1968 and operates through controls on the export of nuclear materials implemented by the International Atomic Energy Agency (IAEA). One major Community state, France, was not an original signatory of the treaty, but its policy approximates that of the regime and it has recently stated its intention of adhering to it. Nuclear proliferation remains a major question in the post-cold war era, with the ability and ambition of an increasing number of third world countries to develop their own nuclear armouries. Yet it is far from being the only non-proliferation issue. Chemical weapons — the poor state's weapons of mass-destruction — and even biological weapons are increasingly widely dispersed,and the proliferation of missile technology is also significant. The Gulf War of 1991 showed how even systems which were out-dated by western standards could be significant threats in regional and local wars.

Arms control, negotiations on arms reduction and confidence-building measures, particularly in the CSCE context refer to the questions arising from the collapse of the Soviet bloc in central and eastern Europe. The signing of the treaty on Conventional Forces in Europe (CFE) in November 1990 opened up the prospect of a CFE II negotiating round in 1992. The CSCE would provide the framework in which all member states could participate in the verification of existing agreements, as well as the negotiation of further reductions and confidence-building measures. Given the more complex environment of current European security than that of the bipolar bloc confrontation, and the necessity for consensus if the CSCE is to be effective, the importance of a coherent approach by what is arguably the most coherent group of states in the CSCE — the Community countries — is likely to be enhanced.

Involvement in peace-keeping operations in the United Nations context is an activity which expanded during the 'new detente' of 1987–1989 (Iran–Iraq, Afghanistan, Central America, Namibia), and again in the aftermath of the Gulf War of January–February 1991. Although the whole role of the United Nations is a matter of political debate in the post-cold war era, the suggestion that peacekeeping be a subject of joint action in the common foreign and security policy indicates a much narrower approach. Peacekeeping refers to activities mandated by the Security Council, such as the supervision of ceasefires and the provision of lightly-armed interpository forces, but not to the measures of military enforcement as implemented,following authorisation by the Security Council,by the American-led coalition in the Gulf War of 1991.

The Yugoslav crisis at the end of June 1991 raised the question of the Community states agreeing to establish peacekeeping missions on their own initiative, or under the aegis of the CSCE. In the event the mandate was agreed in the latter forum, and initially the composition of an observer mission drawn exclusively from Community countries was requested by the Yugoslav federal government. Subsequently the participation of other CSCE states in the observer mission was also considered, but it was noticeable that the Community provided an operational structure which the CSCE simply did not possess. Irish participation in the initial observer mission consisted of a diplomat and two army officers. This marked a new departure but did not involve armed troops. The success of the Twelve's approach was still in the balance two months after the crisis erupted.

Involvement in humanitarian intervention measures is an item which did not appear in the Rome guidelines, but which was a direct response to the situation developing in northern Iraq a month after the end of the Gulf War. The special meeting of the European Council in Luxembourg on 8 April discussed the concept of 'safe havens' or enclaves within Iraq's borders but outside Iraqi authority, in order to protect Kurdish refugees. There were difficulties with the legal basis of this policy, in that the principle of non-intervention in internal politics was in conflict with the principle of human rights of minorities. Nevertheless, it was seen as a demonstration of the Community states' capacity to play a role in a crisis where other agencies, such as the United Nations,were more constrained. It was not surprising, therefore, to find "humanitarian intervention" in the Luxembourg draft text which appeared at this time.

Indeed, this last point illustrates the flexible, incremental, and pragmatic nature of what is envisaged as security policy under the auspices of the common foreign and security policy. The list of topics covered is not exhaustive, nor does it add up to a radical departure from the traditional substance of political cooperation. The items are of a preventive nature, designed to formulate agreements and multilateral regimes in order to control and reduce the scale of military confrontation. In conjunction with economic and general diplomatic measures, they are consistent with the image of the European Community as an important 'civilian power' rather than a military 'superpower' (Duchêne, 1972, 43).

It is arguable that a further element of security policy can be found in a separate part of the Luxembourg negotiating text, which deals with "cooperation on Home Affairs and Judicial Cooperation" (see Brigid Laffan's *The Governance of the Union,* Section 4, The Policy Scope of the Union). In so far as these provisions concern measures to control the external borders of the Community or would-be Union, and include police and judicial cooperation to that end, they potentially cover threats of transnational terrorism arising from regional and local conflicts outside the Community, as well as what could be politically sensitive issues of immigration policy. In this way the spheres of external and internal security inevitably overlap, though political, legal, and administrative competences remain distinct. Indications of how such issues are to be coordinated at the European level suggest a mode of intergovernmental consultation on the lines of political cooperation. Whether the provision of a legal basis for such consultation renders it more effective or accountable remains to be seen.

(iii) Implications for Ireland

The Irish government's position on the agenda of soft security has been generally positive; for example, the Minister for Foreign Affairs was reported to be enthusiastic about Irish participation in the Yugoslav observer mission (The Irish Times, 11 July, 1991). To some extent this represents a move away from the distinction previously insisted on in the Single Act, and reiterated in the national declaration on neutrality which was lodged with the instrument of ratification. By the same token it can be represented as a willingness to accept the "gradual extension" of the Union's role in security, as laid down in the Inter Governmental Conference guidelines. However, the extension is indeed gradual and is relatively tentative in the context of what other Community governments might be prepared to accept. It does not represent a very significant change even for those governments with a minimalist approach to these matters, such as the United Kingdom and Denmark. Moreover, at this stage of the negotiations it is not clear whether these actions will, as the Draft Treaty suggests, be decided on the basis of 'joint action', or by 'cooperation'.

Measured against the yardstick of what is generally considered appropriate behaviour for neutral states, involvement in the field of soft security is not necessarily of itself problematic. The norms of neutrality policy in peacetime (in contrast to neutrality law in time of war) are not codified rigorously. With the end of the cold war they are in the throes of a major reassessment, primarily by each neutral state and not by some omniscient external authority. In the Gulf crisis, for example, the domain of 'neutrality policy' shrank considerably. Finland and Austria served on the Security Council at different stages of the crisis, Switzerland most unusually participated in economic sanctions, and although no neutral state adopted a combatant role each facilitated the coalition's enforcement of Resolution 678 in some way. Even before this current reappraisal it was common practice for neutrals to be actively involved in United Nations peacekeeping, and in negotiations on those aspects of security policy which the alliances would deal with in the CSCE. Neutral states have as authentic an interest in the control of arms production, exports and proliferation as any other state. The opportunity directly to influence such policies within a group of states is not incompatible with a stance of neutrality, so long as the neutral state is not formally bound to alter its own position by the vote of a majority of its partners. In short, so far as soft security is concerned, it is the type of decision-making — not policy substance — which is the crucial factor from the point of view of neutrality. However, in the field of hard security or defence the substance of policy, as much as the form of the policy process, is a bar to neutrality.

6. THE QUESTION OF DEFENCE

(i) "With a view to the future"

The guidelines of the Political Union conference included a heavily qualified reference to defence, indicating that this issue, along with decision making, is one of the central tests of whether the negotiations will lead to incremental change or the 'qualitative leap' so often referred to in the rhetoric of Community integration. The statement is both speculative and tentative: "the European Council emphasises that, with a view to the future, the prospect of a role for the Union in *defence matters* should be considered . . ." Such a consideration is limited in scope, being "without prejudice to Member States' existing obligations in this area, bearing in mind the importance of maintaining and strengthening the ties within the Atlantic alliance and without prejudice to the traditional positions of other Member States". The latter phrase represents a delicately worded acknowledgement of Ireland's military neutrality.

Nevertheless, the guidelines also draw attention to two particular questions related to a defence role. The first is "the idea of a commitment by Member States to provide mutual assistance", while the second serves as a reminder that a west European alliance — the WEU — already exists, within the broader framework of the Atlantic alliance (NATO) and is therefore an inherent element in any consideration of defence (Presidency Conclusions 14–15 December, 1991).

The Luxembourg 'Non-paper', formulated after the tabling of specific proposals and the completion of the controversial war of UN-authorised enforcement against Iraq, served to underline the contentious nature of the defence issue. The proposition that the objectives of the common foreign and security policy should include "the eventual framing of a common defence policy" was encased in the square brackets which in this document indicated an acute divergence of views ('Non-paper' A.2). So too was a more specific commitment to review existing arrangements "with a view to the eventual implementation of a common defence policy", in a report to be submitted to the European Council not later than 1996 ('Non-paper' L.3). The Draft Treaty presented to the European Council in June eschews the bracketing of contentious issues, but it is noticeable that in the corresponding articles the wording is less specific. The eventual defence policy is no longer described as "common", and there is no longer a reference to implementing it (Draft Treaty CFSP–A and L.5). In short, there is no longer the presumption that a defence policy already exists at that stage.

Given the particular problems these proposals pose for Ireland, as a state with a policy of military neutrality, it is necessary to explore their implications in some detail. It is important to consider not only what effects their adoption might have on Irish policy, but also whether they are likely to be realised in the prevailing international context.

(ii) A commitment to mutual assistance?

On 7 March, 1991 the President of the Commission, Jacques Delors, amplified a suggestion already made in the Commission's opinion on changes to the treaties (Political Union, 1990, 14). He argued that the Twelve's solidarity should be made plain in any new Union Treaty: "how better than by taking over Article V of the WEU Treaty and adjusting the wording as follows: 'If any of the Member States should be the object of an armed attack in Europe, the other Member States will, in accordance with the provisions of Article 51 of the Charter of the United Nations, afford the party so attacked all the military and other aid and assistance in their power'" (Agence Europe 9 March, 1991). Such a commitment would represent the legal core of a military alliance, though shorn of the other legal and political conditions of membership which indicate more precisely how the basic commitment is to be implemented.

This proposal has its advocates in the Inter Governmental Conference — especially Italy, which advanced it during the Italian Presidency in the second semester of 1991 — but as such has raised little general interest to date. For most member states the more pressing issue is how their existing alliance commitments and policies, which involve non-Community states, are to be reconciled with a possible Community role in defence. However, for Ireland it causes difficulties at a more fundamental level, simply because it implies a major change — the end of a policy of *non*-alliance. In order to understand what would be at stake in a change of this nature, it is necessary to identify the principal consequences of accepting an alliance commitment. These are most readily observed by referring to the political values associated with neutrality (see above, Part 4 (iii)) to see in what respects and to what extent alliance membership might affect these values.

Independence of decision. The basic alliance commitment, like other Treaty obligations, means a significant loss of sovereignty — the right to say yes or no in certain circumstances. In particular, national autonomy is circumscribed in the event of an attack by a third party against an ally. In that situation the alliance's function as a deterrent has failed, and although there may be a constitutional requirement for the national government to confirm the commitment, the obligation to use force in defence of the alliance seems inescapable. However, in peacetime the policy of contemporary alliances (NATO, WEU) is based on consensus decision-making procedures. In these circumstances — and NATO has experienced no other circumstances — the alliance serves as a deterrent; policy covers issues of expenditure (burden-sharing), strategic doctrine and decision (responsibility-sharing), and military posture and deployment. The constraints on the individual member state in this regard are political rather than legal; for small states they reside in the pressures exerted by their larger allies. In principle, it can be argued that the loss of *formal* independence entailed in such an arrangement is if anything less than that implied by the collective security obligations of United Nations membership. In the latter case the member state which is not one of the five permanent members of the Security Council must submit to the direction of a body on which it is very rarely represented; only the historical disagreement between the permanent members has served to obscure this loss of sovereignty.

Minimal resort to force — the nuclear question. NATO (and by inference the WEU) operates on the basis of deterrence, and in the nuclear age that has implied a political (though not legal) commitment to the doctrines of mutual nuclear deterrence. That entails the risk, if deterrence fails, of a war of mass-destruction. The precise significance of nuclear weapons in such doctrines varies according to circumstances and the evolution of military technology, but it is never wholly absent, even if it is presumed to be a last rather than early measure in armed conflict. The WEU's 'Platform on European Security Interests', adopted in 1987, contains an explicit political commitment to nuclear deterrence (Cahen 1990, 36–44); irrespective of the role of the United States as NATO's nuclear superpower, neither of the two nuclear weapon states in the Community (France and the United Kingdom) has shown any sign of repudiating nuclear armament in the post-cold war era. However, the emphasis on nuclear deterrence has declined in recent years, with the prospect of large cuts in the level of armaments and a more serious attempt to curb proliferation. Even during the cold war partial reservations about nuclear weapons were accommodated in alliance policy; for example, NATO members Denmark and Norway have not been required to deploy nuclear weapons in their territory during peacetime.

Minimal resort to force — the projection of force. An alliance may, as in the case of NATO, be confined to a particular 'zone of application' i.e. a precise geographical area, in which the alliance commitment is restricted to the members' territorial integrity. The WEU, on the other hand, has no such restriction, and can thus envisage the defence not merely of territory but of perceived interests 'out of area'. In theory, this might be seen to increase the risk of any given alliance member becoming entangled or entrapped in military commitments which are geographically remote and which have little bearing on its own interests. However, to date the WEU's 'out of area' operations have been very modest, and always the result of consensus. The coordination of naval policing of the Gulf during the latter stages of the Iran–Iraq War, and the contribution of units to the enforcement of the UN-authorised blockade of Iraq in 1990–1991 represent a commitment of military force on a scale not very far removed from that entailed in a major UN peacekeeping operation.

Credibility as 'peacemaker'. It is obvious that as a member of an alliance an individual state is hardly in a position to play the formal role of mediator between that alliance and any other country or group of countries. However, mediation in disputes which have no bearing on the particular alliance cannot be ruled out. Nor can the possibility of a state exerting more effective conciliatory influence from within an alliance than as a third party without political leverage.

Credibility as 'peacekeeper'. Membership of a military alliance is in itself no bar to contributing to UN peacekeeping operations.Although there is a possibility that it might make an alliance state less politically acceptable in specific circumstances, the peacekeeping records of countries such as Canada and Norway suggest that in practice this is rarely the case for a state with a serious commitment to peacekeeping. A more likely constraint is to be found in the limitations of the military capability of a small state, which might not have the resources to contribute regularly to both alliance and peacekeeping missions.

Crediblity as 'third world developer'. It is sometimes argued that alliance membership would have negative consequences for development cooperation policy. There may be something to this proposition in the sense that expenditure on alliance commitments is clearly not going to development programmes, but the same could be said for other forms of public expenditure. The development policies of alliance states such as Denmark and the Netherlands, which are typically among the most generous aid donors, suggest that what counts in development policy is political commitment to development. From the recipients' point of view whether the donor has alliance commitments or not is a secondary consideration. Although many less developed countries adhere to the Non Aligned Movement, this does not necessarily mean they eschew their own participation in local or regional military alliances.

The question of cost is an essential consideration in the calculus of alliance membership. This can be seen first of all in human terms. It is sometimes assumed that male conscription is a *sine qua non* of the modern peacetime alliance, but in practice the implementation of conscription has been at least as thorough in other European neutrals as it is in European alliance countries. Military service is a pervasive feature in Swiss life, but one of NATO's major members, the United Kingdom, like Ireland relies on a volunteer professional defence force. In the post-cold war era there may well be a general reassessment of the utility of conscription. However, it would be foolish to ignore the financial costs of alliance membership, particularly against the background of the relatively limited resources which Ireland has traditionally devoted to national defence. It is beyond the scope of this paper to indicate what order of cost would be incurred, but the proposition that participation in collective defence could even have positive redistributive effects may not bear close examination, particularly at a time of general retrenchment in defence industries.

It is clear even from this cursory analysis of the implications of a specific and immediate commitment to collective defence that it would have considerable consequences for Irish policy. For those who assume that any direct association with a military alliance is in itself an endorsement of militarism or 'great power politics', these may be *ipso facto* unacceptable. However, the assumption merits closer examination. In the post-cold war era an alliance may not necessarily embody the adversarial connotations or level of armaments experienced since the late 1940s. Moreover, a European alliance might be more balanced in its composition than NATO has been, with its dependence on a dominant leader, the United States.

However, although the question of defence has been raised in the Inter Governmental Conference, there appears to be no serious proposal by even the maximalists to insist that such a commitment be written into the Union Treaty now. This hesitation derives from the larger uncertainties of a volatile international system. The enlargement of the western alliance system is *ipso facto* too sensitive an issue for even its most enthusiastic supporters to contemplate. The Soviet Union has already made it clear that it would regard the extension of NATO security guarantees to its former allies in central Europe (Czechoslovakia, Hungary and Poland) as provocative, and NATO has in fact rebuffed the latters' approaches. Thus the question of alliance commitment is on the agenda of the Inter Governmental Conference as a marker for the medium rather than the short term;the immediate issue is whether a Political Union should incorporate an incremental approach to such a policy by establishing links between the Community and the WEU.

(iii) Links between the European Community and the WEU

The Gulf crisis of 1990 demonstrated the possibility of an operational role for the WEU, in the implementation of the naval blockade of Iraq, and the Italian Presidency used this experience to advocate formal links between the Community and the WEU. Such links could be established at any or all of several levels in ascending order of political significance: between parliamentary institutions (the appropriate committees or in plenary sessions); between the respective secretariats; or in joint ministerial meetings. If regular procedures are formally laid down the links may be described as 'organic' and not merely *ad hoc*. In practice the supporters of this approach in the Inter Governmental Conference look first of all to the European Council acting as a source of 'guidelines' for both the Union and the WEU. These general policy directions, presumably arrived at by consensus, would then be followed through by some form of coordination at the lower levels. A 'dry run' of such a procedure was informally executed during the special meeting of the European Council in Luxembourg on 8 April, 1991. The Community leaders agreed to provide emergency aid to Kurdish refugees, whereupon France (as President-in-office of the WEU) convened a meeting of WEU foreign ministers,who were naturally in attendance, to coordinate the deployment of military personnel to implement the decision (Agence Europe, 10 April, 1991). However, writing such a process into a new Treaty has as yet made little headway in the Political Union negotiations, because of a divergence of views on the broader implications of a formal relationship between the Community and the WEU.

The proponents of new links include most of the major community states. Italy has urged an immediate 'marriage'. The Franco-German partnership — a necessary element in any serious integrative move — is more circumspect with regard to the timing (1996 or 1997, i.e. before the WEU treaty is due for renewal in 1998) and precise nature of such links, but has no difficulty in principle (Agence Europe, 4–5 February, 1991). Their interest is hardly surprising given the changing balance of influence between the two states following German unification; French apprehension and German reassurance are accommodated within a joint concept of 'European' defence. To these considerations of traditional 'high politics' may be added the federalist goal of deepening integration as such; the Commission and Belgium represent that line of argument.

While the sceptics on this issue are undoubtedly in a minority in the conference, they do reflect the concerns of a very important external influence — the United States of America. The traditional 'Atlanticist' orientation, represented most forcefully by the United Kingdom and the Netherlands, rests on the assumption that the American contribution to European defence is still essential and that NATO, and in particular its integrated command structure, represents the necessary operational centre of decision for collective defence. In this view the role of the WEU should not detract in any way from such a consideration; indeed the important links to be reassessed may be those between the WEU and NATO rather than those between the WEU and the Community. The strength of the Atlanticist argument — and it is primarily this argument, not Irish neutrality, which has hitherto kept defence out of the the Community — may be open to question in the post-cold war era, when the dissolution of the Warsaw Pact might be expected to lead to the dilution, at least, of NATO.

However, the latter process is not proving to be as sudden as the former. NATO governments still see a residual Soviet or 'Russian' military threat in the enormous nuclear and conventional capability at the disposal of an increasingly incoherent political leadership in Moscow. Even in the context of continuing significant reductions in military deployments in Europe the United States at present shows no sign of a desire to wind up NATO. Thus it has made it clear that the issue of Community/WEU links can only be approached within the overall Atlanticist *status quo*. The United Kingdom and the Netherlands for their part, while willing to contemplate pragmatic and *ad hoc* cooperation on the lines of the 'Kurdish experiment', reject the proposal that comprehensive organic links be established between the two organisations. Although the Dutch look to an eventual focus on European defence while the British show no such inclination, the reluctance of both governments to do anything which might prematurely 'decouple' the United States makes them, along with Denmark and Portugal, determined advocates of the *status quo*.

During the first six months of 1991 the focus of this debate about the future shape of defence policy has been mainly on NATO, to a lesser extent on the WEU, and barely at all on the European Community. French attempts to reverse this order of priorities during the Luxembourg Presidency, on which they might be expected to have some influence, have proved less successful than American insistence on the centrality of the transatlantic alliance. The communiqué of the NATO foreign ministers' meeting in Copenhagen on 6–7 June, while recognising that other institutions such as the WEU, the Community, the CSCE and the Council of Europe, all have a role in European security describes the transatlantic link as "essential". The accompanying statement on "NATO's core security functions in the new Europe" refers to the "security of North America [as] permanently tied to the security of Europe" (Agence Europe, Documents No. 5508). This position has yet to be endorsed by the NATO summit meeting in November, but it is unlikely that the Dutch Presidency of the Community will encourage any deviation in the context of the Inter Governmental Conference.

Maintenance of the *status quo* is also the position of Ireland in the conference, though for reasons which have little to do with the defence debate between 'Atlanticists' and 'Europeanists'. For Ireland the prospect of WEU/EC organic links raises the question of entanglement in existing defence commitments which would not only negate military neutrality, but which would probably also prejudge the nature of any future defence arrangements. On that basis, opposition to a direct merger between the Community and the WEU is a logical stance.

The difficulty for Ireland, however, lies in the formulation that such a merger should be attempted at some definite point in the not very distant future. Irish government leaders have never — while in government — committed themselves to permanent neutrality. On the contrary, Irish neutrality has been conditional. As the Taoiseach has said: "in general, our position is to maintain our traditional policy in regard to military alliances subject only to the qualification that if the Community develops its own defence arrangement we will favourably consider taking part in that arrangement" (Dáil Debates, 30 April, 1991). Following the European Council on 28–29 June, he commented that "a defence arrangement which the EC works out for itself, and which has Community interests as its primary focus, is clearly different from a system in which existing wider arrangements continue to have primacy and where non-Community members are part of the decision-making process" (Dáil Debates, 9 July, 1991).

The question is whether the Community is in fact developing its own defence arrangement. The answer provided so far by the Inter Governmental Conference might be represented as 'not quite yet', but the question looks set to stay on or near the top of the agenda for the 'foreseeable future'. That in itself is a change from the situation which prevailed in the debate preceding the Single Act. Then the government could justifiably claim defence was not an issue. Now, although there may be no actual commitment to defence, an explicit *aspiration* to such a role for the Union may appear in the Treaty or its preamble.

7. PROSPECTS AND OPTIONS

(i) The prospects for change

Before examining the options facing Ireland with regard to the external action of the Union, it is necessary to assess the prospects for the Inter Governmental Conference. This is bound to be a tentative evaluation, at what is only the half-way stage in the deliberations, but by distinguishing issues where agreement seems likely from those where disagreement is marked an initial appreciation is possible.

The area of *substantial agreement* covers the following issues raised in the Luxembourg Draft Treaty:

(a) the consolidation and amplification of existing arrangements under the EEC Treaty which deal with external economic relations and development cooperation policy;

(b) a rationalisation of the institutional framework, particularly by streamlining procedures in the Council and secretariat. This may improve the coherence between the Community and common foreign and security policy pillars of policy-making, but does not amount to a fusion or merger between them;

(c) an explicit focus on the agenda of 'soft security' issues, thus replacing the previous formula which referred to 'political and economic aspects' of security as distinct from 'other' aspects.

Disagreement persists on three major questions:

(a) the admission of some element of majority voting, seen by some as an issue of principle in the field of foreign policy;

(b) the admission of a commitment to an EC role in 'hard security', i.e. defence in the medium-term future;

(c) the development of transitional defence links with the WEU.

Those governments aiming at acceptance of the first set of issues only may be described as the 'Draft Treaty *minimalist*' camp so far as this part of the negotiations is concerned; those prepared to accept both sets are 'Draft Treaty *maximalists*'. In rather crude terms, the latter includes Belgium, France, Germany, Greece, Italy, Luxembourg, Spain, and, of course, the Commission; the former is composed of Denmark, Ireland, the United Kingdom, and less emphatically, the Netherlands and Portugal. In neither case, and certainly not among the minimalists, is there evidence of a concerted move to achieve a genuine federal union in the current negotiations. 'Gradualism' is the order of the day; thus the overall prospect for the Inter Governmental Conference is a Single European Act Mark II. Against that background, what options does Ireland face, and what questions arise in choosing between them?

(ii) The basis of choice

No consideration of options makes sense without a clear appreciation of what goals are being sought. This is by no means easy in the field of foreign policy; broad policy goals are inevitably open to differing interpretations, may prove difficult to reconcile, and are in the last resort the reflection of subjective values rather than self-evident elements in some mechanistic calculus. That said, questions about goals can and must be raised, even if only at a general level.

The first question may be put thus: do the proposed changes meet Ireland's interests and goals within the scope of the Union's external action as such? This question may be broken down into further queries concerning the compatibility between Ireland and the Union with regard to: national material advantage (balanced against the redressment of international economic injustice); international security; the promotion of human rights and peaceful change; and so on. Merely to list these objectives is to suggest the dilemmas which are likely to arise.

One obvious example concerns neutrality and defence. The former stance, as we have seen, has hitherto been justified on a variety of grounds (independence, limitation of force, and so on). To some extent its persistence reflects an element of deliberate moral choice — to abstain from and oppose the corruption of militarism or power politics which is assumed, in this view, to be an inherent part of military alliances. Yet its survival has also been a consequence of Ireland's location in a backwater of the cold-war maelstrom. In the changed circumstances of recent years the relationship between neutrality and the purposes it is supposed to serve may appear in a different light. Without necessarily repudiating the original moral objectives, the question can be posed whether changed, or even new, forms of collective defence can be established, in which a small state like Ireland can exert a positive influence more effectively as a participant than as an outsider.

It is also necessary to pose another even broader question: how do the proposed changes in the Union's external action, and Ireland's choices in that respect, affect Ireland's interests and goals with regard to the *internal* development of the Union? Are they consistent with the objective of economic and social cohesion, or with the overall requirements of effective and legitimate policy-making? In other words, the options facing Ireland regarding a common foreign and security policy cannot be considered in isolation; they are part of an overall package in the Inter Governmental Conference, and positions adopted in this part may affect the outcome elsewhere in the negotiations.

In that regard, the possibility of the negotiations leading to a formal two-tier system of integration must be taken into account. Hitherto this issue has arisen more acutely in the economic sphere, where it has been argued that such an arrangement would leave peripheral member states in a position of institutionalised underdevelopment, from which it would be difficult to escape (see Brigid Laffan's *The Governance of the Union*, Section 5, Prospects and Options/Graduated Integration). The current conference on Political Union at least implicitly raises that possibility in the sphere of the common foreign and security policy, in the division between minimalists and maximalists noted above. Thus an important question to consider is how Ireland's interests would be affected, both with respect to influence within the common foreign and security policy itself and within the Union as a whole. The costs of opting out of an important activity of the Union may be difficult to calculate at the outset, but they could prove to be significant.

(iii) Options for Ireland

The options presented in this section are not policy prescriptions, ranked in order of preference. Rather they represent an attempt to define the range of choice in very broad terms. Towards the end of the negotiations a much more complex picture will probably emerge, but at this stage the possibilities can only be sketched in, starting with the option of making no change, and then moving up a scale of changes leading to increasing levels of political integration.

Option 1: No change. In theory it is possible for a participant in the negotiations to take the position that the arrangements agreed in Title III of the Single Act should simply be reconfirmed, not for the long term — that might deny the 'ever closer union' aspired to in the founding treaties — but at least for the foreseeable future. The very uncertainties of the current era, it might be argued, require stability and prudence above all. Yet would such a conservative strategy meet Ireland's general diplomatic interests? To continue participating in a mode of collective diplomacy in the face of new challenges and at the same time to deny the possibility of making even incremental institutional adjustments is to argue for inefficiency and complacency in one of the few elements of stability in the current world system. It is hard to see how any of Ireland's foreign policy goals — apart from the possession of formal sovereignty — would be advanced by what would in effect be a renationalisation of foreign and security policy. Although the label of neutrality might be preserved, the goal of security would come no closer.

Such a stance on the common foreign and security policy issues would be likely to invite pressures for formalised two-tier integration. The basic moral argument for economic and social cohesion — that it is required by the solidarity between the peoples of the Community — would be undermined by such an obvious failure to reciprocate, particularly in a multilateral negotiation in which there is little sign of other small states exposing themselves to a similar risk of isolation.

Option 2: Draft Treaty minimalism. This option is based on a willingness to proceed with the issues raised in the 'area of substantial agreement'. It is consistent with a recognition that the international system is faced by new challenges, including those in the field of security, and presumes that a series of incremental adjustments will meet this need. The possibility of eventual federation is not precluded, but neither is it encouraged; the insistence that there can be no measure of majority voting makes this option strictly confederal in nature. Moreover, given its exclusion of defence cooperation, it is a confederation of limited scope.

Ireland's stance at this stage of the conference is close to this option. Under the consensus rule formal sovereignty in decision-making is retained. The long-established emphasis on measures of peaceful change, the focus on the United Nations (especially peacekeeping), and on development policy can continue, and as experience in political cooperation has shown, on occasion Irish positions can influence the member states' collective positions. The dilemma about changing neutrality is dealt with by redrawing the former explicit line between the 'aspects' of security as an implicit line between soft and hard security, which seems to require the exclusion of even the mention of defence. It is not very clear how this situation provides for the state's overall security, as the lacuna with regard to *national* defence persists.

One problem with this minimalist approach to the common foreign and security policy is that it might contribute to a *de facto* two-tier diplomacy by the Union, with a reduction in the influence which states in the second tier could exert. Another serious difficulty might be a linkage between the common foreign and security policy arrangements and Ireland's interests in economic integration. The more Ireland finds itself in the position of '*demandeur*', especially with regard to economic and social cohesion (see Brigid Laffan's *The Governance of the Union,* Section 5, Prospects and Options/Economic and Social Cohesion), the more vulnerable it will be to pressures to concede on other issues, including the experiment on majority voting, a statement of intent on defence, or links with the WEU. To stand firm on all these matters might expose Ireland to the danger of being in a possible second tier on both economic and foreign policy dimensions.

Option 3: Draft Treaty maximalism. The maximalist approach in the conference, by accepting a limited measure of majority voting, a statement of intent on defence, and organic links between the Community and the WEU, hardly represents a fully-fledged federal system. Rather it amounts to a comprehensive confederation in which federal goals at least receive more legitimacy and effect than hitherto. However, the evolution of a centralised federal foreign and security policy would not be guaranteed by these institutional changes since decision-making is still primarily intergovernmental, and the inclusion of defence in the short to medium term is nominal rather than operational.

So far as Ireland's foreign and security policy goals and interests are concerned, this option would permit the continuation of the broad lines of most existing policies. It would, however, seem to put a term to a politically credible position of 'military neutrality', but without making it very clear what exactly would replace that position, since the negotiation of detailed alliance commitments in the current Inter Governmental Conference is not envisaged. Adopting this option does not mean that Ireland joins either NATO or the WEU now, rather that some form of alliance commitment will be considered before very long. The ratification by referendum of Treaty amendments of this type would probably not authorise an Irish government to undertake alliance commitments without a *further* referendum, so long as a statement of intent on defence was in the preamble rather than the main body of the Treaty. However, in the light of ambiguities of this nature, any experimentation with majority voting might be better confined to issues with a minimal security dimension.

So far as Ireland's interests in economic integration are concerned, the increased solidarity implied in adopting this option would at the very least reduce the dangers of two-tier pressures, and might even enhance Irish claims to be included in the first tier on the economic front.

Option 4: Proactive federalism. If there were a wholescale move to majority voting together with the adoption of an immediate commitment to the defence of the Union, it could indeed be said that a federal union was in the making. Though this does not seem a likely outcome of the negotiations, that does not prevent any participant in the conference arguing that it should be. The rhetoric, and in more guarded ways some of the proposals, of some other member states and the Commission reflect this option. Moreover, it is sometimes argued that all the signatories of the various Community treaties have already made an implicit commitment to what is often referred to as 'the finality' of European integration — a United States of Europe.

Irish governments have, from the time of the initial application in 1961, accepted this goal in very general terms; why should they not advance it in the context of the current negotiations? A negative linkage between the foreign policy and economic spheres would be less likely than under the other options, and if Ireland is to undertake alliance commitments the position of being directly involved in the formative stage of a new European alliance might allow a greater influence on the shape of such an alliance.

One difficulty with this position can be seen from the rather narrow ground of negotiating tactics. A premature concession of what the other parties want may engender general goodwill, but it does not guarantee the achievement of one's own objectives, particularly if the ultimate form of Union is unlikely to be agreed at this stage. A broader problem is posed by the issue of defence. The ambiguity about precisely what commitments were being accepted, already seen in the previous option, would be unresolved in the current conference, and given traditional attitudes on this matter a referendum might turn on an issue that was no more than an hypothesis.

The first and fourth options are the least likely to match the eventual outcome of the Inter Governmental Conference, and the realistic range of choice arguably lies between the second and third options. It is of course possible to envisage a final position somewhere between these two. Of the three issues which separate them (majority voting, links with the WEU, a statement of intent on a future defence commitment), the third would seem to be the easiest for an Irish government to concede, if only because such a concession has long been made in informal political terms. It would, however, highlight the defence issue in a referendum campaign, in so far as it gave greater credence to 'thin end of the wedge' arguments about the end of Irish neutrality.

(iv) The context is a moving target

One inherent difficulty in deciding between options resides in the need to balance so many disparate goals and interests, many of which cannot be reduced to quantifiable terms. Another such difficulty is the fact that the Inter Governmental Conference is taking place at a time of major transition in international politics. Many of the questions in the field of foreign and security policy, with which governments are grappling at the same time as they are negotiating in the conference, are likely to remain unresolved well beyond the time frame envisaged for completion of Treaty amendments. The continuing instability in the Soviet Union, and the problems of economic and political reconstruction in central and eastern Europe — to look no further — suggest that the unexpected may be expected to disrupt conventional assumptions in the field of foreign policy. Time is not on the side of the architects of a 'grand design' for the new Europe.

Even at the half-way stage of the negotiations, the major crises in Yugoslavia and the Soviet Union seem set to influence their outcome in unpredictable ways. So, too, could parallel negotiations in other forums, and particularly in the NATO review which is due to be finalised in November 1991. That is all the more reason to suppose that whatever does emerge from the conference is an interim adjustment to the integration process, which will probably have to be reviewed again in the mid-nineties. Such key factors as the intensity of the American commitment to transatlantic defence could well have changed by then, and there will almost certainly be the additional complication of the increasing pressures of further enlargement (see Tony Brown's *The Extension of the Union,* the following paper in this book). The questions raised in 1991 are not going to disappear, whether resolved in the Union Treaty or not.

BIBLIOGRAPHY

Agence Europe

Buzan, B. (1983), *People, States and Fear: The National Security Problem in International Relations,* Brighton: Wheatsheaf.

Cahen, A. (1990), *The Western European Union (WEU) and NATO: Strengthening the Second Pillar of the Alliance,* Washington D.C.: Atlantic Council.

Cardozo, R. (1987), 'The Project for a Political Community' (1952–54), in R. Pryce (ed.), *The Dynamics of European Integration,* London: Croom Helm.

Claude, I. Jnr., (1964), *Swords into Plowshares,* (3rd ed.), London: University of London Press.

Duchene, F. (1972), 'Europe's Role in World Peace', in R. Mayne (ed.), *Europe Tomorrow,* London: Fontana.

Edwards, G. and Regelsberger, E. (eds.), (1990), *Europe's Global Links: The European Community and Inter-regional Cooperation,* London: Pinter.

Hakovirta, H. (1988), *East-West Conflict and European Neutrality,* Oxford: Clarendon Press.

Hogan, G. W. (1987), 'The Supreme Court and the Single European Act', *The Irish Jurist,* XXII.

Keatinge, P. (1984), *A Singular Stance: Irish Neutrality in the 1980s,* Dublin: Institute of Public Administration.

Kruzel, J. and Haltzel, M. (eds.), (1989), *Between the Blocs: Problems and prospects for Europe's neutral and nonaligned states,* Cambridge: Cambridge University Press.

Kuyper, P. J. (1982), 'Community and International Law', in D. O'Keefe and H. G. Schermer (eds.), *Essays in European law and Integration,* Deventer: Kluwer.

McCutcheon, P. (1991), 'The legal system', in P. Keatinge (ed.), *Ireland and EC Membership Evaluated,* London: Pinter.

Millar, D. (1991), 'European Political Cooperation', in C. Carstairs and R. Ware (eds.), *Parliament and international relations,* Milton Keynes: Open University Press.

Murphy, S. (1990), 'The New Europe and Irish Neutrality', *Studies,* 79, No. 316.

Regelsberger, E. (1990), 'The "European foreign policy" in the test', unpublished paper presented at Bruges, 28–30 June.

Rummel, R. and Schmidt, P. (1990), 'The changing security framework', in W. Wallace (ed.), *The Dynamics of European Integration,* London: Pinter.

Salmon, T. C. (1989), *Unneutral Ireland: An Ambivalent and Unique Security Policy,* Oxford: Clarendon Press.

Sundelius, B. (1987), *The Neutral Democracies and the New Cold War,* Boulder, Colo.: Westview.

Temple Lang, J. (1987), 'The Irish court case which delayed the Single European Act'; *Common Market Law Review,* Vol. 24.

Official Documents

Crotty v. An Taoiseach [1987], *Irish Law Reports,* 713.

Draft Treaty on the Union, 18 June: *Agence Europe Documents,* No. 1722/23.

Luxembourg 'Non-paper', 17 April: *Agence Europe Documents,* No. 1709/10.

'NATO's core security functions in the new Europe': *Agence Europe Documents,* No. 5508.

Political Union: Commission proposals at the IGC regarding 'Common External Policy': *Agence Europe Documents,* No. 1697/98.

Political Union: Commission Opinion, 1990.

Presidency Conclusions, 14–15 December 1990.

The Single European Act: A Government Information Booklet, 1987.

THE EXTENSION OF THE UNION

Tony Brown

EXECUTIVE SUMMARY

"The fact is that we are going to be a sixteen or nineteen nation Community by the middle 1990s — even without including the pressure for accession from countries in Central and Eastern Europe". (An unnamed Commission official).

Enlargement on the Agenda

Enlargement is on the agenda of the EC and, together with the question of the Community Budget, will be the next big 'European' issue for debate after the conclusion of this year's Inter Governmental Conferences.

Already five applications are on the table: Turkey, Austria, Malta, Cyprus and Sweden. The Commission has recommended that negotiations with Austria should commence in 1993 and Sweden's application has been cleared at Council level for more detailed assessment. The Turkish application is 'on hold' and those of the two small Mediterranean states are being studied by the Commission.

Other countries are debating membership, for example Norway, Finland, Switzerland, Hungry, Poland and Czechoslovakia. This situation arises from the growing conviction that the Community has become the nucleus of political development in Europe as well as an economic power of major significance. The dramatic process of change now underway in the USSR has added the prospect of membership applications, for example, from the Baltic Republics which have close historic ties with Scandinavia.

Evolution of the Community

The Community today is engaged in the creation of both Economic and Monetary Union (EMU) and Political Union on the basis of the 1992 Programme for the Single Market. Furthermore, the Community exists in the context of a continent in flux as the old bipolar political order and blocs disintegrate. A new European construction is required and the EC will be at its heart.

For, despite the problems inherent in adding to the complexity of working within a Community of Twelve, and in facing up to some weighty political issues such as neutrality, it is becoming clear that the destiny of the Community cannot be delimited by its present boundaries. The Community will extend from Twelve to fifteen and onwards perhaps to as many as twenty four members over the years ahead. It will do so by absorbing most of the present EFTA, together with states from Central and Eastern Europe and from the Mediterranean region.

Deepening versus Widening

The debate in the Community today relates to the balance to be achieved between the completion of the present agenda of greater integration among the

Twelve and the expansion of the EC by the accession of new members, north and south. There are strongly held views on both sides of the argument, reflecting a divide between ideas which may be summed up as 'Exclusive Europe' and 'Open Europe'. As President Delors has put it: "As far as the 'other Europeans' are concerned, the question is quite simple: how do we reconcile the successful integration of the Twelve without rebuffing those who are just as entitled to call themselves Europeans?" (European Commission, 1989, p. 17).

As the debate has developed in recent months it has become clear that practical political considerations and acceptance of the Community's long term vocation have combined to produce a general acceptance of the view expressed by the Vice-President of the Commission, Sir Leon Brittan, addressing the European Parliament: ". . . I think that it is right that enlargement and deepening need not be opposed concepts, and that it is right to say that we can accommodate the changes that are necessary to accept new members of the Community". (Brittan, 1991).

A History of Enlargements

The history of the EC has been marked by successive enlargements with the initial applications to join the founding Six being launched in 1961. Following a decade of struggle with the views of President de Gaulle the first enlargement took place in 1973 (UK, Ireland, Denmark) and this was followed in 1981 (Greece) and 1986 (Spain, Portugal). While in 1973 the primary incentive for expansion was economic, the developments in the 1980s were first and foremost political in nature, being inspired by the need to provide the applicant states with an underpinning of their new and hard won freedom and democracy. Developments today can be seen to relate to both economic and political factors.

It has been strongly argued that: "Historically it is not the case that the entry of new members has led to a slowing-down in the process of European integration, quite the reverse. The process . . . has in fact accelerated in recent years as the membership of the Community has increased, and, when necessary, there have been changes in the way in which we run our affairs". (Brittan, *op. cit.*). So it was that Spain and Portugal became full members of the Community in January 1986 just weeks before the signing of the Single European Act (SEA).

1992 — Creation of the Single Market

The pace of progress towards 1992 and the completion of the Single Market has become irreversible. This reality has led a number of European states at present outside the EC to accept the absolute need to formalise relationships in terms of market access and full integration into a Community whose achievements — and whose advances in areas such as technological standards — would pose severe difficulties for those remaining outside. The initial response of the EFTA countries has been through the ongoing negotiations for a European Economic Area (EEA). But here there is evidence of a dramatic shift in opinions on their part towards a conclusion, in the words of the 'Economist', "that the EEA agreement in-the-making favours the Community more than them, but that the price is slight provided that it is a down-payment on full EC membership".

Central and Eastern Europe

In Central and Eastern Europe profound changes on the political front in 1989 and 1990 were paralleled on the economic front by urgent action to move from bureaucratic, stalinist, command economies to open market structures. The democratic governments coming into power in the former Communist states looked at once to the West and, in particular, to the Community for assistance in political, economic, trading and financial terms. The establishment of the European Bank for Reconstruction and Development and the PHARE Programme of the EC have been designed to meet immediate development and funding needs.

The Community has embarked on Association Agreements with some of these countries but it is clear that the more economically advanced are already thinking in terms of full membership at the earliest possible moment and have stated so. This is true in particular of Hungary, Poland and Czechoslovakia.

Southern Europe

Further south, Mediterranean countries like Cyprus and Malta have already applied for EC membership and Turkey is actively pursuing its application despite serious economic and political obstacles.

USSR

The question of the Community's future relationship with the USSR, whatever its future shape, must arise for consideration. While the initial emphasis is likely to be on economic and financial assistance, it is certain that Europe's future architecture will involve formal and institutional links between the EC and the evolving USSR and/or with its constituent parts.

Forces for Enlargement

Overall, it may be argued that the growing economic dominance of the Community within the wider Europe provides a 'pull' while rapid political and military changes produce a 'push' towards full membership of the Community.

Criteria for Membership

The criteria for membership of the Community are clear and the basis for accession is Article 237 of the Treaty as amended by the Single European Act. Applicants must be (a) democratic, (b) capable of fitting into the Community in economic, political and institutional terms and (c) prepared to accept the *acquis communautaire,* i.e. the full corpus of Community Law and policy put into place since 1957. The applicant must "accept the overall view of the European Union as well as the constraints imposed by its gradual creation". (Tindemans, 1975). A strict process is followed in respect of each application, involving an initial Commission assessment, detailed negotiations and decisions by both European parliament and national parliaments.

The Issues

The enlargement of the Community gives rise to range of major issues which may be summarised as follows:

- *institutional issues:* the necessity to streamline Community structures to cope with enlargement
- *economic issues:* capacity to integrate into the changing and developing Community system
- *structural problems:* the Eastern European economies in their transition to the free market system
- *political issues:* notably the implications of the traditional neutrality of some applicants; prospects for Pan-European security structures
- *expanding Community competences:* their expansion under the terms of Political Union
- *acquis communautaire:* the capacity of applicant states to absorb or accommodate to existing EC legislation
- *budgetary issues:* the need to underpin Community commitments on Economic and Social Cohesion
- *key policies:* implications for critical policies such as CAP, Transport, Environment.

The Options

Bringing together all of the foregoing aspects of the issue of enlargement it is possible to identify a number of scenarios for the future of the European Community. These options have been current in political discussion in recent times and they have been specifically identified and analysed by major commentators. Five such scenarios are discussed in detail:

- Internal Integration and External Partnership
- A Larger Single Market
- A New Intergovernmental Structure
- Multiple Pillars
- Deepening and Sequential Enlargement.

Deepening and Sequential Widening is the option most likely to be implemented, with current integration efforts continuing apace and arrangement for the negotiation of an initial phase of enlargement commencing as soon as the Inter Governmental Conferences (IGCs) and preparations for the Single Market project are completed. The Commission's decision in the case of Austria is very much in line with this approach.

Conclusions

The main issues related to enlargement are indicated above and it is clear that there must be satisfactory progress in respect of each of them. This means that the enlargement issue is more than just an increase in the number of member states. More importantly, it requires confronting and overcoming novel institutional challenges. No enlargement or series of enlargements can succeed if decision-making and representation are not redesigned to achieve effectiveness and efficiency. And it is clear that the Security question, arising from the neutral status of several potential applicants, will require close study as will the linked issues of Economic and Social Cohesion and the future shape and scale of the Community Budget.

Issues for Ireland

A number of issues arise for policy consideration in Ireland:

- first of all it is necessary to take a view on the basic nature and vocation of the Community at this critical point of decision on integration and enlargement. The concept of a European Union with extensive competences in both economic and political terms, and with appropriate policy instruments and institutions, must have a philosophical and inspirational content and strong popular assent; debate is overdue on this aspect of EC involvement despite the strong 'European' commitment on the part of the general public indicated by all current research
- the challenge of further enlargement poses fundamental questions as to our understanding of what Europe is in geographical, cultural and political

terms; what is meant by the description 'European'; what is required at all levels to build a true unity between 400 million people; and what alternative is there to setting out to do so in the circumstances of today's Europe where so many economic, social, ecological and political problems are beyond solution by any individual nation state

- in practical terms it is necessary to ask what should be the pace of enlargement: the Deepening and Sequential Widening Option would appear to have relevance if interpreted as retaining genuine openness over time
- institutional arrangements arising from enlargement are of prime importance; in this connection there arises the debate on inter-governmental as against Community approaches to decision-making. This debate goes beyond the enlargement issue; the crucial issue is the impact of such concepts on a smaller member state — does Ireland stand to gain more from the policy line of the Commission and Parliament or from working largely at the level of Council and European Council?
- specific economic issues arise, notably concerning the impact of enlargement; new markets and additional resources for the Structural Funds as against the demands of the less developed candidates from Eastern and Southern Europe; giving rise to major calculations for Ireland not least on the future EC Budget
- there are also important policy issues on the current EC agenda which are likely to be affected by enlargement; these include the reform of the CAP, Transport and Environmental Policies and arrangements for migration and citizenship
- the sensitive issue of the development of a Common Foreign and Security Policy with the long term perspective of a defence commitment must be confronted: debate on the meaning and future relevance of Ireland's traditional neutrality is required in the context of the changed European political scene and of perceived 'risks'; the prospects of Pan-European developments, possibly in the CSCE framework, offer new opportunities for application of the positive principles of Irish foreign policy
- the enlargement debate will be an item of practical concern in the short-term and part of the second phase of debate on the future shape of the Community. Hence, it is urgently necessary in this country to initiate meaningful debate at all levels on the content and promotion of Irish national policies.

1. INTRODUCTION

"The fact is that we are going to be a 16 or 19 nation Community by the middle 1990s — even without including the pressure for accession from countries in Central and Eastern Europe" (unnamed Commission official).

That prediction would be increasingly endorsed by observers of the Community scene, some of whom point to the fact that the huge office complex now under construction in central Brussels for the future use of the Council of Ministers is designed to accommodate at least eighteen national delegations!

The Next Great Issue

The further enlargement of the European Community — together with the scale and scope of the Community Budget — will be the next great political issue to be addressed by the member states and it is an issue of the most profound long term significance since it brings into focus questions which bear on the prospects for economic advance, peaceful political progress and clear European identity. *Enlargement will happen* and it is essential that this process takes place in a manner which will ensure that it will be a benefit for Europe and its peoples and not a disservice.

The current work of providing a Treaty base for Economic and Monetary Union and for Political Union — together with the final preparations for the opening of frontiers on 1st January, 1993 — represent the completion of a phase of integration designed to create a Community which is at once democratic, effective and efficient. The next phase must be one of extension with the goal, over time, of creating a Community that can truly claim the name of Europe.

Fifty years ago, when many Europeans were waging a bloody war to save their continent — and the world — from fascism, it was the dream of numerous political thinkers and resistance leaders that one day their divided continent would have the gift of unity from the Atlantic to the Urals, from the Arctic to the Mediterranean. Today, in the aftermath of the events of 1989 and 1990 and with the EC as both a model and a nucleus, that hope is being rekindled and, even, spoken of as a realistic political prospect.

Enlargement is on the agenda of the European Community and is moving quickly up the order of priority as, one after another, European democracies outside the Twelve reach the decision that the appropriate form of future relationship with the evolving Community is that of full membership. This fact was recognised by the Commission in its Opinion on Political Union which referred to the need to create "a single institutional structure flexible enough to take account of . . . the likelihood of further institutional change to accommodate enlargement of the Community. Common sense dictates that in a much larger

Community the institutions will have to be radically reformed . . ." (Commission Opinion, 1990, p. 12).

Applications on the Table

Already, five applications are on the table — from Turkey, Austria, Malta, Cyprus and Sweden. More are anticipated. These applications arise from the growing conviction that the European Community is now seen as the nucleus for building the political future of Europe and also as an economic power of such strength and significance that every European nation must have a positive working relationship with it. They give rise to complex questions touching upon the fundamental *raison d'etre* and future vocation of the Community.

The Inter Governmental Conferences reflect the rapid pace of economic integration within the Community and the remarkable transformation of the political life of Europe which has come about over the past two years. The Community is seeking to secure a major leap forward towards the goals of Economic and Monetary Union with a single currency, a 'one-voice' status in international politics, a more effective structure for decision-making and — in an as yet undefined form — a concept of its security identity within the wider Europe.

The Community exists, however, in a continent in flux as the old order and the old blocs disintegrate and a new European construction is sought. Various potential designs, from the minds and ambitions of various distinguished designers, may be considered — from Mitterrand's European Confederation, through Delors' Concentric Circles to Gorbachev's Common European Home. That such concepts lack something in precision is understandable at a time of rapid change and uncertainty, not least in the USSR.

Two Strands of Thought

Yet it is possible to discern two clear strands of thought in relation to the future of the Community itself which are of importance in any attempt to assess the prospects for enlargement. These positions are at times put forward passionately while, at other moments, they are more implicit than explicit in political or bureaucratic comment on relevant developments or options.

First, there is an 'Exclusive Europe' approach, rooted in the conviction that the economic, monetary and political integration of the existing Twelve must lie at the heart of any new European construction and that the present Community has the vocation to become a virtual 'elite' or 'core' around which other states will be grouped in a variety of relationships of varied timespan and intensity. The widely canvassed idea of the Community at the centre of a system of

Concentric Circles — EC EFTA/East & Central Europe/Southern and Mediterranean Europe — is a sophisticated version of this approach.

This idea has surfaced in some misgivings about enlargement and even in open hostility to one or other of the potential applicants — for example, in calling into question the 'European' credentials of Austria because of its treaty-based neutrality. Indeed, there are some who argue that security and defence might become the very core policies of the future Community. This strand of thought is supported by strongly argued economic and institutional considerations and by the view that the Twelve themselves are of such diversity that their full integration remains problematic.

Then there is an 'Open Europe', tendency based on the concept of a Community which, while evolving internally towards greater integration, is always open to new members and sees this openness as an inherent element. The idea of openness extends to an acceptance of applicants from among the EFTA countries and from the newly-emerging democracies of Central and Eastern Europe as well as from a wider catchment area including the Mediterranean region. This viewpoint has been further refined to cover openness on world trade matters and on cooperation for development with the Third World.

An 'Open Europe' has been seen by many strong advocates of European Union as a necessary, and feasible, option despite the many obstacles arising from concerns such as overloaded decision-making and differential levels of economic or political development. It has been characterised as an expression of the deepest aspiration of the original movement for reconciliation and unity among Europeans and its admitted difficulties have been regarded as part of the high price of Europe's ultimate destiny.

Of course, the 'Open Europe' was, for a time, strongly advocated by the UK whose enthusiasm was, in reality, part of an over-riding concern to contain the accelerating drive towards economic, monetary and political integration by placing the emphasis on the simple goal of free trade between a growing number of European states with the minimum addition of common policies and strengthened institutions.

It is clear that elements of both 'Exclusive Europe' and 'Open Europe' exist within the various strands of political thinking on the enlargement issue. It is equally clear that neither simple view can cope with the complex relationships and aspirations now emerging.

Commenting on the on-going talks between the Community and EFTA on the European Economic Area, Wallace and Wessels make the point that ". . . some of the initial EC, and particularly European Commission, enthusiasm for the EEC had much to do with a desire to head off the Austrian application and to deter others. The strategy has not worked . . . so enlargement is on the EC agenda whatever happens to the EES". (Wallace, W., ed. 1991, p. 271). Indeed, the same authors go on to argue that for the EFTA states "full membership is the most honest and clear option", *(op. cit.)*.

Deepening versus Widening

So it is that the debate on enlargement has become focused on a fundamental choice between Deepening and Widening which has generated political controversy since the 1960s: "Should the EC concentrate on its already declared policy agenda since so much remained to be turned into solid legislation? Could the EC pass up the opportunity to embrace new policy areas? Would the whole endeavour be helped or hindered by accepting new members?" (H. Wallace, 1989, p. 1). In this connection it is of interest to consider the thinking of the Commission President, Jacques Delors.

Addressing the European Parliament on 17th January, 1989, he dealt at length with this subject:

> As far as the 'other Europeans' are concerned, the question is quite simple: how do we reconcile the successful integration of the Twelve without rebuffing those who are just as entitled to call themselves Europeans? As you know, the Commission has already adopted a position on this: internal development takes priority over enlargement. Nothing must distract us from our duty to make a success of the Single Act . . .
>
> It is my deep seated conviction, speaking personally, that we shall be in a better position to carry out the hoped-for enlargements once we have consolidated, strengthened our unity and elevated it to the political plane . . .
>
> If I have mentioned this subject it is because I myself have been getting worried about all this airy-fairy talk anticipating a watered-down Community as a wider entity . . . (European Commission, 1989, pp. 17, 22, 23).

A year later, he had the following to say: "But we must be wary of raising unrealistic expectations. Of course, the principle is quite clear: any democratic European country is free to apply for Community membership. But . . . it all comes down to ways and means and, while we do not abandon our basic approach, the substance of practical arrangements can vary over time . . . the question put to every applicant for membership is simple: are you, or are you not prepared to accept the marriage contract in its entirety, with all that it holds for the future?" (European Commission, 1990, p. 7).

President Delors has held firm to this view of Community consolidation and has, on occasion, used rather restrictive language on enlargement. In his 1989 address to the European Parliament he made reference to Gorbachev's idea of a Common European Home and said: "To make the point, I would say that our vision is of a 'European Village' where understanding would reign . . . but if I were asked to depict that village today, I would see in it a house called the 'European Community'. We are its sole architects; we are the keepers of its keys; but we are prepared to open its doors to talk with our neighbours", *(op. cit.)*.

Yet, commenting on the themes of the Rome meeting of the European Council in December 1990, he felt able to speak of the prospect of a Community of twenty-four member states and to speculate, in some detail, about the institutional and decision-making implications of such enlargement. Clearly, the debate goes on.

Opening

And, in the European Parliament on 14th May, 1991, Commission Vice-President Sir Leon Brittan, replied to the debate on the Planas Puchades Report on Community Enlargement and stated, *inter alia*, that ". . . we should recognise that the interest in joining the Community is a reflection of our success . . . Mr. Planas Puchades himself covered most of the main issues in his opening speech. He started by saying that enlargement and deepening are not opposed concepts and I am sure that he is right. It was reflected by what many other speakers said; by Mr. de Clerq when he said that the Community must be open, that we should not be a fortress or a rich man's club. That is indeed the case . . ." (European Parliament, 1991, p. 110).

In summary, enlargement of the European Communities has now become a significant agenda item. Although the idea of expanding the Community from Twelve to as many as nineteen or twenty member states gives rise to misgivings or to actual hostility among the present members, it has become clear that political imperatives, coupled with a clear view of economic realities and power relationships, have become dominant.

The Deepening versus Widening debate remains a factor in the overall discussion of enlargement. Indeed, it is the vital issue. In this debate may be summed up the concerns and interests of the present member states and the disquiet of some about the Community's capacity to survive enlargement. The debate equally focuses on the interests of the potential and actual applicants. And, it gives rise to consideration of the Community's long term vocation and optimum shape and capacity. So rapid is the pace of change and development in Europe today that the argument is shifting from a direct confrontation of two opinions to a more nuanced consideration of the correct balance of opportunity and advantage for Europe as a whole.

The 1993 Moratorium

One important aspect of the enlargement debate which reflects the dilemma of Deepening or Widening is the widely held view that there should be no negotiations on any of the applications until 1993, after the formal achievement of the Single Market and subsequent to the ratification of the Treaty provisions arising from the work of the Inter Governmental Conferences. This view has been endorsed by the Commission — and is contained explicitly in its recommendations to the Council on the Austrian application.

The Movement towards Enlargement

The movement toward further enlargement springs from many causes, as will be discussed below, but it fully reflects the fundamental ideas behind the concept of a United Europe. ". . . we must hold on to two simple ideas: the imperative need to unite to meet the challenges of history, and the extraordinary stimulus provided by the prospect of a united Europe, as Jean Monnet imagined it. He said, and I quote: 'Gradually to create among Europeans the broadest common interest, served by common democratic institutions to which the necessary sovereignty has been delegated. This is the dynamic that has never ceased to operate, removing prejudices, doing away with frontiers, *enlarging to continental scale,* within a few years, the process that took centuries to form our ancient nations'." (Delors, 1989, *op. cit.*).

2. THE BACKGROUND

The argument about Widening or Deepening has always been central to debate about the Community's future. It first emerged in the late 1960s when the young Community, having completed the Customs Union and initiated the CAP and other common policy projects, was confronted by the persistent efforts of the UK, Ireland, Denmark and Norway to get long-stalled talks on accession underway. Many voices were heard to argue that the Six should concentrate on its own evolving agenda and put negotiations for enlargement on the 'long finger'.

However, the Hague Summit of December 1969 saw a number of key decisions facilitated by the departure from the scene of President de Gaulle. President Pompidou agreed during the Summit to accord budgetary powers to the European Parliament, obtained a fresh financial package from the CAP and gave his assent to the opening of accession talks with the four applicant countries. In effect, Widening and Deepening were accepted as simultaneous goals. *"Le Marche Commun, sans attendre le conclusion des negotiations avec la Grande-Bretagne, va realiser de nouveaux progres d'unite, les plus vastes depuis l'echec de la Communaute de defence"*. ("The Common Market, without waiting for the results of the negotiations with the UK would seek to bring about new advances towards union, far greater than anything attempted since the collapse of the EDC"). (Van Helmont, 1986, p. 137).

The First Enlargement

The subsequent period saw significant progress on both fronts, with the eventual accession of the UK, Ireland and Denmark on 1st January, 1973 and the development of Community policies in key areas. These included monetary policy (Werner), political cooperation (Davignon) and culminated in the seminal Paris Summit of 1972 at which the leaders of the candidate member states joined those of the Six in agreeing a number of major policy initiatives not least in the field of social policy which had been largely ignored up to that point. Despite many frustrations and delays arising from the constraints of the first Oil Crisis following the Yom Kippur War in 1973, the groundwork had been laid for important progress in the enlarged Community. The one setback was the decision of the people of Norway, in a Referendum, to reject the terms negotiated for accession and to stay outside the Community.

The first enlargement proved the capacity of the Community to tackle deepening and widening in parallel but it did not do away with the underlying concerns in this connection. The 1975 Tindemans Report on European Union which, in many particulars, was the precursor to the major policy developments of the mid-eighties had a strong flavour of this unease. Dealing with the overall impact of his wide-ranging proposals for institutional and policy changes the author of the Report continued:

> The progress achieved as a result will gradually transform the nature and intensity of relations between our States. It is foreseeable that other European democratic states will want to join the undertaking. This will be open to them, on condition that they accept the overall view of the European Union as well as the constraints imposed by its gradual creation. New accessions must not slow down the development of the Union nor jeopardise it. (Tindemans, 1975, p. 34).

The first enlargement worked well with the Nine showing the capacity to work together even in a period of external economic difficulties and of internal fiscal problems, although the UK provided an element of uncertainty especially at the time of its 1975 Referendum on remaining within the EC. In the field of policy development, progress was slow since originally attractive concepts such as a Social Action Programme embracing worker participation, equality legislation and designs for common activity in the field of social security became unacceptable because of cost implications. However, these setbacks were tackled together and the institutions of the Community were further developed, most significantly by the agreement to introduce direct elections for the European Parliament. The democratic nature of the enlarged EEC was thus underlined.

The Second and Third Enlargement

In the 1970s, three nations on the southern flank of the Community returned to the democratic fold after periods of harsh fascist dictatorship. The new democracies in Greece, Spain and Portugal were initially frail and uncertain and their leaders looked to the Community as an established centre of freedom. It looked inevitable that these countries would seek to adhere to the Community as a guarantee of democratic development and as a firm support for economic renewal and social advance. Despite the Tindemans comments, and the known reluctance of more than one member state, political realities gave the applications of the three southern states an impetus that could not be repulsed. The Community took on the role of nursery for fledgling democracies.

Consequently, Greece entered the Community in 1981, followed by Spain and Portugal in 1986. Despite early difficulties of integration on the part of Greece, whose government found itself out of sympathy with certain political tendencies in the EC, a Community of Twelve was established with a population of 320 millions and a predominant role in world trade. At the same time the Community became an entity of sharp difference in economic and social development. Ensuing political arguments about, *inter alia,* Regional Policy and its funding, the various crises of the CAP and the scale and structure of the overall Community Budget led to successive UK governments attempting to shift the focus of Community policy from the grand design of monetary and political union to a more modest goal of free trade among a growing circle of European states along the lines of EFTA but with a degree of political co-operation on a limited basis. This strategy coincided with a period in Community history when the combination of world economic difficulties — high inflation and stagnant growth leading to high levels of unemployment — and internal adjustments due to the two enlargements led to a series of events destined to revolutionise the EC and to reopen the enlargement question for totally new reasons.

The Tindemans Report of 1975 had been, to a considerable extent, ahead of its time. But its publication had occurred at the moment when European voters were about to be given a direct say in the election of the Community's Parliament. And it was within the European Parliament that the blueprint for European Union emerged under the charismatic leadership of Altiero Spinelli and his 'Crocodile' group. Parliament's 1984 Draft Treaty for European Union must be seen as the decisive step forward leading as it did to the Declaration of Fontainbleau, the report of the Dooge Committee, and the Single European Act.

It is important to note that these events, including the Stuttgart meeting of the European Council in late 1983, occurred at a time when enlargement was very much in the air. Greece had joined and negotiations with Spain and Portugal were underway. Commenting recently on those historic times, Commissioner Vice-President Brittan has argued that "historically, it has not been the case that the entry of new members has led to a slowing-down in the process of European integration, quite the reverse. The process of European integration has in fact accelerated in recent years as the membership of the Community has increased, and, when necessary, in order to accommodate those new members, there have been changes in the way in which we run our affairs. There has been an increase in majority voting, and it is no coincidence that the Single European Act came about at a time of increasing membership of the European Community. So I think that it is right that enlargement and deepening need not be opposed concepts, and it is right to say that we can accommodate the changes that are necessary to accept (states) who are eligible and who wish to become members of the Community". (Brittan, 1991, *op.cit.*, p. 110).

So it was that Spain and Portugal became full members of the Community in January 1986 just weeks before the signing of the Single European Act. The Single Act asserted that the member states of the Community intended to "transform relations as a whole among their States into a European Union . . . on the basis, firstly, of the Communities operating in accordance with their own rule and, secondly, of European Co-operation among the signatory states in the sphere of foreign policy and to invest this union with the necessary means of action". Thus, the Community solemnly recommitted itself in 1986 to the paths of closer integration in the economic and political spheres.

The Single European Act

In the words of the Irish Government of the day, "The Single European Act represents the culmination of a process of debate and negotiation within the European Community in recent years on how the impetus towards progress on European integration could be restored and strengthened. There was a general recognition of an increasingly urgent need to equip the Community with the means to face the obligations and challenges arising from its recent enlargement to Twelve Member States, the growth in competition from its main trading partners, notably the United States and Japan, and the increasingly intensive development of high technology. The decision-making procedures of the Community obviously needed to be improved and provision made for an enhanced role for the directly-elected European Parliament. It was also evident that, despite the progress which had been made in removing tariff barriers, a wide range of non-tariff restrictions still remained which prevented Community industry and exporters from taking full advantage of a common market which had grown to 320 million people — the largest in the world". (Government of Ireland, 1987, p. 8).

The Commission had set out its detailed views on the implications of enlargement in a Communication to the Council in April 1978, occasioned by the progress towards the second — Greek — enlargement and by the prospect of Spanish and Portuguese membership:

> The process of enlargement has already begun, and it has been the Commission's intention . . . to show the risks that the Community may run if the steps necessary to ensure the success of the operation are not taken . . .
>
> The institutions and organs of the present Community cannot ensure that the process of integration will continue in an enlarged Community: on the contrary, there is reason to fear that the Community decision-making procedures will deteriorate . . . the institutions and organs of the enlarged Community must accordingly be decisively strengthened . . . (European Commission, 1978).

The Commission went on to outline a range of necessary changes in the institutional area, stressing the need to make more use of majority voting in Council and arguing that "the challenge of enlargement can and must be the start of a new Community thrust towards the objectives set by the authors of the Treaty".

Looking at the experience of the enlargements to date, it is relevant to point out the significant differences between them. The first enlargement — UK, Ireland and Denmark — was driven largely by economic considerations while the subsequent ones were essentially political in nature and a clear Community response to three European nations "inspired by the desire both to consolidate democracy and to become part of a forward moving Europe". (Commission, 1978).

Towards the Single Market

The Delors Commission entered office in 1985 and the new President declared before the European Parliament that "it may not be over-optimistic to announce a decision to eliminate all frontiers within Europe by 1992 and to implement it. That gives us eight years, the term of office of two Commissions". (Delors, 1985, p. 6). The Commission at once commenced work on the White Paper "Completing the Internal Market" which set out the legislative programme needed to secure the 1992 target date. The White Paper was published in July 1985 and established the concept of '1992' as a political driving-force of unique power and influence.

At the same session of the European Parliament, President Delors made a significant reference to the issue of further enlargement of the Community and to his approach thereto: "Another marked characteristic of Europe has been its desire for universality and, of course, when I say Europe I am not confining myself to 10 or 12 countries as I have been accused of doing. But we must start with those who want to be together, with those who want to live and work together". (Delors, 1975, p. 19).

There then commenced the extensive programme of legislative preparation for the Single Market in 1992 with a list of up to 300 draft Regulations and Directives scheduled for adoption by the Council after consultation with the European Parliament, many of them to be dealt with under the terms of the Cooperation Procedure laid down in the Single Act. The pace of work on this programme and the emerging profile of the Single Market gave rise, at an early stage, to fears that the reality of 1992 would be that of a closed and inward-looking Community content to develop and exploit its own strengths but unmindful of the needs and aspirations of its European neighbours and dependents — and of other areas including the struggling countries of the Third World. This idea of an 'Executive Europe' continues to be part of debate on the Community's future shape and relationships.

An Irreversible Process

The 1992 process has been driven forward with such pace and determination by the Community Institutions and by the commitment of both national administrations and organised business interests that it has, for a long time, been recognised as irreversible. This recognition is fully shared by the people and governments of a number of countries outside the Community and, in particular, by those within EFTA who have come to accept the absolute need to formalise relationships in terms of market access and full integration into a Community whose progress "could pose serious problems for countries remaining outside — not only as regards obstacles to trade, but also through the imposition of new technological and industrial standards which the internal market process will determine". (Palmer, 1988, p. 174).

Economic and Monetary Union

The process of development towards the Single Market has been so fast and comprehensive that it has been possible to return to the long-cherished goal of Economic and Monetary Union and to set its completion — to include a unified and consistent monetary policy, a Community Central Bank and a single currency — as a realisable political objective within the decade of the nineties.

The growing debate on the 'architecture' of Europe has been given added impetus by the revolutionary events in the USSR and Central and Eastern Europe during 1989 and 1990 and by the reduction of Cold-War tensions. This shift in political and economic power and relationships has been paralleled by the re-emergence of the drive towards the goal of Political Union as advanced by the 'founding fathers' of the EEC and discussed by Tindemans. The perceived need is to match the Community's progress on the economic and monetary fronts with a quantum leap in terms of political integration and united response to the new world around it.

Decisions taken at the Dublin and Rome sessions of the European Council during 1990 to establish two parallel Inter Governmental Conferences on Economic and Monetary Union and Political Union moved the issue of the long term construction of Europe significantly forward. The terms of reference of these Conferences, the volume of Commission and national submissions and communications on a wide range of future Community policies and structures, together with the comprehensive Treaty drafts of the Luxembourg Presidency have combined to give the clear impression that the Community means to intensify the process of integration even if the pace is faster on EMU than on Political Union. These lessons have not been lost on the Community's neighbours.

European Economic Area

The member states of EFTA have become more and more dependent on the Community as a market, as a target for external investment and as the centre of European technological and financial development. It is no longer possible for these small yet prosperous and technically advanced countries to stand aloof from the drive towards economic and monetary unity. Recognition of these facts led to the EFTA acceptance of the invitation from the European Commission, in 1989, to enter into negotiations on creating a structured relationship between the two organisations in the form of the so-called European Economic Area (EEA). These talks have proved difficult and at times appeared likely to fail because of problems related to major issues such as the involvement of the EFTA states in the Community decision-making system, on the one hand, and the future of fishing — in which Ireland has emerged as a significant protagonist — and freight transit, on the other.

However, on 13th May, 1991 the Ministers of the Community and EFTA met in Brussels where they "confirmed their commitment to conclude, before the summer, negotiations on a comprehensive EEA agreement, based on equality which should ensure the greatest possible mutual interest for the parties concerned as well as the global and balanced character of their cooperation". (Joint Declaration, 1991, p. 1). As discussions have continued it has proved increasingly difficult to achieve finality in this important project. The pressures of the talks were reflected in the reported comments of the Finnish Trade Minister, Pertti Salolainen, after one session with EC representatives that the meetings had far from fulfilled the expectations of the EFTA countries. The negotiations are continuing.

The EEA development, and the conclusion of a draft agreement after much difficulty may be seen as significant in itself but it has become clear that the months of tough negotiation have brought about a significant shift in opinion on the part of the EFTA states. In the words of the 'Economist': "Their unwritten conclusion was that the EEA agreement-in-the-making favours the Community more than them, but that the price is slight provided that it is a down-payment on full EC membership". (Economist, May 1991, p. 27). The new situation was summed up in a statement by the Leader of the Finnish Social Democratic Party and former Foreign Minister, Pertti Paasio, who argued that Finland must now apply for full membership of the EC "as the likelihood that the EEA . . . cannot become a permanent integration solution for Finland has increased. Membership should be considered since the difficulties in attempting to find an acceptable form for the EFTA countries to take part in the decision making of the area of integration have been insurmountable, despite other progress made in the EEA negotiations". (Paasio, 1991).

At the outset, it was widely argued that the offer by the Commission to negotiate the EEA was designed to deflect the EFTA countries from the course of membership application. If so, it has had precisely the opposite result. "Mr. Delors may have believed he was stamping on the brake two years ago. It was in fact the accelerator". (Economist, 1991, p. 28).

Central and Eastern Europe

In Central and Eastern Europe the past two years have seen the former German Democratic Republic (GDR) disappear into a unified Federal Republic, and hence directly into EC membership. At the same time, Hungary, Poland and Czechoslovakia were transformed from Communist to liberal democratic republics while Bulgaria, Romania and, latterly, Albania began the painful transition to democracy. Yugoslavia has been faced with the linked dramas of democratic demands and ethnic/nationalist confrontation.

These changes on the political front were paralleled on the economic front by urgent action to move from bureaucratic, stalinist command economies to open market structures. This transformation necessarily involved great strains and difficulties as the Comecon trading system disappeared and industries within inefficient centrally-planned economies were exposed to international competition. The newly elected governments looked at once to the West, and in particular to the Community for assistance in political, economic, trading and financial terms. The establishment of the European Bank for Reconstruction and Development and the launching of the EC PHARE Programme have been designed to meet the immediate economic and funding needs.

But it is recognised that, for the long term, more permanent relationships between the EC and the countries of Central and Eastern Europe must be established. It has already been made clear by their governments that Hungary and Czechoslovakia mean to pursue the goal of full membership and Poland sees membership as a future option. The Community is already undertaking the negotiation of new and advanced Association Agreements with these three countries which will provide a basis for an evolving relationship and, most likely, for eventual full membership.

In the consideration of the future position of the Central and Eastern European states the point is made that the second enlargement of the Community was strongly influenced by the willingness of the member states to give newly emerging democracies the benefit and political support of the Community system. This experience has been without doubt most positive and is widely recognised as having an historic significance. It is argued that the new Central and Eastern European democracies must be similarly assisted.

All of these arguments apply with equal force to the USSR in the aftermath of recent dramas. The process of political change and of economic restructuring which is now underway has totally altered the situation in Europe and demands a range of short and long term responses from the Community in both political and economic terms.

The Southern Flank

On the Southern flank of the Community there are also indications that the economic strength and potential of the Community are proving irresistible. Yugoslavia has for years attempted to build a meaningful working relationship with the EC although its current crises have deflected attention from closer association with the Community. Turkey, which has applied formally for EC membership, has been struggling with the restoration of effective democracy and of full human rights after a prolonged period of authoritarian and, at times, brutal rule. At the same time, Turkey has been seeking to reassert its European vocation, for example, through its contribution to the prosecution of the Gulf War.

Turkey

The Commission has issued its Opinion on the Turkish application for accession to the EC. The Opinion, published in December 1989, argued that "it would be inappropriate for the Community — which is itself undergoing major changes while the whole of Europe is in a state of flux — to become involved in new accession negotiations. Furthermore, the political and economic situation in Turkey leads the Commission to believe that it would not be useful to open accession negotiations with Turkey". (European Commission, 1989). The Opinion then stated that the Community should undertake a series of measures to strengthen the relationship between Turkey and the EC under four headings: Customs Union; financial cooperation; industrial and technological cooperation and political and cultural links.

Cyprus and Malta

The applications of Cyprus and Malta reflect a mixture of economic interdependence, European identity and a desire for political stability based on the Community's visible strength. The tragic continuation of the Turkish military occupation of a part of Cyprus, reflecting as it does, a very real crisis of intercommunal strife is an obstacle to a positive Community reaction to the applications of both Turkey and Cyprus.

Even on the Southern side of the Mediterranean the attraction of membership or the perceived disadvantages of exclusion from the EC has led some Maghreb countries, notably Morocco, to raise the possibility of a future membership application.

Factors of Attractiveness

Other factors influencing the attractiveness of membership include:

- changing military alliances with consequent alteration of political perspectives
- removal of perceived military 'threat' leading to rethinking of traditional neutralist positions in certain pivotal countries, e.g. Austria, Sweden
- impact on economic perspectives of protracted and controversial world trade negotiations within the Uruguay Round of the GATT.

Also of significance has been the emerging debate on the so-called 'architecture' of Europe. This debate has led to a plethora of models of greater or lesser precision, among which may be counted:

- the Mitterrand vision of a European Confederation to which President Delors has added the idea of the EC as a discrete member of the Confederation
- the Gorbachev concept of a Common European Home with its picture of Pan-European peace and sharing but with no details as yet specified
- the Delors concept of a Europe of 'Concentric Rings' with the EC as the central element and with EFTA, the Central and Eastern European states and the smaller so-called 'orphans' in the other circles
- various ideas of Eastern origin relating to the creation of European Security and Co-operation bodies of one kind or another, reflecting the disappearance of both Comecon and the Warsaw Treaty Organisation (WTO)
- proposals from within the European Parliament aimed at developing a federal structure in Europe wider than the present Community or at achieving a gradual opening of the EC membership specifically to the North and Centre/East
- proposals for new and broader Security structures based on NATO/WEU/CSCE.

The fundamental question arising from all of these proposals is that there must be a political choice between:

- enlarging the Community so as to become the framework for future European cooperation; or
- establishing some new framework in which the EC will participate as a cohesive but restricted grouping.

Assessment

From the foregoing discussion seven key considerations emerge:

- enlargement of the Community has now occurred on three occasions and has, in general terms, proved to be a positive element in its historical development
- the current moves towards further enlargement arise from a mixture of 'pull' and 'push' factors related to the internal working of the Community and from major European and world trends in the political, economic and military spheres not least in the USSR
- the growing economic dominance of the Community provides a 'pull' towards full membership which has been growing more and more difficult to resist even for such traditionally-independent states as Switzerland and Finland

- the rapidly changing face of Europe, notably in the East, and the collapse of the certainties of the Cold War have produced ‘push’ factors arising from the need on the part of most countries to find new political or security relationships and, insofar as the neutral countries are concerned, to redefine their particular standpoints
- the debate on these matters has so far produced a number of options for future structures and relationships none of which has yet won acceptance
- economic dependence must be recognised as central to the discussion and must be looked at in the light of fears expressed about the possible creation of a ‘Fortress Europe’
- the Widening and Deepening debate is nothing new having surfaced initially in the early days of the UK/Irish/Danish/Norwegian applications when President de Gaulle dominated the Community’s vision of itself.

3. THE POTENTIAL APPLICANTS

A Growing List

The 'push' and 'pull' forces referred to above have led to the emergence of a growing list of countries of Europe which may be considered to be serious or persistent applicants over the next few years. Were all the currently identified candidates to become full member states the Community would have doubled its membership from 12 to 24 and its population would total more than 480 millions.

Any assessment of the potential applicants must be made against the background of (a) the criteria for membership generally accepted within the Twelve, (b) the degree of 'fit' between those guidelines and the situation within each potential candidate, (c) the likely process of application, scrutiny and negotiation and (d) the likely timetable.

Criteria

The criteria for membership require that an applicant must:

- be a fully functioning democracy with clear respect for human rights
- "accept the overall view of the European Union as well as the constraints imposed by its gradual creation". (Tindemans, p. 34)
- accept the *acquis communautaire,* e.g. the entire corpus of Community law and policy put in place by the existing member states since the inception of the EEC in 1957
- be able to demonstrate the capacity, economically and otherwise, to fit into the Community system or to have the clear potential to do so within the terms of an agreed programme of adaptation and development
- contribute positively to the maintenance and advancement of the European Identity.

Each application for membership of the Community will be treated in its own right since each country has its own history, political structure and traditions, economic and social situation and potential.

Each potential applicant brings with it a number of strengths and problems, opportunities and challenges. It is equally the case that each applicant brings with it particular issues which require close attention. For example, among the current line-up, Austria gives rise to debate on Transport and Environmental questions while Norway provokes consideration of Energy and Fisheries.

Procedure

The procedure for dealing with membership applications is set out in Article 237 of the Treaty as amended by the Single European Act:

> Any European State may apply to become a member of the Community. It shall address its application to the Council, which shall act unanimously after consulting the Commission and after receiving the assent of the European Parliament which shall act by an absolute majority of its component members.
>
> The conditions of admission and the adjustments to this Treaty necessitated thereby shall be the subject of an agreement between the Member States and the applicant State. This agreement shall be submitted for ratification by all the Contracting States in accordance with their respective constitutional requirements. (Treaty, Art. 237, p. 315).

In practice, after the receipt by the Council of a formal application for membership, the Commission proceeds to prepare an Opinion on all aspects of the application, taking into account the specific political and economic situation of the applicant. The Opinion will indicate the views of the Commission on the compatibility of the applicant with the Community, on the economic and social circumstances of the applicant, on any particular issues requiring special attention and on the range of matters which would become the subject of negotiation. On the basis of the Opinion, the Council will decide on the opening of formal negotiation or on any alternative approach such as deferment pending economic or political developments or offering an alternative outcome (e.g. Association Agreement).

Should the decision be made to open negotiations these are conducted by the Commission on behalf of the Community with the aim of drawing up an agreement providing the basis for accession and dealing with all matters of mutual concern. In the light of previous experience such an agreement would identify areas in which the circumstances of the applicant might necessitate provisions such as derogation or transitional arrangements; specify the modalities of inclusion of the applicant into Community structures and policies (seats in Parliament, membership of the Commission, quotas, percentage contributions to funds, etc.); indicate any adjustments needed on the Community side; and specify relevant time-scales and schedules.

The European Parliament is accorded a crucial role in the process of application and ratification. The Council can act only with the assent of Parliament which, in turn, must make its decision by an absolute majority of its total membership — at present 260 votes out of 518. The Parliament, under the terms of the recent Planas Puchades Report on Enlargement, is now seeking to be involved at all stages of the process from the moment the Council agrees on the negotiating mandate of the Commission so that "Parliament's views were taken into consideration at an early stage". (Planas, 1991, p. 11). Parliament is also calling for the right to appoint a Rapporteur to monitor all stages of the negotiation.

Categories of Applicants and Potential Applicants

It appears appropriate to divide the list of applicants into a number of categories, each of which have certain characteristics in common:

- the *EFTA States:* developed and stable states; advanced economic and social systems; advantages gained through the detailed EEA negotiation process; effectively part of the economic heartland of Europe: Austria; Sweden; Norway; Finland; Switzerland; Iceland
- the emerging democracies of *Central and Eastern Europe:* taking their first, hesitant steps towards the market economy; urgently seeking a security 'anchor' and firm political underpinning within the EC framework: Hungary; Poland; Czechoslovakia
- countries in the *South and Mediterranean* which are in a different phase of economic development; serious problems of integration into an advanced market system; particular political and security issues: Turkey; Malta; Cyprus.

In addition to the group of countries which may be identified as the likely applicants in the present decade, it is necessary to point out that there are other nations in which membership of the EC is a matter of political debate or speculation. In this category must be included Yugoslavia (or, one or more of its constituent republics) and the three Baltic Republics — Latvia, Estonia and Lithuania. And, the remaining countries of the former Communist dispensation — Bulgaria, Romania and even Albania — must be taken into account. As indicated above, the widely acknowledged need to develop closer relations between the Community and the Maghreb States of North Africa has led to the suggestion of EC membership at some future time and even to serious discussion of the possibility of an application by Morocco. Some commentators also include Israel in the extended list of possible future members.

While the individual circumstances of the twelve principal candidates are very different, and their prospects of accession must be seen to vary greatly, it is relevant to consider each of them and to point out some of the most significant issues which arise.

Austria

Austria applied formally for membership in July 1989 in a letter which stated that: "in making this application Austria proceeds from the assumption that it will maintain its internationally-recognised status of permanent neutrality, based on the Federal Constitutional Law of 26 October, 1955 . . ." (H. Wallace, p. 133). This application was received coolly in Brussels where emphasis was placed on Community moves towards a common security policy. The application was passed to the Commission for preparation of an initial Opinion by the autumn of 1991. Public opinion in Austria moved sharply in favour of membership in recent years largely for economic reasons but more recent soundings indicate a continuing large volume of support for the traditional independence of Austria in international affairs. Austria's close contacts with the Central and Eastern European countries points to a crucial role in any evolving system of Europewide security. It is in the context of a changing security scene and of a redefinition of neutrality in new circumstances that the final decision on Austrian membership will be made.

It is accepted that Austria meets all the normal requirements for EC membership in political and socio-economic terms having already made significant adaptations of tariffs, technical standards, etc. The Austrian Schilling has a stable parity with the DM and is regarded as a *de facto* participant in the EMS.

The European Commission adopted and published its Opinion on the Austrian application on 31st July, 1991. The Opinion concludes that the Community should accept Austrian accession which is seen to be beneficial to the Community. However, a number of important points were made by the Commission:

- in line with long-standing Commission policy the Opinion recommends to the Council that actual negotiations should not commence before 1993
- it is stressed that all applicants must accept the *acquis communautaire* as it will be following the conclusion of the two Inter Governmental Conferences now underway
- in economic terms, Austria is seen to pose no problems other than in the areas of road transit and agriculture
- particular reference is made to Austria's 'perpetual neutrality' which is seen to pose political problems which are, however, not regarded as insurmountable and which will be resolved in negotiation.

(see Appendix One for more detailed text).

Sweden

Sweden applied formally for EC membership in July 1991. Earlier the Swedish Premier, Ingvar Carlsson, had addressed the Riksdag on 14th June, 1991 indicating that ". . . the EC is regarded as a major driving force for cooperation and development on our continent. As a member, Sweden's possibilities of influencing this future cooperation — in political, economic and social terms — would be improved". (Carlsson, 1991, p. 9). On the crucial issue of security, the Prime Minister argued that "if, in the future, a durable European security order is established, based for example on the CSCE, the foundations on which Sweden's policy of neutrality has rested hitherto will change".

Sweden has moved towards practical integration into the economic system of the EC with widespread Swedish investment in Community countries. Sweden's business interests have long argued for membership on the grounds of obtaining a real say in EC decision-making. For some time Sweden has been developing efficient structures for adapting the vast range of EC rules, standards and directives into Swedish legislation and practice.

At its meeting on 29th July, 1991, the General Affairs Council instructed the Commission to commence preparation of its Opinion on the Swedish request and informed the government of Sweden of this decision.

Norway

Norway's reactions to current developments is coloured by the memory of the decision taken by Referendum in 1972 to reject the terms for accession negotiated at the same time as the UK, Ireland and Denmark. Discussions have been taking place between the Norwegian government and the Commission on the subject of a possible application but the timing of such a move remains uncertain. As a NATO member, Norway has no problems on security.

Political attitudes in Norway are still divided on the question of applying for membership and it seems likely that the progress of the Austrian and Swedish cases will be watched with interest by all parties. Prime Minister Brundtland has indicated that her ruling Labour Party will debate the whole matter at a Conference in 1992.

Finland

Finland has for many years argued that membership was ruled out by the very strict interpretation of the country's neutrality. The rapid evolution of the country's economic relationships with the Community together with a rethinking of its traditional political attitudes has led to an increasing evidence of serious consideration of the membership option. A growing disenchantment with the EEA process has added to the attractions of full integration, an outcome desired by Finland's aggressive and successful industrial sector. However, Finland will move with caution, watching both Sweden and the USSR very carefully. Security considerations will prove significant because of the particular historical experience of the Finns, not just with the USSR but with its western neighbours during World War II.

Switzerland

Switzerland remains outside the UN, the IMF and the World Bank. It traditionally follows a most independent and almost isolationist policy in international relations. But general economic and political developments in Europe and the realisation that the EEA negotiations add up only to an interim arrangement have led debate in Switzerland to the point of considering full membership. Parliament has given the government freedom to consider the membership option and the influential Social Democratic Party has taken a Conference decision in favour of an early application. ". . . Switzerland is not a social and ecological island . . . if we are not to be integrated into Europe, we shall become more and more a place for dubious deals, a European area to circumvent European law . . . Isolation is not, and cannot be, an option . . ." (SPS, 1991).

Iceland

Iceland, although geographically isolated, is a stable democracy with strong external links through its NATO membership and trade relations with the United States. Its living standards are close to those of the Scandinavian nations. Iceland was not one of the founder members of EFTA, joining only in 1970. Dependence on the US because of security ties are thought to be weakening with a parallel increase in interest in 'European' issues and relationships. Fishing remains a major trade policy issue, as has been made clear during protracted arguments within the EEA talks but the initiative on membership lies very much with the active business community whose opinions remain divided.

Hungary

Hungary had sought to reform its economic system for some years prior to the rejection of the Communist regime in 1989 and the election of a democratic government in 1990. However, this effort was largely unsuccessful due to the country's external payments crisis. Hungary has the highest foreign debt of the countries of Central and Eastern Europe. But the positive effect of past liberalisation attempts has been reflected in success in avoiding some of the traumatic experiences of other former Comecon states in the move towards a market economy. Private foreign investment is underway and there is an extensive privatisation programme. The government has placed a high priority on full membership going as far as to designate 1995 as their target date for entry.

Poland

Poland set the pace in the 1989 revolution following the long struggle between Solidarity and the Communist regime. Democratic government has been introduced and is in its early stages, with the charismatic but controversial Solidarity leader, Lech Walesa, as directly-elected President. Poland's economic restructuring has had a serious social impact in terms of unemployment and living standards. The programme has been successful in improving food supplies on the domestic market, restoring balance to the external accounts and bringing down inflation.

Czechoslovakia

Czechoslovakia is more advanced industrially than the other East European countries. It had a pre-war tradition of democratic government and of industrial achievement with many high-quality craft and precision enterprises. These provide a basis on which a market economy may be constructed relatively smoothly. The democratic political system introduced in 1990 has seen the Communist regime hand over power to a government led by Civic Forum, with Vaclav Havel as President. The peaceful and harmonious handover of power, the strong international reputation of Havel and the country's industrial background combine to give Czechoslovakia a positive rating in western economic, banking and political circles.

Turkey

Turkey applied formally for membership in 1987. The Commission Opinion on the application was published in 1989 and, as indicated above, concluded that the political and economic situation of Turkey meant that it would not be useful to open negotiations on accession. Turkey is a huge country geographically and has a large and rapidly-growing population. It has a level of overall development much lower than the Community average and very serious problems in areas such as structural imbalances in the main economic sectors and macroeconomic variables, massive protectionism and inadequate social provision.

There are also significant issues in respect of the stability of Turkish democracy, of human rights and ethnic differences, most notably in respect of the position, rights and treatment of a large Kurdish minority. The problem of the occupation of Cyprus by Turkish forces remains unresolved and means that the country's application will be vetoed by Greece for the foreseeable future. Close economic and financial relations with the Community are provided for under a formal Association Agreement signed in 1963. Developments under this agreement have been characterised by stop-and-start situations related to political and human rights issues.

It is recognised that Turkey, now receiving much praise in some western circles for its cooperation in the Gulf War, is unhappy that its aspirations for 'inclusion' in Europe continue to be rebuffed. The recent statement by US

President Bush that the USA would back Turkey's EC application has given rise to disquiet insofar as it appears to be an interference in EC business from the most powerful NATO member. Turkey's application will remain a difficult and emotive issue, not least because of unquestionable cultural differences between a predominantly Moslem society and a community of the Judaeo-Christian tradition.

Malta

Malta applied for membership of the Community in July 1990 and a study leading to a Commission Opinion is underway. Malta has had an Association Agreement since 1970, and is recognised as a stable European democracy, but the Commission will have to assess carefully the economic status and living standards of the island in arriving at a judgement on its capacity to take on the full range of responsibilities of Community membership.

Cyprus

Cyprus formally applied for Community membership in 1990. While the general circumstances of Cyprus are similar to those of Malta, the over-riding consideration must be that of the impact of the division of the island following the Turkish military intervention. It is widely accepted that Cyprus's application will not be given serious consideration until the partition problem has been dealt with politically. Recent moves under U.S. influence may give rise to hope in this connection.

Yugoslavia

Yugoslavia has had formalised trade relations with the EC since 1980 and there exist important financial protocols. The changing political situation in Yugoslavia and the evolution of Central and Eastern Europe have led to expectations of moves towards closer relations with the EC. Yugoslavia is, however, in a phase of serious ethnic and nationalist confrontation between and within the constituent republics and must deal with the crisis caused by the independence declarations of Croatia and Slovenia.

There appears to be no serious prospect of membership of the EC in the case of Yugoslavia as a whole but rather for one or more of the present constituent republics in some future dispensation. The economy has not performed well despite the major economic reform programme introduced last year.

Other European States

While the countries listed above are those accepted as the probable and possible candidates for Community membership in the period ahead, it is relevant to mention a number of other states whose future relationships with the EC will be of importance:

- *Bulgaria, Romania* and, eventually, *Albania* are at a different stage of both political and economic development but are of significance in regional terms
- the *Baltic Republics* have won recognition of their independence and are already looking to the west — and to the EC — for economic and political ties and Association Agreements and, in all likelihood, for Community membership in due course
- the *Maghreb States of North Africa* are of long term importance for the EC since stability in the Mediterranean is a critical factor; relations with these developing states must be put on a sound and evolving basis; for the same reasons future relations with *Israel* must be taken into consideration even if membership seems an unlikely outcome.

Soviet Union

The Soviet Union cannot be looked upon as a potential member of the EC but the entire future of the European construction must depend on the future of the USSR itself and on the nature of EC/USSR relations in economic and political terms. Closer USSR involvement in the western economic system and in the CSCE, with formal agreements on trade, finance and commercial relations will build an appropriate basis for the future. The recasting of the internal relationships of the USSR, with a new emphasis on the integrative forces of the marketplace may lead in time to the existence, alongside the EC, of another economic and political community of great scale and importance and to intriguing new issues of cooperation.

Central/Eastern Europe — A Confederation?

The potential applicants from Central and Eastern Europe are faced with daunting problems of economic restructuring as they move towards a full market economy and integration into the wider European system. Consideration of their difficulties may lead to recognition that membership will be a long term prospect.

Three options for the interim may be considered:

- the current negotiation of Association Agreements between the EC and these countries can "help create a climate of confidence and stability favouring political and economic reform and allowing the development of close political relations which reflect shared values". (Commission, 1990)

- the Vice-President of the Commission, Frans Andriessen, has on two recent occasions put forward the concept of a new form of relationship through giving these nations the status of 'affiliate' or 'associate' member of the Community which would give such members the opportunity to contribute to the formulation of policy development in areas considered to be of joint interest
- the Mitterrand/Masowiecki concept of a European Confederation would involve the federative phase of the EC and a progressive confederal phase for the other states. The final Declaration of the special Dublin European Council is relevant in this connection: "The movement to restore freedom and democracy in Central and Eastern Europe — and the progress already made, and in prospect, in arms negotiations — now make it possible and necessary to develop a wider framework of peace, security and cooperation for all of Europe. To this end, the Community and its member states will play a leading role in all proceedings and discussions within the CSCE process and in efforts to establish new political structures or agreements based on the principles of the Helsinki final act while maintaining security arrangements of member states". (Dublin, 1990). This option places a significant emphasis on the CSCE but would also imply new relationships in policy areas such as transport and the environment.

In considering these possibilities, it is necessary to dwell on the likelihood that the future structure of the Soviet Union may resemble a Community of autonomous or independent nations, along the lines of the EC itself, rather than a centralised empire. This prospect merits close assessment in terms of political, trade, financial and institutional relationships.

THE EXTENDED COMMUNITY — SOME BASIC DATA

Country	Area 1000 km²	Pop/'87 mill	GNP/cap/'87 $
Germany (United)	357	78	16,600
UK	244	57	14,500
Italy	301	57	14,400
France	547	56	17,000
Spain	505	39	8,700
Netherlands	41	15	15,400
Belgium	31	10	15,400
Greece	132	10	5,200
Portugal	92	10	4,000
Denmark	43	5	21,000
Ireland	70	3.5	9,200
Luxembourg	3	0.4	18,000
	2366	340.9	—
Sweden	450	8	21,100
Austria	84	8	16,700
Switzerland	41	7	27,700
Finland	337	5	21,200
Norway	324	4	21,700
Iceland	103	0.3	23,600
Eighteen	3705	373.2	—
Poland	313	38	5,500
Czechoslovakia	128	16	7,600
Hungary	93	11	6,500
	4239	438.2	—
Turkey	781	53	1,400
Cyprus	9	0.7	7,700
Malta	1	0.3	5,000
	5030	492.2	—
Yugoslavia	256	23	2,300

Source: Eurostat; The Economist

4. THE ISSUES

The Central Issue — What Kind of Community?

It is widely recognised that the enlargement issue is far more than a technical or economic matter. This is something which goes to the very heart of the Community's destiny, identity and self-perception. While the technical, economic and short-term political questions summed up in the dilemma of Deepening or Widening are of great practical importance and must not be ignored in any analysis, the central issue is that of the Community's fundamental purpose.

The three enlargements so far undertaken have identified the EC as an open Community, sensitive to the aspirations of other European States and peoples and — in the case of the Greek, Spanish and Portuguese accessions — ready to play an historic role in underpinning basic democratic values at moment of great drama and change. The spirit in which such enlargements were planned and carried out was one of considerable generosity coupled with a capacity to envisage a European entity stretching from the Nordic fringe to the Aegean and from Donegal to the Algarve. That is the spirit enshrined in Monnet's concept of a Community "enlarging to continental scale".

The Debate on Enlargement

Debate on enlargement at present takes place against the background of change and evolution sketched out above and, for this reason, has tended to lack a certain spirit of openness. The debate has been marred by a real concern that the new Community structures and policies emerging from the IGCs should not be too easily open to alteration after an enlargement. It is also an observable fact that the decision-making processes are concentrated on the current IGC issues and not influenced too much by considerations of enlargement. Indeed, enlargement is being seen as next year's business and psychologically put aside. In the minds of some, the experience of 1972 will also be influential — at that moment of EC development there was an unseemly rush to finalise Community fishery and sugar policies before the entry of new members and this led to subsequent difficulties and to residual bad feeling.

However, there are signs of awareness. The European Parliament debate on the Planas Puchades Report on Enlargement in May 1991 provided reassuring evidence, across political dividing lines, of commitment to a wider, more inclusive Community and to the commencement of a process of enlargement which — while it might take a great deal of time and trouble — would end in the creation of a greatly expanded EC including as many as twenty four member states.

And, the Commission's Opinion on the Austrian application has provided further evidence of a greater openness, arguing that the Community "must unhesitatingly and in accordance with the procedures laid down in Article 237 of the EEC Treaty confirm its openness towards applicant European countries whose economic and political situation are such as to make accession possible".

Institutional Change

Such an expanded Community would require major institutional changes to operate democratically, effectively and efficiently. It is essential to face up to this fact now and to recognise that the nature of the response will depend on the vision of the Community's future which prevails. Taking on board these concerns in addressing the European Parliament, Commission Vice-President Brittan has argued that "if we . . . say that at some stage later we will make the institutional changes necessary to accommodate an expanded Community we will never make those changes because the only thing that leads the Community to make the institutional changes that are so difficult to make is imperative political necessity, and that necessity will make itself felt if we are faced with membership applications which in all conscience we cannot and do not want to refuse . . ." (Brittan, 1991, p. 111).

Europe — A Zone of Peace?

Another important element in the discussion of the future shape and identity of the Community relates to the potential economic and political power of the Twelve and, even more so, of an enlarged EC. Will the EC become a major civilian power or move on to establish itself as a political/military power? And, if so, will it be able to use such power in a positive manner? Basically, will the new Europe be seen as a Zone of Peace or as yet another grouping of powerful and armed self-interest.

Francois Duchene has argued that, if security and military issues were to become less central, the Community could be ". . . the first major area of the Old World where the age-old process of war and indirect violence could be translated into something more in tune with the twentieth-century citizen's notion of civilised politics. In such a context, Western Europe could in a sense be the first of the world's civilian centres of power". (Laursen, 1991, p. 28). He later developed this argument to emphasise the very constructive role that a civilian power in Europe could play in moving the world away from traditional ideas of "empire and prestige", suggesting that ". . . the European Community will only make the most of its opportunities if it remains true to its inner characteristics. These are primarily: civilian ends and means, and a built-in sense of collective action, which in turn express, however imperfectly, social values of equality, justice and tolerance". (Laursen, 1991, p. 28).

In the same vein, the 1989 Manifesto of the Socialist parties of the Community had argued that the objective of the Community "is not to create a new military super-power but, rather, to contribute, through political action, diplomatic initiatives and economic and ecological cooperation, to the reduction of tension and the creation of areas of freedom, democracy and autonomy in the world". (Confed., 1989).

These are serious and basic considerations. They must be taken into account. For there are still those who can argue that the future Community might have a military/security policy as its very kernel. The Gulf crisis saw more than one leading European politician speaking as if the absence of a Community military dimension, with troops to review and 'situation rooms' to visit indicated some form of weakness.

And, clearly, they have been so considered in many European states inside and outside the EC. Discussing the "Dynamics of European Integration", William Wallace has put the future enlargement into clear perspective:

> The dynamics of European integration thus depend both upon the informal pressures of undirected economic and social forces and on the formal channelling of those forces into particular directions . . . but the emergence of a more tightly integrated and institutionalised core area has pulled the region more closely together: a gravitational force which has attracted the peripheral countries of the European region towards it . . .
>
> Confusion between 'Europe' and the 'European Community' may thus gradually resolve itself in a progressive identity between the two, with other non-Community countries concluding, as did Spain, Portugal and Greece on the establishment — or re-establishment — of democratic government that 'any European state must apply to join the European Community. (Wallace, W., 1990, p. 20).

(i) Impact on Community Institutions

Perhaps the most important issue of all is that connected with the institutional capacity of the Community. This concern arises from consideration of the question of 'critical mass' within a decision-making body such as the Community. Given the variables of optimum size for efficiency and effectiveness, cultural and language differences and different political traditions it is essential that preparations for any enlargement should confront the implications of the inherent complexity of Community Institutions catering for up to twenty four member states.

Commenting on the prospects of enlargement, President Delors has been reported as arguing that enlargement could lead to the Community becoming no more than a weak intergovernmental organisation. To avoid this, Delors suggested that it would be necessary to give greater powers to the centre with greater delegation of capacity to the Commission and with less frequent meetings of the intergovernmental bodies. The Commission has debated these aspects in some detail and will revert to them prior to the end of the deliberations of the IGCs. It has also established new specialist policy units to deal with these, and related, issues.

At the time of the proposed accession of Spain and Portugal the Community authorities set out in some detail the many institutional implications arising from enlargement thus enabling adequate responses to be made in advance of the actual date of accession. The Commission's Communication of 20th April, 1978 argued that "experience in the changeover from six to nine members has already revealed difficulties and deficiencies in the capacity to act and react jointly, with twelve members . . . the Community will be exposed to possible stalemate and dilution unless its practical modus operandi is improved". (Commission, 1978).

The next enlargement of the Community will pose more fundamental questions which must be answered in advance. A structure must now be conceptualised which will be capable of accommodating a Community of twenty four and this must be put in place in such a way as to facilitate gradual but certain enlargement over the next decade and to avoid all incoherence in performance and planning. The great 'jump' in institutional terms must be made at the outset and there must be a strategic approach rather than an *ad hoc* response to pressures. Central to any such development must be a recognition of the special needs and fears of smaller member states at such a moment of change. The accession to the EC of a number of predominantly small member states could lead to a concentration of power and influence in a virtual *directoire* of the larger states and economies. This could be brought about by recourse to such approaches as 'group' or 'regional' representation or voting rights at Council or in the Commission. The smaller states, including Ireland, have a profound interest in resisting such moves.

These key institutional questions include:

- *the structure of the Commission:* on present rules a Community of 24 member states would imply 29 or 30 members of the Commission making the college unwieldy and unlikely to achieve any cohesion in policy or action; a reduction to one Commissioner for each member state would still produce a Commission of 24; any solution involving less than one member per state is certain to create serious political difficulties and tensions; suggestions of representation based on regional considerations will be resisted firmly by several member states

- *the size and structure of the European Parliament:* one projection of the Parliament's likely size with 24 member states indicates as many as 870 MEPs; this gives rise to major questions such as the appropriate national quotas, the principles on which they would be based and the optimum relationships between the European Parliament and both national and regional parliaments or assemblies

- *the structures and voting methods within the Council:* what balances would be required between majority and unanimous voting in Council in order to achieve real efficiency and at the same time a proper protection of the interests of individual member states and of regional and other minorities affected by centralised decision-making
- *the Presidency of the Council:* six-monthly changes of Presidency could lead to a position where each State in a Community of 24 member states would hold the Presidency once every twelve years thus making it almost inconceivable that any individual Minister could hold a Presidency role more than once in a political lifetime and removing any element of continuity; the same problem of loss of any continuity within national civil services
- *the appropriate size and working structures of the other Community bodies* such as the Court of Justice and the Economic and Social Committee.

These issues are now widely debated. For example, former French President Giscard d'Estaing has proposed an approach to the Presidency involving a strengthening of the office by the election of a four-year Presidency while balancing this with a second chamber of the European Parliament representing the national parliaments and acting as a form of Senate. This idea is opposed by others on the ground of undue concentration of power in the larger, more economically-advanced member states.

The Planas Puchades Report on Enlargement deals in detail with these issues:

> The theory of political union . . . shows us that an increase in the number of participating states presupposes an increase in the decision-making capacity of the centre, which is the EC level. Otherwise the complexity of rules designed to protect national interests will lead to paralysis. Again, theory shows us that the danger of partial coalitions to maximise gains from a minority increases with the number of players . . . It has been demonstrated that the institutional mechanisms, firstly of the six nation and then the twelve nation Community have prevented the formation of coalitions designed to produce deadlock. But it is more than uncertain whether the same applies to a larger group . . .
>
> . . . the major challenges facing a government of the Community with new members would be the need to increase the capacity to decide and the ability to arbitrate to ensure the effectiveness of the new entity . . . progress towards European Union would not be completely out of the question but would be more difficult and certainly far slower . . . political energies would have to be concentrated initially on strengthening the centre with a view to securing effective convergence of the Community as a whole, on intermediate economic and social objectives. (Planas, 1991).

Such an approach would presuppose:

- reinforcement of the central Community institutions to implement common policies and assure coordination
- giving the European Parliament and the Commission the range of powers and prerogatives 'necessary to correspond to the increased demands for problem solving, differentiation, coordination, political action and democratic control'.

A Hierarchy of Competences?

In this connection, President Delors has argued that "... a significant enlargement of the Community would make it more imperative than ever to devise an effective decision-making process, the price being a hierarchy of competences and transfers of sovereignty. It would also be necessary, in the interests of preserving the Community spirit, to invent novel forms of democratic control. Failure to do this could mean the end of the ideal defined by the founding fathers and a return to a classic inter-governmental organisation". (Delors, CEPS, 1989).

The counterposing of a centralised 'Community' type organisation for an enlarged EC to an intergovernmental style of policy-making and administration raises fundamental issues which will be debated in the medium term, centring on such points as effectiveness, protection of the interests of smaller states and capacity to pursue the longer-term goals of European Union.

Technical Consequences

Apart from these fundamental institutional issues a number of what might be called technical consequences will also have to be addressed:

- the complexity of language combinations within all Community institutions
- the technical capacity to cope with multiple transitional periods and derogations arising from applicants with varying economic and infrastructural circumstances
- the relationship between participation in EPU and lengthy transition to EMU, etc.
- the complexities of span of control and of monitoring the implementation of Community legislation.

Community Budget

Parallel to these institutional and technical issues consideration will have to be given to the basic question of financing Community activity. The present agreement whereby the proportion of member states' GNP devoted to the EC Budget is fixed at 1.2% and is to be reviewed in 1993. The Commission wants to raise the key figure to 1.4% of GNP in 1997 and to 2% by the end of the century.

This proposal involves large sums of money in absolute terms but still falls short of the conclusions of the MacDougall Report of 1978 on Community finances which foresaw a level of 2.5–3% of GNP as the minimum figure for effective Community redistribution and for attaining Economic and Social Cohesion.

Closely related to this argument is that concerning the impact of enlargement on the Community's regional policies and, in particular, on the Structural Funds. It has been suggested that the accession of the Central and Eastern European countries and those of the Mediterranean basin could demand as much as a tripling of the present financial requirements of the Funds not to mention necessary assistance to the USSR. The potential impact of such developments on the relative position, and on the attitudes, of the present poorer member states must be borne in mind. The scheduled review of the Structural Funds, including their size and criteria, will now take place in 1993 within the context of enlargement.

(ii) Economic Issues

While the negotiations on the EEA were drawing to a close, it was argued by 'The Economist' that "Like the Grand Old Duke of York, the countries of the EFTA have learned that if you are halfway between two places you are nowhere". ('Economist', 1991, p. 27). Having been drawn into those talks because of their growing realisation of economic inter-dependence with the EC the EFTA states had come more and more to accept that the pace and depth of EC economic integration was such that full membership would represent by far the best option.

"Their dependence economically on the EC as a partner and supplier is great and the alternatives are simply non-existent. Their vulnerability to the extra-territorial impact of EC legislation is beyond question and the patchwork of free trade agreements and supplementary bilateral agreements cannot possibly keep pace with the volume or content of new EC rules". (Wallace, H., 1991, p. 269).

As it became increasingly evident that the EEA process could not deliver any meaningful involvement for the EFTA countries in the decision-making on those very rules the message became clear that, however favourable the technical agreement might be, the dependency factor would not be offset by worthwhile political gains. Outside the Community the EFTA states would feel that they were sitting in the 'waiting room' of the European Station. The time had come to consider buying a one-way ticket.

The economic issues facing the EFTA states also confront the other potential applicants and there is a long and expanding economic agenda connected to enlargement and some of the areas of immediate concern are:

- the imminence of 1992 and of the full realisation of the Single Market with its legislative framework demanding the capacity for rapid integration
- specific policy areas such as Competition and State Aids rules and their compatibility with existing practice in non-EC countries
- sectoral problems such as those highlighted by the impasse between Iceland and Spain over the issue of fishing rights; equivalent issues such as transport, transit and energy policy
- the prospect of an early move towards the practical implementation of Economic and Monetary Union with consequent implications for key policy-making areas including taxation and budgetary strategy
- the future of European agriculture as the reform of the CAP becomes a central issue on the Community agenda within the context of the GATT negotiations
- the potential benefits of membership for the new adherents and the possibility of contributions by them to the Structural Funds as a matter of solidarity.

Issues in Eastern Europe

These issues, and others like them, are common to all the potential applicants. But for some there are even more basic economic questions to be faced, in particular for those now emerging from Communist bureaucracy:

- transition from bureaucratic planned or 'command' economy
- lack of competitiveness of traditional state firms emerging from the strait-jacket of central planning and Comecon-controlled external trade
- particular problems of centralised, collective farm structures and marketing arrangements; here also a counter-balancing factor of low-cost production of some products which can offer prospects of entry to markets within the EC to the detriment, and with the opposition, of Community farming interests
- problems of reconstruction and indebtedness within the former planned economies, requiring massive financial assistance, for example, through the European Bank for Reconstruction and Development.

Cyprus and Malta

In the case of the small Mediterranean economies of Malta and Cyrpus, the main issues arising under this heading relate to their small scale and to their relatively narrow economic and financial bases. Both have enjoyed the advantages of long-standing arrangements with the Community in the shape of Association Agreements which have combined market access provisions with financial and technical assistance and have significantly benefited the two small republics.

The very small size of these two economies may well mean that their addition to the Community would have little or no economic 'fall out'. Problems are, however, likely to arise in relation to the capacity of such small countries to cope with much of the more bureaucratic aspects of EC involvement having particular regard to their distance from the centres of power, influence and action. Luxembourg is no larger but is strategically positioned at the heart of the Community and can rely on traditional links with its neighbours and on such well-established systems as the Benelux agreements and, latterly, the Schengen accords.

In the case of *Iceland,* dependence on the Fishing Industry gives rise to particular problems in respect of aspects of the Community's fisheries policy and these have surfaced as one of the most tricky aspects of the EEA negotiations, not least because of Irish concerns.

"There is no question as regards the EFTA countries about whether their legal and political systems could in practice deliver compliance with the emerging EC economic regimes or meet the accompanying environmental and social provisions. Indeed they are already well on the way to having congruent policies in place and, in some areas, setting the standards for the EC to follow". (Wallace, H., ed., 1991, p. 281). The same cannot be said of the countries of Central and Eastern Europe although crash programmes of training and initiation are being undertaken under varied auspices but largely within the framework of the EC PHARE Programme.

(iii) Political Issues

But, of course, it is in the area of political concerns that many of the most pressing issues arise. Economic and financial questions are soluble provided that the appropriate level of political will exists. Political difficulties are in many cases more problematical because of deep-seated attitudes, traditions and ideologies. For a continent such as Europe, with its divided and often bloody history, the Community's growth and harmony over the past forty years must be seen as quite extraordinary. Franco–German leadership in so many areas of Community development represents a change in relationship little short of miraculous, given the history of the previous hundred years. To a considerable degree this success stands as one of the real pointers to the future potential and progress of the Community enterprise.

Political Attraction

Whatever may be the economic attractiveness of the EC to the potential applicants "it would be wrong, however, to underestimate the overtly political appeal of the Community to the remaining non-members in Western Europe and . . . to those in Eastern Europe as well. The development of EEC political cooperation — and with it the prospect of a common foreign and security policy — is itself a magnet, though of course there are contradictions in this process". (Palmer, p. 176). While the neutrality issue, discussed below, remains a significant point for several countries, it is clear that the development of the political capacity and standing of the Community is seen as important by political leaders in the non-member states and that they see it to be important to be able to participate in this development.

"By and large the EFTA countries have been spectators only at the scenes of reform in Central and Eastern Europe, with the exception perhaps of Austria and Finland where history and geography have preserved at least seats in the front row . . . the governments of the EFTA countries . . . have been involved at the margins and recruited as extras for the G24 exercise in channelling economic aid; they have voices in the CSCE discussions. But no one else needs to know what their views are before acting . . ." (Wallace, H., ed., p. 270). For the EFTA states, and by extension, for the countries of Central and Eastern Europe, there exists a power relationship which is seriously asymmetrical.

At present, for many European countries the only real focus of political influence within Europe is the EC and the prospect of ever closer Political Union will add to the certainty that it is only through full membership of the Community that meaningful involvement and influence can be achieved.

Central and Eastern Europe

In the case of the countries of Central and Eastern Europe, one of the main policy imperatives is the requirement to avoid chaos in the aftermath of the fall of Communism and of the withdrawal of the Soviet Union from its former European empire. Gaps in both the economic and political areas must be filled.

For the countries of Central and Eastern Europe, a major political issue is their urgent requirement to find a new and credible framework of international relationships — in economic and security terms — to replace the structures of the Warsaw Pact and of Comecon which had provided a rigid but predictable and understood context for over forty years.

The EFTA States

A parallel issue of importance relates to the situation of the EFTA states. The EC member states have worked within the structures of the Community for many years and have jointly developed the twin concepts of EMU and Political Union — summed up in the concept of European Union — and given it a constitutional standing in the Single European Act. The EFTA states have not had the experience of working within such a framework and it will be a significant challenge to them to adapt. However, the experience of the intensive EEA talks and the parallel development by some of the EFTA states, notably Sweden, of internal structures for adaptation and integration in technical matters will already have had a positive impact.

Competences of the Community

One of the central elements of the Political Union project under discussion within the IGC is that of the extension of the Competences of the Community. The drive to expand the areas in which the EC states act together to develop common policies, to raise standards and to harmonise provisions or controls has been accentuated as the idea of a Community capable of meeting its present economic and commercial challenges while fulfilling more demanding popular expectations has increased.

The Luxembourg Presidency in its Draft Treaty on the Union of 20th June, 1991 has indicated a wide range of policy areas — twenty one in all — with significant revisions or entirely new Treaty provisions:

> Elimination of Customs Duties/Quantitative Restrictions; Single Market; Common Commercial Policy; Common Transport Policy; Competition Policy; Approximation of Laws of Member States; Social Policy (revision); Economic and Social Cohesion (revision); Environment Policy (revision); Strengthening Industrial Competitiveness; Technology and Research Policy (revision); Energy Policy (new); Trans-European Networks (new); Health (new); Education Training and European Culture (new); Development Co-operation (new); Association of Overseas Territories; Consumer Protection (new); Civil Protection (new); Tourism Policy (new); Common Agricultural Policy.

Submissions from member states have sought to add to this long list such issues as Road Safety and Animal Welfare. The implications of such an extension of the Community's policy powers are considerable even for the existing member states — implying new legislation, new rules, new control and new financial outlays. But for new member states they will involve a massive amount of adaptation and preliminary planning.

Towards a Common Foreign and Security Policy

The issues surrounding the Community's search for a common Foreign and Security Policy will, of their very nature, give rise to important considerations for potential applicants. In particular, this is a matter of central concern for those states which have followed a policy of neutrality over many years.

There has long existed a view that the creation of a true Political Union among the member states must involve the establishment of a Foreign and Security Policy with a view to giving the Community a 'single voice' in international affairs and that this Policy should be developed over time into a common European Defence System. The Single European Act took a number of significant steps in this direction in its Title III which provided that the member states "shall endeavour jointly to formulate and implement a European foreign policy". It went on to lay down that member states "consider that closer cooperation on questions of European Security would contribute in an essential way to the development of a European identity in external policy matters. They are ready to coordinate their positions more closely on the political and economic aspects of security . . . nothing in this Title shall impede closer cooperation in the field of security between certain (member states) within the framework of the Western European Union or the Atlantic Alliance". The final phrase of this extract from the SEA was seen to be an indirect but deliberate acceptance of Irish neutrality.

In the next phase of European integration the question of Security will have a priority place in the agenda for a number of reasons:

- the end of the cold war and collapse of the Warsaw Treaty Organisation
- the revolutionary political transformation of Central and Eastern Europe
- the systematic process of nuclear and conventional disarmament initiated by the superpowers
- the perception of an emerging agenda for common policy in the foreign/security area involving such questions as disarmament; arms control; peace-keeping — even within Europe in the context of emerging ethnic and nationalist confrontations; nuclear non-proliferation; economic aspects of security; coordination of positions in international bodies — the regional or spatial dimension of security as evidenced in the Baltic or Balkan situations.

The Gulf War gave an added urgency to the Security and Defence debate within the Community. In the words of Commission President Delors: "the Gulf War has provided an object lesson — if one were needed — on the limitation of the European Community. It is true that giant steps have been taken along the path of economic integration and the last two years have seen advances on foreign policy cooperation. But the Community's influence and ability to act have not kept pace. We should interpret this as yet another argument for moving towards a form of political union embracing a common foreign and security policy". (Delors, IISS, 1991).

Discussion of these points was given particular emphasis by the emergence of a Franco–German initiative in the context of the IGCs. This joint position advanced the argument that a common policy "will have as its objective the defence of the fundamental interests and common values of political Union in its external relations. It should in particular reinforce the security of Member States, contribute to maintaining peace and international stability, develop friendly relations with other countries, and promote democracy, primacy of law and human rights as well as the economic development of all nations . . .

. . . political Union should implement a common security policy in the aim of setting up a common European defence system in due course without which the construction of European Union would remain incomplete". (Agence Europe Document 1690).

The European Council, meeting in Rome in December 1990, laid down the guidelines for the IGCs. In its Conclusions it dealt specifically with the issue of Security and Foreign Policy. It indicated that the "gradual extension" of the Community role in Security should be considered and that "with a view to the future, the prospect of a role for the Union in defence matters should be considered, without prejudice to Member States' existing obligations in this area . . . and without prejudice to the traditional positions of other Member States".

As the IGC developed its work on Foreign and Security Policy the Luxembourg Presidency's Draft Treaty of June 1991 contained a lengthy section on the subject providing that the Union and its member states "shall define and implement a common foreign and security policy with the aim of reinforcing the identity and role of the Union as a political entity on the international scene. The policy of the Union may extend to all areas of foreign and security policy". The Draft Treaty defined the goals of the Common Foreign and Security Policy in terms of: safeguarding the common values and interests of the Union; strengthening the security of the Union, including "the framing of a defence policy"; preserving peace in line with the United Nations Charter; promoting international cooperation and human rights across the world.

It went on to provide for the extension of Security Policy into the area of Defence where relevant decisions — to be taken at the level of the European Council — "may be wholly or partly implemented in the framework of the Western European Union insofar as they also fall within that organisation's sphere of competence". It then, rather opaquely, referred to decisions in this connection not affecting "obligations arising for certain member states from the Treaties establishing the Atlantic Alliance . . . and the situation of each member state in that connection". It went on to provide that concrete steps towards a defence policy will be taken "on the basis of a report to be submitted by the Council to the European Council in 1996 at the latest".

A variety of options exist in this area which have given rise to serious controversy between member states and between the Community and the USA over the future shape of defence arrangements involving NATO members within the EC Community and members of the WEU. The likelihood now is that the Treaty amendments to emerge from the IGC will defer any final decision on the specific Defence issue for some years, leaving these matters for the moment within the NATO/WEU ambit. However, it is clear that the spectrum of policy issues covering foreign, security and defence questions are firmly on the agenda but without any finality in terms of structures, institutions and decision-making.

Neutrality

The issue of Neutrality arises as an important element in the enlargement debate because of the traditional stance of one member state of the Community — Ireland — and of a number of the potential applicants — Austria, Sweden, Finland, Switzerland, Cyprus and Malta — each of which has espoused neutrality in the context of the cold war era and in some cases over a much longer period.

Each neutral state has arrived at its policy on the basis of its own history and political experience and there is no common philosophy or legal basis other than fairly academic 'definitions' of neutrality and the rather dated provisions of the Hague Convention of 1907. Neutrality varies in definition and practice from the century-old positions of Sweden and Switzerland to the assertion of new Irish independence in 1939 and the post-World War II constitutional arrangements in Austria and Finland. "Ireland's neutral stance in the Second World War was, in the first place, an assertion of the new nation's independence. It did not represent a deeply-thought-out political philosophy. Nor did it imply a lack of conviction as to the rights and wrongs of the global conflict". (Brown, *Studies*, 1988). Both Cyprus and Malta arrived at their neutral status in the context of their search for a post-colonial identity.

One of the most striking characteristics of the neutral states is their individuality which places them, in terms of their national attitudes and political thinking on the issues of security, in contrast to most of their European neighbours who have participated in military and security alliances.

Over the years the neutral countries have acted internationally in different ways ranging from what has been described as 'convenient invisibility' to high-profile involvement in world movements for peace and for the assertion of human rights and self-determination in many regions of the world. Neutral countries have had a particular role in the evolution of the CSCE process and have played a significant part in the work of the UN, not least in the sphere of peace-keeping.

Traditional neutrality — whatever its origin or expression in practice — is now confronted by a changed world order, particularly in Europe. The Cold War is ended. The political map of Europe is changing with the collapse of the Soviet Empire. At a global level the superpowers are committed to disarmament and arms control initiatives and are working together satisfactorily to solve regional crises, as in the case of Angola, or to permit UN action as in the Gulf. The old certainties of bloc confrontation and simply defined 'threats' and 'risks' are seriously reduced and it is opportune to rethink attitudes and policies in both alliance and neutral countries.

NATO and WEU

The countries of the Community have responded by opening up their current rather confused and diffuse debate on the future of NATO and the WEU and on the security role, if any, of the EC itself. At the same time, neutral states are engaged in their own debates and are arriving at their own perspectives on the new situation, for example, in Sweden:

> Over the least two years, Europe has undergone vast political changes. The climate between the superpowers . . . has improved considerably. The previous division into two rival power blocs is a thing of the past . . . cut-backs in both nuclear weapons and conventional forces have been initiated, and further disarmament negotiations are in progress. The Summit meeting of the CSCE in Paris in November 1990 laid the foundations for a new system of security and cooperation on our continent . . . Important aspects of Sweden's security policy situation have thus improved markedly . . .
>
> Members of the Community also seem inclined to gradually extend their security policy cooperation, a term which in EC usage is not as directly linked with defence policy and military cooperation as it is in the Swedish context . . . there are no prospects for the transformation of the EC into a defence alliance with operative military responsibilities at this Inter Governmental Conference . . .
>
> . . . in a longer perspective, we cannot exclude the possibility that cooperation between members of the EC may also be extended to defence questions. It is the view of the government that any decision on this would be based on unanimity between member countries and that there would be a continued readiness to find solutions for states which do not wish or cannot participate in such cooperation. As far as Sweden is concerned, this would imply that we would not be obliged to participate in a possible future defence alliance between EC states or in possible collective security commitments . . .
>
> If, in the future, a durable European security order is established, based for example on the CSCE, the foundations on which Sweden's policy of neutrality has rested hitherto, will change. (Carlsson, 1991).

That statement of view by the Swedish Prime Minister to the Riksdag, when explaining his government's announcement of its decision to apply formally for EC membership has led to an extremely guarded response from Commission President Delors who stated that: "I consider that neutrality poses a problem as it does for all neutral countries unless we abandon the idea that the Community may have a defence policy some day; I have not given up on this idea". (Agence Europe, 5526).

A somewhat similar view is expressed by a Swiss expert:

> The future security of Europe depends mainly on the developments in the former communist countries and the USSR. If they do not succeed in solving their ethnic and economic problems by peaceful means . . . it is to be expected that Switzerland will keep up its strict neutrality in security questions and will see itself forced to uphold a high degree of military readiness . . .
>
> If Europe remains stable and the antagonism between East and West continues to diminish, Switzerland will really be faced with the question of the future of neutrality . . . there might be a point when it will be favourable to give up the status of neutrality in order to establish an operational European system of collective security . . . (Brunner, 1991).

Debate on Foreign and Security Policy

For all the neutrals, the debate on Foreign and Security policy is of crucial importance. The move towards a common position, including defence, is clearly part of the long term blueprint as seen by many interests but it is becoming obvious that no decision will be taken at this stage which would lock all member states into a defence pact — indeed there are now many voices calling for a prudent and step-by-step approach in this connection both because of the enlargement question and because of the many uncertainties and discontinuities in the European and world security scene.

The Irish position was indicated by the Taoiseach, Charles Haughey, speaking in the Dail on 9th July, 1991. He reiterated the long-standing formulation that "if the Community were to develop its own defence arrangements for its security then Ireland as a committed member state would consider participating". But he went on to take a new and interesting standpoint, arguing that "a defence arrangement which the EC works out for itself and which has Community interests as its primary focus, is clearly different from a system in which existing wider arrangements continue to have primacy and where non-community members are part of the decision-making process". (Haughey, 1991).

The neutrals can — and will — agree to participate fully in the elaboration of a Foreign and Security Policy for the Community in the realms of so-called 'soft security' and they consider that such a policy can serve important world and regional interests. Security based on sound, agreed principles and on a realisation that peace is achieved by political rather than military means is gaining greater credibility. In these circumstances it is likely that the neutrals will seek, initially from outside but ultimately as members of the Community, to influence thinking in the direction of a Pan-European security system. The present phase may be seen as an interim stage in the movement towards common European Security. Over the next few years the Community will intensify debate on that objective as the implications of the events of 1989 and 1990 are assessed.

Central and Eastern Europe

For the countries of Central and Eastern Europe, the position is different. They have been members of one of the military blocs and have seen that system disintegrate and disappear. Already agreements have been put in place for the removal of Soviet forces and military equipment from the former WTO states. While these developments must be seen as positive from the overall peace and disarmament standpoint it is also true that they have resulted in the creation of a vacuum in Central Europe at a time of considerable instability and uncertainty in the former communist states and in the countries which have still not yet entirely cast off the old system, such as Romania and Bulgaria. In these circumstances the new governments in the East are seeking acceptable external security links or props and have turned to the Community, NATO and the WEU. While the question of any form of adhesion to NATO or WEU must be recognised as a matter for the long term it is clear that these countries must be offered some form of meaningful reassurances at a time of new and largely undefined risks and challenges. Future discussions between the Community and these countries will inevitably have a significant security component which, in turn, will affect the nature of the political union to be decided later in this century.

(iv) The *Acquis Communautaire*

The agreed conditions for acceptance of new members to the Community include acceptance of the *acquis communautaire*, i.e. acceptance of the entire corpus of Community law and jurisprudence built up since the inception of the EEC in 1957. New members must join the 'club' as it is subject only to the result of entry negotiations which may lead to special consideration for particular problems and concerns. Thus, Ireland on entry in 1973 was allowed specified periods of derogation in certain areas (e.g. in relation to the protection of the car assembly industry) and was given a special Protocol recognising the underdeveloped state of the Irish economy and, in effect, permitting the whole country to be classified as a single entity for regional policy purposes.

Acceptance of more than thirty years of Community legislation now implies the assimilation into national legal and administrative frameworks of some 1,400 separate laws and of the associated jurisprudence and implementing rules and systems. For any state this would be a daunting prospect but for some of the present prospective applicants — and notably the Eastern European states — it must be seen as a cause of considerable delay in arriving at the point at which entry to the Community would be feasible.

EFTA and EEA

In the case of the EFTA countries three factors exist to reduce the impact of this particular element in the overall enlargement file:

- the EFTA states have advanced and sophisticated economies and, in many key areas — environment, social policy, etc. — have attained standards which equal or excel those set down in EC law
- the EFTA states have, over a number of years, set out to align many of their industrial standards and other relevant regulations to those pertaining in the Community and some — e.g. Sweden — have set up specific institutions to achieve this goal
- the EFTA states have been involved in more than a year of detailed negotiation with the Community in the framework of the EEA talks and have, thus, covered a great deal of the groundwork at least in general terms.

Association Agreements in the case of some other states will have gone some distance to prepare them for the strict framework of laws and rules which will apply in the case of accession. Such arrangements will also have given them some familiarity with EC bureaucracy in action.

It has been commented that, during the EEA negotiations, ". . . EFTA members were asked to identify which parts of the 'acquis' would cause them problems and need detailed examination. Their careful efforts to do this meant that the EFTA countries were put through much of the work that would be required of all candidates for full membership not least because it is in practice so difficult to determine what is relevant". (Wallace, H., 1989).

For example, a major snag arose concerning the problems foreseen by Iceland in respect of Spanish fishery interests in the North Atlantic. For a time this issue — relatively small in economic or financial terms and undoubtedly soluble within normal EC 'package deals' — had the potential of stalling the entire negotiation since it was raised on both sides to the level of principle.

Among other significant points to be taken into account in respect of the *acquis* may be listed:

- alignment of policies in certain sensitive areas; social protection (pensions in Sweden); education and training; environmental protection
- protection of higher standards already achieved in some areas by EFTA countries; a cause of very serious concern and perhaps a major barrier to eventual application in the case of Norway
- institutional aspects such as involvement in the standards-setting bodies such as CEN and CENELEC where much has already been achieved through joint efforts
- application of EC policies on Competition and State Aids in countries with different traditions and Structures
- possibility of acceptable transition arrangements and sectoral derogations in the case of Central and Eastern European states where industry is decades behind in terms of technology and productivity; this will depend on the effectiveness of current plans for aid, technical assistance and market access
- likely adverse reactions in certain cases from present EC members fearing enhanced competition; this is being tackled to a large extent within the EEA talks
- particular problems of adjustment to the comprehensive Community system in the case of Turkey whose economic structures are seriously out of line with those of the Community as a whole (GDP per capita below that of some Eastern European countries).

5. THE AVAILABLE OPTIONS

Bringing together all of the foregoing aspects of the issue of enlargement it is possible to identify a number of basic strategies which the Community could pursue.

These would include:

- Internal Integration and External Partnership
- A Larger Single Market
- A New Intergovernmental Structure
- Multiple Pillars
- Deepening and Sequential Widening.

(i) Internal Integration and External Partnership

This may be characterised as the 'Exclusive Europe' option. It would involve a determined and rapid drive towards the completion of the entire integration programme which is now underway — Single Market, EMU, Political Union — with a clear decision to defer consideration of membership applications until the unspecified moment in the future when the Community would have arrived at its chosen degree of union. However, during the period of consolidation the Community would pursue a policy of good relations or partnership with the other groups of European nations including those which have indicated a desire to become full members. This way forward has been advocated at times by Commission President Delors in his regular references to a Europe of Concentric Circles centred on the EC and has been favoured in certain statements from Bonn.

At the heart of this approach there is a commitment to build the economic and political strength of the Community to the point where it would be the unquestioned power centre of the continent in the shadow of which all other relationships would exist. It may be seen as the epitome of the views and interests which have led many outside the Community to speak of an 'Exclusive Europe' and to argue for immediate applications for membership and pressure to get inside the Community as soon as possible.

The proponents of this option have identified three specific forms of partnership to be followed:

- a comprehensive agreement with the EFTA states as potentially realised in the outline EEA package
- a range of nation-specific agreements with the various Central and Eastern European countries designed to meet the particular needs of each and to provide incentives for necessary change

– *ad hoc* association agreements with a number of Southern European and Mediterranean countries, including Turkey.

It is argued that this approach would not rule out eventual full membership but it would enable the Community to test the possibilities of various future arrangements. It would equally ensure that the Community could take certain hard decisions on controversial issues such as Defence without having to consider the sensitivities of countries such as Austria or Sweden.

(ii) A Larger Single Market

This scenario foresees the Community adapting its programme in order to permit early entry of a number of EFTA states and to deal, in one way or another, with the Turkish application. The EC would press ahead with the 1992 project for the Single Market but would not expand its policy agenda in areas likely to complicate accession negotiations and, in particular would soften its political, institutional and defence/security aspirations. The central theme of Community development would switch from the present concept of integration to that of European 'architecture'. Only as the enlarged Community came to realise its own identity would it return to the difficult integration portfolio.

This approach would see a switch of emphasis from the process of continuing integration which has characterised the Community in recent years towards an increasing range of negotiations with the long list of applicants for membership. It would, in all probability, become a stage of intense negotiation with EFTA countries which would have the considerable advantages of their current economic and financial strength and of the detailed discussions already undertaken within the EEA framework. The countries of Central and Eastern Europe might well be the losers in such a scenario and the Southern European candidates might also be relegated to the back of the lengthening queue.

The question has been raised of the degree to which "the entrepreneurial dynamics of economic integration might be less confined and might operate in ways that did not correspond to the politicians' intentions or the institutional map". (RIIA, 1989, p. 25). 1992 without some of the intended flanking policies and institutional changes could be characterised by an undesirable free-for-all.

(iii) A New Intergovernmental Structure

This is an 'Open Europe' scenario with a strong Pan-European flavour. The 'greater good' of an approach to all European countries would be given priority over the current concentration on integration within the Community itself. The thinking behind this option has been summarised along the following lines:

> . . . the EC had well served European interests for forty years, but . . . the new political map and historic transformation need *de novo formulae*. Either a

recasting of the EC or a new European framework would have to be designed to which virtually all European states could belong. Political access would be open, institutions would be intergovernmental, not supranational, and economic and industrial issues would be a matter for coordination not common policies. (Wallace, H., 1989).

The former British Premier, Margaret Thatcher, expressed a strong perference for this approach arguing often that there were only two important issues to be addressed — the removal of barriers to trade and capital movement and the early inclusion of other European states, notably the new Central and Eastern European democracies. However, there exist a number of crucial questions arising from this approach:

- what would be the future of the EC Budget; would resource transfers become an *ad hoc* matter?
- what would be the security dimension of such an arrangement; would the new construction become linked in some way to the CSCE?
- would it not be the case that some of the present EC member states would wish to continue their integration efforts and, if so, how could this be achieved?
- how would a political impetus be maintained and a degree of cohesion assured?
- could the newly-united Germany be bound satisfactorily into such a loose arrangement?

It is clear that this variant represents a very untidy and unpredictable approach. It has been advanced as an attempt to concentrate some attention on the position of the Eastern Europeans and on the serious institutional vacuum created by the disappearance of Comecon and the WTO from the European scene. Consideration of this approach must give rise to the thought that it would permit "all European countries to shelter under a common European roof, but it does not necessarily correspond to Mikhail Gorbachev's 'common European home', a notion that currently emphasises security frameworks. There is also a testing question . . . of whether the USSR would be taking shelter under the same common roof". (Wallace, H., 1989).

(iv) Multiple Pillars

Commenting on recent developments within the IGCs and the EEA negotiations, the 'Economist' magazine came forward with what is, in effect, an additional scenario of the future Community:

> . . . the train is rolling; but its destination is changing. The European Commission's preferred terminus remains a quasi-federal European Community,

> ringed by a European Economic Area for the members of EFTA, ringed in turn by aspiring associates, mainly former inmates of Comecon. In place of this rises the prospect of a Europe of many spires — a wider EC in which all members form part of a supranational market, but within which one elite pools its foreign policies, another elite its immigration and policing policies, a third its currencies and the elite of all elites, all three. The flat-topped earthwork of Chateau Delors is being replaced by a Mont Saint Michel ('Economist', 1991).

This is the pragmatists' option, reflecting the thrust of all the varied opinions on how to proceed with controversial and divisive questions such as NATO/WEU relationships (shorthand for Atlanticist/Eurocentrist attitudes to security); fast-track or step-by-step progress to EMU; intergovernmental or federalist approaches to integration as a whole and, of course, Deepening versus Widening on the enlargement issue. Using this approach there can be something for everyone and an umbrella concept of European advance to reassure those who insist on demonstrable progress towards unity, however defined.

It is argued that such a compromise method would permit the early accession of countries like Austria and Sweden without a confrontation on security and neutrality. While this was being organised a different pace of integration could be followed in respect of the countries of Central and Eastern Europe without formally excluding or long-fingering their applications. The Schengen Agreement could be used as the framework for a step-by-step move towards a fully frontier-free Community while the WEU would provide a suitable focus for those countries feeling the urgent need to develop rapid-response forces.

Clearly such an approach has the serious disadvantages of being diffuse and of lacking a single, cohesive centre of policy development and collective decision. On the other hand, the 'Economist' argues ". . . there is little wrong with some Europeans creating structures, showing that they work and then allowing others to join them if they wish. The EMS was not harmed by Britain's shilly-shallying; it was Britain that was hurt". ('Economist', 1991).

(v) Deepening and Sequential Widening

For many observers, the most acceptable option — and the one with most political attractiveness — is that described as Deepening and Sequential Enlargement. This would involve the undiminished continuation of the present broad programme of economic, political and institutional transformation of the Community but with a selective element of relatively rapid enlargement.

The capacity to succeed in adopting this approach would be dependent on three elements:

- accession candidates which fulfil strict conditions and criteria

- political will on the part of the existing members to make necessary adaptations in attitude and in practice
- institutional flexibility permitting "strengthening the centre with a view to securing effective convergence of the Community as a whole, on intermediate economic and social objectives". (Planas, 1991).

This option reflects the widespread opinion that it is now impossible to rule out some element of enlargement if the Community is to be true to its long-term vocation. The fact that the former GDR has been assimilated into the EC and that its representatives are already sitting as observers in the European Parliament — with no formalities of the kind envisaged for Austria and no potentially endless delays such as those experienced by Turkey have given rise to the reflection that "it appears *de facto* easier to integrate a country into the Community that, in its present state, shows a large similarity in its economic, financial and political structure with the EC, as is the case for Austria or Norway — despite all remaining questions — than a country or territory which during the last 40 years has taken a completely different orientation and development, as is the case of the GDR". (Planas, 1991).

The most difficult issue arising in this case is that of how a selection is to be made as between the many applicants now lining up to become EC members. What interpretation is to be put on the expression 'sequential' — two, three, six more members? And at what pace? Perhaps the answer lies in the institutional area with the rate of expansion being limited to what can be accommodated within the main Community institutions in terms of purely practical considerations such as translation capability. In the recent European Parliament debate on the Planas Puchades Report, the senior Belgian MEP, Fernand Herman, asked whether the Community was doing enough in practical terms so as to be able to welcome new members. Can simultaneous translation work effectively in decision-making meetings with as many as twelve languages?

This particular approach appears to have had one significant political supporter in the person of Italian Foreign Minister, Gianni de Michelis, who has been arguing that political union should come in stages, like EMU, with Stage One based on the likely modest achievements of the current IGC and starting in 1994 with the arrival of, say, Austria, Sweden and Norway. Stage Two, in 1998, would be linked to the arrival of the first Central or Eastern European member states and to important developments in the area of security (e.g. major revisions of the WEU Treaty). It might also see big increases in the powers of the Parliament. Stage Three would be scheduled for the early years of the next century and would, in effect, see the arrival of the Pan-European Confederation. Mr. de Michelis has warned specifically against seeking to do too much too soon: "To move too quickly in a federal direction — such as a common defence policy — would make it harder for East European and EFTA countries to join". ('Economist', 1991).

The Commission Opinion on Austria's application may also be interpreted as reflecting this general approach since it asserts an overall openness to enlargement while expressing great caution about its impact on Community development and on common institutions.

Assessment

These options have been the subject of a great deal of close scrutiny and debate and pick up most of the main currents of political debate. Looking at them with a view to practicality it can be argued that:

- Internal Integration and External Partnership is no longer a real option since the pressure for enlargement is irresistible
- A Larger Single Market ignores the degree to which the Community is already committed to integration
- A New Intergovernmental Structure has its advocates but is seen as a long term departure from present trends within the Community towards unity and not as a *de novo* option
- Multiple Pillars may yet turn out to be what happens but it tends to fly in the face of the Community's proven capacity to retain basic cohesion and to respect its unique institutional system even at a time of crisis
- Thus, by elimination and having regard to the long pragmatic and flexible history of the EC, the option most likely to emerge as the model for the decade ahead is that of Deepening and Sequential Widening. In other words, this implies a step-by-step approach which at no point allows the Community to close its doors or to refuse other European countries the hope of eventual membership.

6. CONCLUSIONS

The enlargement issue goes to the heart of the debate on the precise nature of the European Community. It poses a choice between two broad views:

- Monnet's concept of a particular European dynamism which could give reality to a common interest through common institutions and shared activity was to be enlarged over time to 'continental scale'. A Community which is not exclusive in either its attitudes or its practices but which recognises that, because the successive enlargements of the past twenty years have enriched the EC in many ways, it is essential that it should remain open to other European States which wish to participate in the creation of a genuine Union
- and that exemplified by the comments of the former British diplomat, Sir Michael Butler, writing in 1986: ". . . one thing is certain; it will be best if there are no more enlargements for quite a long time . . . Meanwhile, the Twelve, besides being an auspicious number, can be said to include all the traditional Western European cultures and to represent the vast majority of Western European people. It was perhaps presumptuous of the Six, or even the Nine, to speak of the Community as though it was Europe . . . But when we talk of Europe's importance in the history of our millennium, especially the cultural history, it is primarily about develop-ments in the Twelve that we are thinking. The Twelve are not far from representing the Continent of Europe as we normally conceive of it". (Butler, 1986).

The latter viewpoint may be justified in terms of efficiency. It is however often advanced as the basis for promotion of a 'power-bloc' concept which would see a future Community as an economic, political and even military world power.

The reality of a much enlarged Community does give rise to genuine concerns over decision-making capacity, cohesiveness of day-to-day operation and single-minded pursuit of an ultimate vision of integration. Nevertheless, the case is made by many commentators that a Community which calls itself European and which defines for itself a long term role in economic, political and social integration within Europe cannot refuse full participation to countries such as Austria, Sweden or — eventually — Hungary and Czechoslovakia. The Commission, in the light of its Austria Opinion, now recognises the force of this argument.

The enlargement question divides opinions within the Community and strong views are held on both sides with many highly influential voices raised in support of either exclusivity, at least in the medium-term, or of a very restrictive approach to admission of any new members. However, it cannot be denied that over the past three years or so a remarkable change has taken place in relations between the Community and its neighbours. It was possible for knowledgeable figures in Community diplomacy to write only five years ago that no applications for membership were to be anticipated for at least ten years and that the whole enlargement issue could be easily deferred for as long. That is no longer the case for reasons within and without the Community.

The so-called 'push' and 'pull' factors arising from the pace of economic change across the continent and from the pace of the Community's own progress towards 1993 have forced a reassessment of the economic and hence political relationship with the EC and with other European countries. It is certain that a number of European states have reached the decision that to be excluded from the post-1992 Community would be detrimental to their hopes of development and progress and that EC-offered alternatives such as the European Economic Area can be seen as no more than a short-term 'waiting room' prior to formal negotiations and entry into the 'club'. The pressures from these countries will grow — Austria is already busily promoting its case for negotiations to commence as soon as the work of the IGCs is satisfactorily concluded — and the need to arrive at a coherent Community strategy is now evident.

The potential applicants may conveniently be divided into four categories or sub-groups:

- *EFTA Members* (Austria, Sweden, Norway, Finland, Switzerland, Iceland); all of which are highly-developed economies with strong democratic, participatory and progressive systems which have produced in particular advanced policies and structures in areas such as social protection and ecology. These countries are all well above the Community average for GDP per capita. Economically and politically they would be integrated with little difficulty
- *Central and Eastern Europe* (Hungary, Poland, Czechoslovakia); countries in transformation from communist to market economies and from tyranny to democracy; all characterised by weak and uncompetitive economic structures in both industry and farming; requiring massive assistance both financial and in terms of skills and restructuring if they are to be realistic EC candidates; in economic terms they will need a prolonged period of transition
- *Southern Flank* (Turkey, Malta and Cyprus); these three have already applied for membership but all face serious investigation of their economic and infrastructural capacity to take on the full responsibilities and challenges of full membership; serious political issues arise in connection with both the Turkish and Cypriot applications which will require delicate handling
- *Others* (Yugoslavia, Baltic States, etc.); there are some other states whose future relationship with the Community must be considered seriously.

Yugoslavia has long sought to develop closer relations with the EC not least because of geographical considerations, but present political upheavals and uncertainties tend to rule it out as a short-term candidate; the future shape and degree of internal cohesion of the USSR is clearly in question, thus it is not unrealistic to raise the question of possible future approaches from, for example, the Baltic republics which have considerable ties and shared concerns with Western countries such as Finland and Sweden. The nature of future relations with the USSR itself must also be borne in mind since its restructuring will demand effective support from the EC and the successful implementation of its economic reforms will have a major impact on the overall European economy.

The question of enlargement gives rise to consideration of a number of major issues which must be assessed in terms of their significance, their susceptibility to solution or containment and their priority. These have been discussed under the headings of:

Institutional Issues

Economic Issues

Political Issues, including Neutrality

Acquis Communautaire

Taking account of these points it is possible to identify a range of specific conclusions on the enlargement issue:

- the current debate will determine the future pace and shape of Community development; it is necessary therefore that there should be a coherent and realistic strategy based on a clear set of basic principles and on practical assessment of pluses and minuses
- the previous experience of enlargement must be taken into consideration: the Community had no control over the facts and pace of previous enlargements which may be described as voluntary (economic) or unavoidable (political)
- whatever the weight of the arguments for deferral or slow movement in respect of enlargement it must now be accepted that there will be new member states in the EC within a few years; the pressure to enlarge can now be regarded as irreversible
- the Inter Governmental Conferences may be expected to point the way forward to a form of European Union but it is not likely to arrive at finality in respect of the shape of that Union nor of the pace of advance towards it; nonetheless the substantial extension of competences and progress on decision-making will provide the framework for negotiating future applications; as each new entrant will bring with it its own special

concerns, needs and contributions the relevance of the new 'acquis' will be significant

- the IGCs will almost certainly provide for a further phase of work on the evolution of the EC following 1993: the fact that the negotiation of entry terms for at least some of the candidate states will commence shortly after the end of the present IGCs means that enlargement will be a central element of the next stage of development in the Community requiring clarification of unresolved questions
- while practical economic considerations would point to an early opening of negotiations with EFTA member countries whose level of economic development would mark them out as being easily able to adapt to membership, it will be necessary to lay the foundations of future membership for those countries of Central and Eastern Europe which desire to enter; the special position of the Southern European applicants must also be considered, including the particular position of Turkey
- conclusions will be required on the Institutional structure of the Community in the light of enlargement and here the main emphasis will be on the identification of a workable model of decision-making for an extended Community; in this regard there is a conflict between approaches which may be summarised as either 'Community' or 'Inter-Governmental' in nature. This conflict already exists in the current debate on Political Union where it is argued that certain sensitive matters such as security and civil protection should be subject to Inter-Governmental decision with a major role for the European Council
- dealing with the question of decision-making in an enlarged Community, Commission President Delors has argued for a form of centralisation of administration within the Commission on a delegated basis with major policy orientations being made through the usual Institutional system. Thus, the Commission would be given the responsibility for the dual task of carrying forward the whole process of integration while ensuring that the day-to-day processes of economic, social and regional development could go forward as efficiently as possible; a significant point of controversy in this connection would be the role and representation of the smaller states of the Community within any revised or adapted system of administration following enlargement
- the European Parliament's role: the Planas Puchades Report argues strongly for a central Parliamentary role throughout the process of negotiation and decision on each application as well as in the assessment of the longer-term implications of the extension of the EC
- the Security issue remains controversial and difficult; the IGC process is likely to produce a working compromise and deferral of decisions directly

dealing with defence for a number of years; thus the security/defence issues will be entwined in the parallel processes of entry negotiation and integration; it will be possible for the neutral EFTA states to influence EC thinking and to argue for the creation of a genuine Pan-European security structure based on the CSCE

- the impact of new entrants in the area of Economic and Social Cohesion; the possible accession of East European countries and, especially, of Turkey will demand serious analysis of structural policy and financing requirements; the EFTA applicants will be seen to bring the possibility of additional resources for the various Community Funds
- the future scale and structure of the Community Budget: the present funding of the Community is inadequate to allow the type of redistribution characteristic of most political and economic unions and a more realistic budget system is needed to ensure balanced development.

Policy Options for Ireland

For Ireland, the basic question relates to the very principle of further enlargement. While the initial response to the Austrian application was lukewarm, the general line on the enlargement position has been positive. For Ireland, the prospective membership of Austria and Sweden — relatively small states — is now seen as desirable for reasons of extended market opportunity, potentially increased Community Funds, advanced social concepts and positive input to political debate, not least on security and development policy.

A positive approach is indicated for reasons of Ireland's own experience of integration into the Community and of awareness of the political and economic imperatives leading to the present applications. Indeed their potential addition to the range of political insights in the Community should be of significance as debate on further integration gathers pace.

The negative side of the argument is in terms of possible dilution of the integration strategies of the EC and of the institutional impact. Also, the greater the number of member states the more danger of the reduction of influence for a smaller member like Ireland.

Given Ireland's positive approach to the principle of further enlargement a number of points arise for policy consideration:

- political terms, and with appropriate policy instruments and institutions, must have a philosophical and inspirational content and strong popular assent; debate is overdue on this aspect of EC involvement despite the strong 'European' commitment on the part of the general public as indicated by all current research

- the challenge of further enlargement poses fundamental questions as to our understanding of what Europe is in geographical, cultural and political terms; what is meant by the description 'European'; what is required at all levels to build a true unity between 400 million people; and what alternative is there to setting out to do so in the circumstances of today's Europe where so many economic, social, ecological and political problems are beyond solution by any individual nation state

- in practical terms it is necessary to ask what should be the pace of enlargement: the Deepening and Sequential Widening option would appear to be most relevant if interpreted as retaining genuine openness over time

- Institutional arrangements arising from enlargement are of prime importance; in this connection there arises the debate on intergovernmental as against Community approaches to decision making. This debate goes beyond the enlargement issue; the crucial issue is the impact of such concepts on a smaller member state — does Ireland stand to gain more from the policy line of the Commission and Parliament or from working largely at the level of Council and European Council?

- specific economic issues arise, notably concerning the impact of enlargement; new markets and additional resources for the Structural Funds as against the demands of the less developed candidates from Eastern and Southern Europe; giving rise to major calculations for Ireland not least on the future EC Budget

- there are also important policy issues on the current EC agenda which are likely to be affected by enlargement: these include the reform of the CAP, Transport and Environmental Policies and arrangements for migration and citizenship

- the sensitive issue of the development of a Common Foreign and Security Policy with the long-term perspective of a Defence commitment must be confronted: debate on the meaning and future relevance of Ireland's traditional neutrality is required in the context of the changed European political scene and of perceived 'risks'; the prospects of Pan-European developments, possibly in the CSCE framework, offer new opportunities for application of the positive principles of Irish foreign policy

- the enlargement debate will be an item of practical concern in the short term and part of the second phase of debate on the future shape of the Community. Hence, it is urgently necessary in this country to initiate meaningful debate at all levels on the content and promotion of Irish national policies.

APPENDIX

European Commission Opinion on Austria's Request for Membership to the European Community (Foreword and Conclusions).

Foreword

The Commission is giving its opinion on Austria's application for accession at a time when four other applications have already been presented.[1] Applications from other European countries could follow in the near future.

These developments demonstrate the pull exerted in Europe by the Community. The role played by the Community is further strengthened by the profound changes now underway both within the Community (with its move, through the Inter Governmental Conferences, towards political union with a common security policy) and also at international level (as a result of German unification and of the fundamental changes at work in the economic and political systems of the countries of Central and Eastern Europe, including the USSR).

The Community has to reconcile two requirements. First, it must unhesitatingly and in accordance with the procedures laid down in Article 237 of the EEC Treaty confirm its openness towards applicant European countries whose economic and political situation are such as to make accession possible. In addition, the Community must take care to strengthen its own structures sufficiently to maintain the impetus of its own integration. This forward movement must be safeguarded, even in an enlarged Community.

The Community is at present engaged in completing the single market and is seeking, at the same time, through the two Inter Governmental Conferences that are now underway, to establish an economic and monetary union and a political union. By 1st January 1993, the single market will be completed and the results of the two Inter Governmental Conferences should also have been approved. The Commission is therefore convinced that no negotia-tions on a fresh enlargement should be initiated before that date — a view which it had already expressed in its opinion on Turkey's accession request. Once that date is passed, the Community should be ready and willing to open negotiations with applicant countries meeting the economic and political conditions for accession. It is clear that in this context the Community will have to take account, where some of the countries which have already applied or may apply are concerned, of the implications of the concept of neutrality. This concept of neutrality is, moreover, steadily evolving in the light of developments in Europe and worldwide.

In the accession negotiations, the Community will have to take as a basis the Community rules and structures as they emerge from the two Inter Governmental Conferences, following completion of ratification procedures, including the results concerning foreign policy and security, which will have the effect of establishing a stronger identity to which the applicant countries will have to adjust.

The Community's development will not end, however, with the two Inter Governmental Conferences currently underway. The Community must consequently seek in its future partners the necessary willingness to join with it in the further continuation of the integration process.

Furthermore, in the Commission's view, enlargements of the Community will entail, when the time comes, institutional adjustments according to the nature and number of the accession.

Conclusions

From both the economic and the political points of view, Austria's application for accession is in a quite different category from those of previous applicants.

From the economic point of view, no previous applicant has started from a position where, by virtue of numerous agreements, it already had completely free trade in industrial products with the Community, or had already committed itself to apply a substantial part of the *acquis communautaire,* or where its degree of economic integration with the Community was so advanced. There is also Austria's long experience of monetary stability and the special relationship between the schilling and the German mark, and through it with other EMS currencies.

After accession there should not be any fundamental shift in the direction of Austria's economic policy. As regards the *acquis communautaire,* which Austria will have to apply as a new member of the Community, much of this, as had been noted above, will already have been applied by virtue of the future EEA Agreement. Of the areas which remain, only agriculture and transit seem likely to give rise to a need for anything other than technical adjustments. For agriculture, substantial changes will be needed. As for transit, the position taken by the Austrian authorities raises an important question of principle which will have to be addressed in the accession negotiations. These few difficulties should, however, be resolved in the negotiations.

The Community will on the whole benefit from the accession of Austria, which would widen the circle of countries whose economic, monetary and budgetary performance will speed Economic and Monetary Union on its way. The Community would also benefit from the experience of a country whose geographical position, history and the ties it has retained and forged place it right at the heart of the new Europe that is taking shape.

On the basis of the economic considerations, therefore, the Commission considers that the Community should accept Austria's application for accession.

From the political standpoint, the application must be situated in the general context of the future development of the Community and of Europe in general, as indicated in the Foreword of this Opinion.

In this connection, Austria's permanent neutrality creates problems for both the Community and Austria. The first issue which arises is that of the compatibility of permanent neutrality with the provisions of the existing Treaties. In addition, developments in the negotiations within the Inter Governmental Conferences on political union would also require the Community to seek specific assurances from the Austrian authorities with regard to their legal capacity to undertake obligations entailed by the future common foreign and security policy.

Subject to possible future developments in the discussions under way in the Inter Governmental Conference, these problems should not however prove to be insurmountable in the context of the accession negotiations.

---

[1]Agence Europe Document No. 1730, 3rd August, 1991.

BIBLIOGRAPHY

Agence Europe

Brown T., 'Irish Foreign Policy after the Single European Act', *Studies,* Vol. 77, No. 305. Dublin, 1988.

Brunner, H-P., 'Switzerland: Changing Attitudes'. Paper for Labour Party/FES Seminar. Dublin, 1991.

Butler, M., 'Europe More Than A Continent'. London: Heinemann, 1986.

Carlsson, I., Statement to the Riksdag, 14th June, 1991, on *Sweden's Application for Membership of the EC*. Stockholm, 1991.

Commission of the European Communities:

'European Union'. Report by Mr. Leo Tindemans. *Bulletin of the European Community,* Supplement 1/76. Brussels, 1976.

'Enlargement of the Community'. *Bulletin of the European Community,* Supplement 1/78. Brussels, 1978.

'The Thrust of Commission Policy'. Statement by President Delors to the European Parliament. *Bulletin of the European Community,* Supplement 1/85. Brussels, 1985.

Commission Opinion on Turkey's Request for Accession to the Community, SEC (90) 2290. Brussels, 1989.

Statement on the 'Broad Lines of Commission Policy' by President Delors to the European Parliament. *Bulletin of the European Community,* Supplement 1/89. Brussels, 1989.

'Political Union'. Commission Opinion. Brussels, 1990.

'Commission Programme for 1990'. Statement by President Delors to the European Parliament. *Bulletin of the European Community,* Supplement 1/90. Brussels, 1990.

Association Agreements with the Countries of Central and Eastern Europe: A General Outline. COM (90) 398 final. Brussels, 1990.

'Commission Programme for 1991'. Statement by President Delors to the European Parliament. *Bulletin of the European Community,* Supplement 1/91. Brussels, 1991.

The Community and Its Eastern Neighbours. Luxembourg, 1991.

Confederation of the Socialist Parties of the European Community.

Manifesto. Brussels, 1989.

Council of the European Communities:

Joint Declaration of Ministerial Meeting between the EC, its Member States and the Countries of the EFTA. Brussels, 1991.

Delors, J.:

'European Integration and Security'. Alastair Buchan Memorial Lecture. *Institute for Strategic Studies*. London, March, 1991.

Inaugural Address to CEPS Sixth Annual Conference CEPS. Brussels, 1989.

'The Economist':

'Pocket World in Figures'. London, 1991.

'An Eruption of Pragmatism'. 20th April, 1991.

'Many Spired Europe'. 18th May, 1991.

'EC and EFTA: Inner Space'. 18th May, 1991.

European Council:

Presidency Conclusions. Dublin, April 1991.

Presidency Conclusions. Rome, December 1990.

European Parliament:

Draft Treaty Establishing the European Union. *Bulletin of the European Community*, Supplement 2/1984. Brussels, 1984.

Planas Puchades Report on Community Enlargement. Session Documents, PE 141/136 final, 1991.

Verbal Report of Proceedings, Strasbourg 13th–14th May, 1991. Strasbourg, May 1991.

Haughey, C. J., Statement by the Taoiseach to Dail Eireann, *Dail Debates*, Vol. 410, No. 6, 9th July, 1991.

van Helmont, J., 'Options Europeennes 1945–1985'. *Commission of the European Communities/Perspectives Europeennes*. Brussels, 1986.

Government of Ireland:

Single European Act. Information Booklet. Dublin: Stationery Office, 1987.

Laursen, F., 'Towards a Common EC Foreign and Security Policy'. Paper for 2nd International Conference of the European Community Studies Association, George Mason University. Fairfax, Virginia, 1991.

Luif, P., 'EPC and the Neutrals: an Austrian Perspective'. Paper given to ECSP Seminar on Neutrality and EPC. Dublin, 1991.

Government of Luxembourg:

Draft Treaty on the Union. Luxembourg, June 1991.

Government of Malta:

Malta: *Weekly Review,* No. 155. Valletta, April 1991.

Paasio, P., Statement on Finland and the EC, Social Democratic Party of Finland. Jyveskyla, April 1991.

Palmer, J., 'Trading Places'. London, Century Hutchinson, 1988.

Swiss Social Democratic Party. Report of Party Congress, 1991.

Statistical Office of the EC:

Eurostat: Basic Statistics of the Community. Luxembourg, 1991.

Treaties Establishing the European Communities. Luxembourg, 1987.

Wallace, H., ed., 'The Wider Western Europe'. London, Pinter and RIIA, 1991.

Wallace, H., 'Widening and Deepening'. RIIA Discussion Paper 23. RIIA, 1989.

Wallace, W., ed., 'The Dynamics of European Integration'. London, Pinter and RIIA, 1990.

ACKNOWLEDGEMENT

I wish to express my gratitude to Brendan Halligan for his uniquely helpful response to my first draft.

AN OVERVIEW OF THE COMMUNITY'S INSTITUTIONAL SYSTEM

Brigid Laffan

1. INTRODUCTION

The European Community is much more than a traditional international organisation although it is based on a series of inter-state treaties. Conventional models of states such as unitary, federalist or confederalist, do not capture the complex and messy reality of the Community's political system. However, such models can be useful in probing why political authority is shared between different levels of government. Federalism is typically associated with diversity and heterogeneous societies. Historically, confederations, which are characterised by a high degree of autonomy for the participating states, have been stepping stones to federations. A fully developed federation implies one sovereign state with the focus of external sovereignty at the highest level. Put simply, the federal government represents the state in the international system.

Because federalist principles have been part of the debate on the nature of the Community from the outset, it is appropriate to list the main characteristics of federal systems of government. These are:

- a legislative and administrative separation of powers between different levels of government guaranteed in a constitution
- a bicameral legislature
- a rigid constitution that can only be modified by super-majorities of the participating states
- a highly developed process of judicial review.

The Community's political system has some federalist attributes but is more akin to a confederation in its present stage of development because of the high degree of autonomy retained by the member states.

The foundation Treaties created the basis for a new legal order, independent of the legal systems of the member states. The principles of direct applicability, direct effect and the supremacy of Community law over national law, form the core of the Community's federalist legal order. Community law creates rights and imposes obligations on states and on individuals and companies. The Community's policy scope and autonomous financial capacity is also unique. Moreover, the Community was endowed with a robust institutional system consisting of the European Commission, the Council, the European Parliament and the European Court of Justice. Although there has not been a smooth or automatic transition from independence to integration, the Community represents a high degree of economic interdependence and an emergent polity above the level of the nation state. European integration has created a new dynamic in inter-state relations and in international politics more generally.

Since its inception, the European Community has assumed some of the characteristics of a political system. At Community level, interests are aggregated and articulated, laws are passed, policies are administered, and public goods distributed. The Community is an arena for public-policy-making; participation in the Community adds an additional layer to Western European government and administration. But the Community's political system is supported by the political systems of the member states. However, it is more simply the projection of twelve national political systems on to another level.

The Community represents a new type of political entity characterised by a willingness to pool or share sovereignty in an unprecedented manner. Bulmer and Wessels describe the intermeshing or intermingling of the national and Community levels as "cooperative federalism". According to these scholars, in a system of cooperative federalism, "both levels share in the responsibility for problem solving because neither has adequate legal authority and policy instruments to tackle the challenge they face" (Bulmer and Wessels, 1987, p. 10). This view is shared by Teague when he argues that "the process of integration with regard to the EC is not about the trade-off between member governments losing power and Community institutions gaining it. Instead, it involves a symbiosis between the national and Community level whereby one depends on the other and each is mutually reinforcing" (Teague, 1991, p. 399).

The main goal of cooperation in the European Community is profoundly political: to "transform relations as a whole among their States into a European Union" according to the Preamble of the Single European Act (SEA, Preamble 1987). Jacques Delors, President of the Commission in drawing the distinction between cooperation and integration, spoke of the "intergovernmental Council of Europe as guardian and advocate of democratic values throughout Europe and the integrationist Community working for European Union with all who unreservedly accept the full contract" (speech to Council of Europe Assembly, Strasbourg, 26 September, 1989). Although the precise nature of a European Union has never been clearly articulated, and although there is considerable divergence among the existing member states about the object of integration, this notion of a'full contract' underlines the open-ended nature of the commitment when a state opts for Community membership.

The decision by any state to pool or share sovereignty is thus not a single commitment with clearly established boundaries but a commitment to participation in intensive and dynamic joint decision making. Community membership therefore has profound consequences for sovereignty. The notion of sovereignty in international law implies that a recognised state has jurisdiction over a particular people and territory and that within its jurisdiction, state authorities have control over the legitimate use of coercive power. States have three characteristics, namely a territorial base, a population and a 'sovereign government' (Hocking and Smith, 1990, p. 46). When states agree to participate in advanced political and economic integration, they cede some part of their individual sovereignty in favour of its joint exercise. However, because the Community is an evolving polity, there is a constant tension between the degree of sovereignty that states are willing to share and the desire to maintain as much national sovereignty as possible. Some states in the Community are more attached to traditional notions of sovereignty than others but all states are sensitive to issues arising from historical experience and political culture that impinge on their core values. In the context of European integration, it is important to distinguish between formal legal sovereignty and autonomy: autonomy in this sense relates to the degree of freedom of action that any state can exercise in a highly interdependent world. Loss of autonomy drives states into cooperation and integration as a means of maintaining influence and managing interdependence. It forces them to cede some law-making powers to a political system that transcends their geographical boundaries.

The Community's political system is a curious mixture of intergovernmental and supranational characteristics in which political authority and legitimacy is highly diffuse. Whereas in the political systems of the member states there is a reasonably clear separation of powers in which executive power rests with an accountable government, the Community's political system has no government and therefore no opposition. It is the absence of clear lines of political authority based on a centre of governmental power that makes the EC such a hybrid political system. Its unusual nature is also reinforced by the fact that diplomatic or intergovernmental bargaining constitutes such an important part of the policy process. Sectional or sectoral interests are frequently endowed with the mantle of the national interest in Community law making.

The absence of a European government in turn raises difficult questions about how to ensure adequate political accountability and hence legitimacy in the system. The Commission has executive powers and delegated legislative powers but is not a government in any sense of the word. Although accountable to the European Parliament, the Commission is not appointed by it. Nor do Commissioners have any electoral mandate. The European Parliament's role in taxation, legislation and budgetary matters is heavily constrained. Although directly elected since 1979, the Parliament does not have the reservoir of legitimacy found in national parliaments. European Parliament elections are akin to 'second order' national elections because governmental office is not at stake. Heretofore, such elections have been characterised by uneven turnout.

In 1989, turnout ranged from 90 percent in Belgium (where non-voters are fined) to 36 percent in the UK. In six member states the turnout was less than 60 percent, considerably lower than in national elections (Lakeman, 1990). The Council, a negotiating arena ruled by confidentiality, is the main legislative body in the Community, responsible for the representation of state interests, and the juncture of the policy process where the national and Community systems meet. Ministers sitting in Council are individually responsible to their national parliaments and governments but are not collectively accountable. The judicial function of the European Court of Justice is perhaps the only direct parallel with the national level.

2. THE INSTITUTIONAL SYSTEM

The nature and powers of the Community's institutions have been determined by the original Treaties, subsequent modifications, and the evolutionary nature of the Community enterprise. Since 1958, the Community's policy process has evolved in a dynamic fashion, and not always according to the expectations of the founding fathers.

The Commission is both a collegiate body and a bureaucracy organised along functional lines to carry out the work of the Community. It is thus a political body and an administration. The college of Commissioners has seventeen members drawn from the member states, who are in theory independent of them. The role of the Commission is laid down in the Treaties where its European vocation is emphasised in the stipulation that it must act "in the general interest of the Communities" (Merger Treaty, 1965, Article 10). The Commission fulfils a number of functions in the policy process. It is obliged by the Treaties to exercise the sole right of initiative: put simply, the Commission must suggest proposals and programmes for action to the Council. The Council cannot reach binding decisions without a Commission legislative proposal. Furthermore, according to Article 149 of the Rome Treaty, the Council cannot amend a Commission proposal except by unanimous agreement. However, the reality of policy formation and the drawing up of policy proposals is considerably more complex than is portrayed in the Treaties. First, once the detailed provisions of the Treaties were implemented by the end of the transitional period (1968), the Commission found itself attempting to develop new policies without a strong Treaty basis; it was not until the ratification of the Single Act that the Commission was given a new Treaty framework for the development of policies. Second, the preparatory stages of policy formulation in the Commission involve widespread consultation and discussion with Commission working groups, advisory committees and Brussels-based interest organisations.

Working groups consist of national civil servants whose task it is to react to Commission draft proposals at an early stage. These officials may subsequently negotiate on the proposals under the aegis of the Council. Advisory committees usually involve non-governmental experts. Given the small size of the Commission, such consultation is invaluable as a source of expertise and as a barometer of how individual governments will react to proposals in Council. However, there is the constant danger that the Commission will be drawn into pre-negotiations. Third, as the Presidency of the Council assumed a strongly mediatory role in the Community, the Commission found itself translating political consensus in the Council into Draft Directives.

The Commission's role in the initiation of policy and its normative function as the "conscience of the Community" gives it an important potential in strategic goal setting (Ludlow, 1990, p. 20). The extent to which the Commission can actually exercise this role depends very much on the calibre of the Commission

President and his team and the Community's political environment. The Veto crisis of 1965-66 undermined the Commission as a motor of integration (see page 247). During the 1980s, the Commission regained a role in strategic goat setting: it played a critical part in the budgetary conflict of the early 1980s with a series of papers on the issues including the May mandate report of 1980; the Cockfield White Paper on the completion of the single market, with its calendar technique, is another example of strategic goal setting. The Commission's potential as a think-tank organisation should not be underestimated.

The Commission's role as 'guardian of the Treaties' makes it responsible for ensuring that the member states implement, observe and enforce community laws and that private agents adhere to Community competition policy, for example. The Commission tends not to engage in confrontation with national governments about the implementation of law, and they are usually given a period of grace before the Commission will begin infraction proceedings against them. The infraction process itself is lengthy; the Commission first sends a formal notice to the national authorities pointing out that a Directive had not been translated into national law; if this does not elicit action, the Commission follows with what is known as a 'reasoned opinion' under article 169 of the Treaties, and finally a case is taken before the European Court of Justice. The implementation and enforcement of Community law is receiving considerably more attention since the mid-1980s. The Commission prepares an annual report for the Parliament on the issue, and states with a good record on implementation will press lagging countries to avoid them getting an unfair competitive advantage from non-implementation. The critical role of the national administrative systems in implementing policies is an important feature of the Community's policy process.

The Commission exercises a range of executive functions under the Treaties. These functions are conferred on it by the Council but the Council retains the right even under the Single Act to "impose certain requirements in respect to the exercise of these powers" (Article 145, SEA, 1987). In practice, this means that the Commission is surrounded by a plethora of committees consisting of national officials, which oversees its implementing role to a greater or lesser extent depending on the policy field in question. The Commission's executive functions cover the common policies, notably the Common Agricultural Policy, the Budget including the Structural Funds, programmes on research and development, education, training and the environment. The Commission also has important powers of negotiation in matters of external trade.

Although the Council is legally one institution, in practice the appropriate Ministers meet to negotiate on Commission proposals that fall within the ambit of their responsibilities at national level. Neither does the term Council do justice to the complexity and extent of the Council's hierarchy. At the apex of the hierarchy is the European Council which was finally given Treaty recognition in the Single Act. The Council is in reality a series of separate ministerial fora, whose substructure is made up of numerous committees and working groups, the most important of which is the Committee of Permanent Representatives (Coreper). The Committee of Permanent Representatives has a two-tiered structure, usually known as Coreper 1 and 2. The latter consists of meetings of the permanent representatives of the member states, the ambassadors of the national governments who have been accredited to the Community; their deputies, senior diplomats, meet in Coreper 1. The Antici Group was added to the institutional framework in 1975 to prepare meetings of Coreper 2; the group does not engage in substantive discussions, but highlights areas of difficulty for the ambassadors by giving them an annotated agenda. Some 200 working groups are responsible for examining Commission proposals at the initial stages of the negotiating process.

The key role exercised by Coreper and the Council substructure in the Community's policy process was not anticipated in the Treaties. It was not until the Merger Treaty of 1965 that Coreper was given the task of preparing "the work of the Council and of carrying out the tasks assigned to it by the Council" (Merger Treaty, 1965, Article 4). The pace of Council deliberations has intensified greatly. It is a permanent negotiating forum, where business is managed by a small secretariat and the office of the Presidency.

All member states of the Community hold the Presidency on a rotating basis for a period of six months. Initially, the Presidency was viewed as an equitable means of ensuring that the work of the Council was planned and meetings chaired. Over time the Presidency assumed a more central political role, as all member states wanted to ensure that the Community worked reasonably smoothly during their term and that some important decisions were taken. The highlight of any Presidency is the European Council which takes place at the end of each term of office, though because of pressure of international events, most recent presidencies have held two European Councils during their period in the chair.

The scope of the European Council has never been established by a treaty. In other words, the European Council does not have a precise constitutional role. The Stuttgart Declaration on European Union, adopted in 1983, outlined five activities for the European Council:

- giving general political impetus to the construction of Europe
- issuing general political guidelines for the EC and European Political Cooperation
- initiating cooperation in new areas of activity
- ensuring consistency among different aspects of European Union
- issuing common declarations on matters of external relations (Solemn Declaration, 1983, point 2.1).

The European Council acts in all of these areas. It is now the forum where the main priorities for integration are established. Summit communiques are important statements of political and policy intent. The European Council regained this role in the latter half of the 1980s; until the Fontainebleau European Council in 1984, when the contentious British budgetary dispute was finally resolved, the Council appeared more like a final court of appeal for distributional issues not solved at Council level.

The Council is the arena where the national and Community levels of the policy process formally meet. The task of the Council is to legislate. The Council takes legislative decisions on the basis of:

- a simple majority
- a qualified majority voting
- unanimity

The Treaties make provision for the kind of voting allowed in different situations. A simple majority can be used only for procedural matters and not legislation. Unanimity, which implies consensus in the Council, is self-explanatory. The original Treaties prescribed qualified majority voting as the norm in the policy process once the transitional period was over. Weighted voting is based on the allocation of a pool of votes among the member states. In the Community at present, the total pool of votes is 76, which is divided on a proportionate basis among the member states (see Table 1). A qualified majority is 54 votes out of 76.

Table 1

Distribution of Votes in the Council of Ministers

France	10 votes
Germany	10 votes
Italy	10 votes
UK	10 votes
Spain	8 votes
Belgium	5 votes
Greece	5 votes
Netherlands	5 votes
Portugal	5 votes
Denmark	3 votes
Ireland	3 votes
Luxembourg	2 votes
Total	76 votes
Qualified Majority	54 votes

The use of weighted voting has a chequered history in the Community. The move to qualified majority voting at the end of the transitional period was part of the so-called Luxembourg crisis in the Community in 1965 when President de Gaulle withdrew all French officials and ministers from the Council for a period of six months. The crisis was resolved in 1966 by a 'gentlemen's agreement' whereby on matters of vital national interest a country could request the other member states to continue discussions until a consensus had been achieved. In practice, this introduced the so-called veto into EC policy making. The European Parliament is the Community's representative institution. The organisation of Parliament reflects its intrinsic nature as an assembly. At present there are 518 directly-elected European parliamentarians divided among several major political groupings and a small number of independents who remain outside the group structure. The European Parliament has a highly developed committee structure, derived from continental parliamentary tradition. The European Parliament has a number of powers in the Community's policy process, notably in the budgetary field, in the legislative domain, in matters of external relations and related to the control of the Commission.

The European Court of Justice as the judicial organ of the Community has a reserve role in the policy process. The Court of Justice is composed of thirteen judges and six advocates general, who have the task of investigating cases and giving opinions to the Court. Article 164 of the Rome Treaty (EEC) states that the "Court shall ensure that in the interpretation and application of this Treaty the law is observed" (Article 164, EEC Treaty). The Single Act made provision for an additional Court – the Court of First Instance. The Court hears cases involving:

- disputes between member states
- disputes between the EC and the member states
- disputes between the institutions
- disputes between the Community and individuals and economic agents
- opinions on international agreements
- preliminary rulings on disputes before national courts.

The Court has played a very important role in providing judicial cement to the integration process. It has interpreted the Treaties in a dynamic rather than a legalistic manner. The Court's legal activism has strengthened the federal character of the Community's legal system.

The Community's policy process has a number of additional organs that do not have the status of full Community institutions. The multipartite Economic and Social Committee (EcoSoc) stems from continental tradition that favours the formal incorporation of economic interests into the policy process. In the Community of Twelve, the EcoSoc has 189 members drawn from national interest organisations. Its role in the policy process is merely consultative. The Court of Auditors is a recent addition to the Community landscape, which was established in 1977 to take over responsibility for the audit function. Each year, the Court of Auditors publishes a report on the activities of each institution which includes analysis and comments on the utilisation of the budget. Like the Commission, the Court is a collegiate body, consisting of one member from each member state.

3. THE COMMUNITY'S POLICY STYLE

Three decision-making systems can be identified in the Community's policy process:

- the Community method, based on the Treaties
- European Political Cooperation (EPC); foreign policy cooperation: intergovernmental in format codified in the Single Act
- policy cooperation in areas such as immigration, terrorism, and criminal matters that takes place between the member states in an intergovernmental forum without any Treaty codification (see Appendix 1).

The relationship between Council and Commission forms the central core of the policy process in what can be called the 'Community method' of policy making. The dynamic between these two institutions was designed by the founding fathers of the Community as the main impulse to decision making. The Commission is entrusted with the responsibility of making legislative proposals to Council which possesses the power to transform proposals into law. The European Parliament, especially since it gained its democratic credentials in 1979, has had some success in transforming the Council/Commission dyad into a triad by expanding the Parliament's role. The central core is surrounded by a number of other bodies, notably the Economic and Social Committee which is consulted on major policy proposals. The EcoSoc has declined in importance since the Single Act. Over the years the existence of the Community, with important powers in certain areas of public policy has led to the formation of many transnational interest organisations which have become formally involved in the policy process, albeit in a consultative fashion. As a consequence of the single market, for business there has been a proliferation of professional lobbying companies in Brussels representing the interests of individual firms. Producer groups are more heavily represented in Brussels than other societal interests.

The Community's policy process is multilevelled and multicultural involving as it does twelve member states. What takes place in Brussels is only a fraction of Community related activity in the member states. Most areas of public policy now have a European dimension. Like public policy making at national level, the Community's policy process is divided into a series of policy communities or sectors consisting of the relevant commissioner, directorate general, national ministers, council working party, European Parliament committee, advisory groups, and interest organisations. The Commission in the 1980s has also deliberately fostered the development of networks among private companies, educational establishments, professional bodies and groups operating in the social domain. A distinctive feature of the Community's policy process is the important role exercised by negotiations. Community legislation emerges from a process of bargaining, coalition building, cooperation and conflict resolution. The Council is the centre of a vast negotiating arena involving EC institutions and national administrations. Servicing the Brussels machine is a major part of contemporary government in the Twelve. The Community's unique institutional system has contributed to the establishment of an intense system of joint-decision-making between twelve states and extra-national bodies. Established 'rules of the game' and norms of behaviour are essential in the constant search for agreement among such a diverse range of states.

Because the Community is an evolving polity in which the institutional balance and the power relationships are not fixed, questions of competence and legality impinge on the policy process in a more persistent manner than found in the national political systems. One of the first things the Parliament does when it receives a Commission proposal is to examine its legal basis. The Commission for its part is ever vigilant of its right of initiative. It sees its role as expanding the authority of the Community's political system and in fashioning a common interest from the interests of the member states. Representatives of state interests, both civil servants and politicians, are more concerned with determining the balance of advantage and possible problems that lie in any set of proposals. Domestic political considerations are ever present. Politicians from all member states are sensitive to each others' political problems.

4. CONCLUSIONS

The purpose of this paper was to provide an overview of the Community's political system as background to the substantive papers on the Inter Governmental Conference. The paper draws attention to the basic functions of the Community's major institutions. Moreover, it was concerned to draw attention to the hybrid nature of the Community's political system, characterised as it is by a mixture of federal and intergovernmental features. The Community is an arena where individual states and Community institutions come together in a well-established policy process. The inter-meshing and inter-mingling of the national and Community levels means that political authority and legitimacy is highly diffuse. The absence of a European Government makes both authority and legitimacy highly problematic in the Community.

Appendix
Community Policy Making: three models

Model 1	Model 2	Model 3
Community Method	Member States	Inter Governmental
Decision-Making System Established by Treaties	Political Cooperation Codified in SEA	Immigration Trevi Drugs Coordination 1992 Coordination (Free movement of persons)

BIBLIOGRAPHY

Bulmer S. and Wessels W., (1987), *The European Council: Decision-Making in European Politics,* London, Macmillan.

Hocking B. and Smith M., (1990), *World Politics,* London, Harvester Wheatsheaf.

Lakeman E., (1990), 'The European Elections, 1989', *Parliamentary Affairs,* 43, pp. 77-89.

Ludlow P., (1990), 'The European Commission in a Changing European Community', CEPS Working Paper, No. 52.

Teague P., (1991), Review Article, *Administration,* 38, pp. 373-403.

LIST OF ABBREVIATIONS

ACP	African, Caribbean, Pacific States
ASEAN	Association of South-East Asian Nations
CAP	Common Agricultural Policy
CEN	European Standards Authority
CENELEC	European Electrical Standards Authority
CFE	Conventional Forces in Europe Treaty
CFSP	Common Foreign and Security Policy
COMECON	Council for Mutual Economic Aid
COMETT	Community Action Programme in Education and Training for Technology
COREPER	Committee of Permanent Representatives
CSCE	Conference on Security and Cooperation in Europe
EBRD	European Bank for Reconstruction and Development
EC	European Community
ECHR	European Convention on Human Rights
ECJ	European Court of Justice
ECOFIN	Council of Finance and Economic Ministers
ECOSOC	Economic and Social Committee
ECSC	European Coal and Steel Community
EDC	European Defence Community
EEA	European Economic Area
EEC	European Economic Community
EES	European Economic Space
EFTA	European Free Trade Association
EMS	European Monetary System
EMU	Economic and Monetary Union
EP	European Parliament
EPC	European Political Cooperation

EPU	European Political Union
ERASMUS	European Action Programme for the Mobility of University Students
EURATOM	European Atomic Energy Community
EUROFED	European Central Bank
EUROPOL	Central European Criminal Investigation Office
EUT	European Union Treaty
GATT	General Agreement on Tariffs and Trade
GDR	German Democratic Republic
IAEA	International Atomic Energy Agency
IGC	Inter Governmental Conference
LINGUA	Programme for the Promotion of Foreign Language Knowledge in the European Community
MEP	Member of the European Parliament
NATO	North Atlantic Treaty Organisation
NESC	The National Economic and Social Council
OECD	Organisation for Economic Cooperation and Development
PHARE	EC Phare Programme: Poland, Hungary — Aid for Economic Reconstruction
SEA	Single European Act
SEM	Single European Market
TREVI	Terrorism, Radicalism, Extremism, Violence International (Consultation procedure among EC Ministers of the Interior or Justice)
UN	United Nations
WEU	Western European Union
WTO	Warsaw Treaty Organisation

AUTHOR'S BIOGRAPHIES

James Dooge is a civil engineer and hydrologist. He has been President of the Institution of Engineers in Ireland, the Royal Irish Academy, and the International Association for Hydrologic Sciences. He is the current President-Elect of the International Council of Scientific Unions. His political career began when he was elected to Seanad Eireann in 1961, and he was Leas Cathaoirleach from 1965–73, Cathaoirleach from 1973–77, and Leader of the Seanad from 1983–87. In 1981–82 he was Minister for Foreign Affairs, and in 1984–85 was Chairman of the *ad hoc* Committee of personal representatives of EEC Heads of Government on Institutional Reform and European Union. He has subsequently been involved in EC evaluation of environmental research, and the impact of research and development on policy formation.

Brigid Laffan, Ph.D., is Jean Monnet Professor in European Politics at University College, Dublin. She is a graduate of the University of Limerick, and the College of Europe in Bruges. She is author of numerous articles on European integration and has contributed to *Making European Policy Work* (H. Siedentopf and J. Ziller (eds.), 1988), *Ireland and EC Membership Evaluated* (P. Keatinge (ed.), 1991). She wrote a book on *Ireland and South Africa: Government Policy in the 1980s* (1988), and her text on *Cooperation and Integration in Europe* will be published soon by Routledge.

Edward Moxon-Browne was educated at the universities of St. Andrews and Pennsylvania; and is now Reader in Politics at Queen's University, Belfast where he has lectured on the European Community since 1973. In January 1992, he takes up the Jean Monnet Chair in European Integration at the University of Limerick. His main research interests are the European Parliament, Spanish membership of the European Community, the Community's peripheral regions, Irish politics, and the ethnic roots of political violence. Among his publications are *Nation, Class and Creed in Northern Ireland* (1983), *Political Change in Spain* (1989) and a monograph for the Irish Council of the European Movement entitled 'Relations Between the Oireachtas and Irish Members of the European Parliament after Direct Elections' (1979). He is currently writing a book on Spain's membership of the European Community.

Patrick Keatinge, Ph.D., is Associate Professor in Political Science at Trinity College, Dublin, where he teaches international politics. He is a graduate of TCD and the London School of Economics and Political Science. His publications include *The Formulation of Irish Foreign Policy* (1974), *A Place Among the Nations: Issues of Irish Foreign Policy* (1978), *A Singular Stance: Irish Neutrality in the 1980s* (1984), and many articles on Irish foreign policy. He recently edited *Ireland and EC Membership Evaluated* (1991).

Tony Brown is an economist and European Affairs consultant, and a graduate of University College, Dublin. A Council Member of the Institute of European Affairs, he is Visiting Lecturer on European Institutions at St. Patrick's College, Maynooth. He has been active in EC industrial affairs, social policy and political bodies since the mid-1960s. He was a member of the Royal Irish Academy Committee on International Affairs from 1980–85, and is an Executive Member of the Irish Council of the European Movement. Since 1978 he has been International Secretary of the Labour Party and Council Member of the Socialist International.